Circular 17/96

EN\

Circular from the
Department of the Environment
2 Marsham St, London SW1P 3EB

5 December 1996

Private Sector Renewal:
a Strategic Approach

HOUSING GRANTS, CONSTRUCTION AND REGENERATION ACT 1996, PART I

1.   Part I of the Housing Grants, Construction and Regeneration Act 1996 is due to come in to force on **17 December 1996**. It provides for grants and other measures for securing the renewal of privately owned housing and replaces Part VIII of the Local Government and Housing Act 1989. This circular includes updated advice on private sector renewal generally and on the provisions that will apply following the enactment of the 1996 Act in particular. It replaces the circulars listed in paragraph 12 below.

2.   Local housing authorities are best placed to determine priorities for private sector renewal in their areas within the constraint of available resources. The new legislation will make it easier for local housing authorities to develop local private sector renewal strategies. The following chapters give advice on the development of such strategies within the context of authorities' wider strategies for housing, economic development and regeneration, and community care. The Government will have regard to the effectiveness of local strategies in determining the allocation of resources for private sector renewal.

MAIN CHANGES TO THE PRIVATE SECTOR RENEWAL PROVISIONS

The Housing Grants, Construction and Regeneration Act 1996, Part I
3.   The main features of the 1996 Act are:

- mandatory renovation grants, common parts grants and HMO grants have been replaced by discretionary grants;

- mandatory disabled facilities grants (DFGs) are retained; discretionary DFGs may be paid above the grant maximum for mandatory DFG purposes;

- grants to landlords will be available at local authorities' discretion with the exception of mandatory DFGs;

- a new 3 year residence/ownership condition is introduced for renovation grants to owner occupiers and tenants;

- the provisions setting out when grant is required to be repaid have been strengthened and rationalised;

- the scope of group repair schemes has been widened;

- Minor Works Assistance has been replaced by Home Repair Assistance with wider scope and higher grant limits;

- the housing fitness standard and the duty to enforce it have been retained and a new 'deferred action' enforcement option has been introduced;

- a new relocation grant is being introduced to help owners of houses which have been cleared to acquire another property (in Part IV of the 1996 Act, not expected to come into operation before April 1997);

- the Act contains transitional provisions on the way in which applications for main grants which are outstanding on the commencement date shall be dealt with.

Test of resources

4.   The means test is retained for grants to house owners and tenants. In the case of applications for DFGs, only the means of a disabled person for whose benefit the grant would be given and of the disabled person's spouse (or parents in the case of a minor) will be tested. There will be no specific means test for grants to landlords, the amount of which will be at authorities' discretion.

Exchequer support

5.   The arrangements for exchequer support for private sector renewal are being changed for 1997-98 and subsequent financial years. Separate resource allocations will be made to authorities for DFGs and for expenditure under the other private sector renewal provisions:

- For **DFGs**, specified capital grants (SCG) (which are not cash limited but on receipt of which authorities are required to make equivalent reductions in credit approvals) are being retained.

- **Other private sector renewal expenditure** will be supported by a new specific grant, 'private sector renewal support grant', up to an annually determined cash limit.

Guidance on the financial arrangements is given in *Chapter 8*.

Transitional provisions

6.   The attention of local authorities is drawn to the Housing Grants, Construction and Regeneration Act 1996 (Commencement No 2 and Revocation, Savings and Supplementary and Transitional Provisions) Order 1996 which sets out transitional and supplementary provisions and effects necessary revocations and savings. Authorities should note in particular that, under article 6 of the order, they are required to send a notice to each person from whom they have received an application for a mandatory grant, and whose application will, after commencement, be treated as one for a discretionary grant.

THE GUIDANCE

Structure

7.   The following chapters give advice on the development of private sector renewal strategies, on the use of the statutory powers, and on the financial arrangements. More detailed guidance on the individual elements of provisions is given in the Annexes. The bibliography lists some Department of the Environment sponsored research publications relevant to private sector renewal.

8.   In this guidance the following expressions have the meanings given, unless the context requires otherwise:

Secretary of State	Secretary of State for the Environment
1985 Act	Housing Act 1985
1989 Act	Local Government and Housing Act 1989
1996 Act	Housing Grants, Construction and Regeneration Act 1996

Status

9.   The guidance in *Annexes B* (Fitness enforcement); *C3* (Neighbourhood renewal assessment process); and *D3* (Economic appraisal for group repair) has statutory force. In accordance with section 604A of the 1985 Act and section 85 of the 1996 Act, Annex B was laid before Parliament in draft on 23 October 1996. **Local authorities are required to have regard to the guidance in *Annexes B*, *C3 and D3* in the way explained in each Annex.** *Annexes C1, D2, E2, J3 and J4* include various statutory approvals, consents, directions, determinations, regulations and specifications with which authorities are required to comply. All the statutory elements of the guidance come into force on 17 December 1996. The remainder of the guidance is advisory. *Chapter 7 and Annex I* have been prepared in consultation with the Department of Health.

10.   The guidance does not represent a definitive interpretation of the law; only the Courts are empowered to provide that. In cases of doubt authorities are strongly advised to seek their own legal advice.

Other subordinate legislation

11.   A number of statutory instruments have been made under the provisions in Part I of the 1996 Act. A list of these by title and number together with a brief description is given in *Annex L*. Throughout the body of the guidance statutory instruments made under Part I of the 1996 Act are referred to by title only.

Withdrawal of circulars

12.   The following DOE circulars are hereby withdrawn: 4/90, 6/90, 10/90, 12/90, 5/91, paras 19-21 of 5/93, 7/93, 8/94, 4/95 and 9/96. However they continue to be relevant to orders made or notices served before 17 December 1996; applications for grants and minor works assistance submitted before that date; and group repair schemes approved before that date.

Format

13.   This circular and the guidance are issued in A4 format, 4-hole punched. It may be converted into loose-leaf format for keeping in a ring binder by guillotining the binding edge. Supplementary/updating material may be published from time to time in a similar form.

Copyright

14.   The contents of this circular are Crown copyright. Extracts of up to ten percent of this publication may be photocopied for non-commercial in-house use, subject to the source being acknowledged.

C L L BRAUN
Head of Housing Renewal Policy Division

The Chief Executive
    County Councils
    District Councils
    London Borough Councils
    Council of the Isles of Scilly
The Town Clerk, City of London

HRP 12/2/101

Contents

Chapter 1: The need for private sector renewal strategies and their wider context

1.1   Local housing authorities should, as part of their overall housing strategies, establish and keep up to date strategies for private housing renewal in their areas. These strategies should :

- have regard to overall housing need and to the authority's housing policies and the role of other housing providers;

- be set within the context of the wider economic, planning and regeneration policies for the area, and of policies for community care and public health;

- cover the problems facing all private housing, both owner-occupied and rented;

- define priorities and identify the most appropriate means of tackling problems, using the available powers;

and in turn enable authorities, as part of the implementation of their private sector housing renewal programmes, to:

- identify available resources and how best to use them;

- set realistic targets which are capable of being achieved with the resources available;

- make provision for monitoring progress; and

- keep strategies and programmes under review.

1.2   Local authorities are required to review the housing needs of their areas periodically (1985 Act, section 8). As part of that, they must, at least once a year, consider the condition of all housing in their areas, irrespective of tenure (1985 Act, section 605). This requires the compilation and updating of reliable information. Local house condition surveys are an effective means of achieving this. Guidance on stock condition information is set out in *paragraph 2.13 of Chapter 2.*

1.3   In preparing a private sector renewal strategy, an authority should have regard to the needs and wishes of the owners and occupants as well as the condition of the properties. The primary responsibility for maintenance and repair of privately owned housing rests with owners. The provision of advice to owners, both on the steps they can take to repair their properties and on the assistance that may be available from the local housing authority or other sources, is likely to be an important part of any private sector renewal strategy.

Types of strategy

1.4   A private sector housing strategy is likely, in practice, to comprise a variety of approaches, including some or all of the following:-

- **area based**, appropriate where there are geographical concentrations of unfitness and disrepair. In such cases considerable use may be made of clearance areas, renewal areas and group repair;

- **based on property type**, giving priority to the repair of particular kinds of property such as houses in multiple occupation or blocks of flats;

- **based on meeting particular kinds of property condition**, for example to encourage the repair of empty properties so that they can be brought back into use either in owner occupation or in the private rented sector;

- **issue based**, giving priority to dealing with problems of particular local concern, such as tackling the most unfit housing, poor energy efficiency, lead water pipes, radon, means of escape, crime prevention;

- **client based**, concentrating on the needs of particular groups such as older or disabled people, people in community care or families with young children.

All strategies should give a clear indication of how authorities will deal with requests for assistance that fall outside the priorities identified in the strategies – *see Chapter 5, paragraphs 5.2- 5.3.*

1.5   Private sector renewal strategies should have regard to, and be consistent with, related policies including the following:

1.5.1   **Other housing renewal and regeneration policies**, including

- authorities' work with their own stock;

- the Housing Corporation's Approved Development Programme for the district and the renovation and new build work of housing associations, including reinvestment in their own stock, where relevant;

- schemes supported by funds from the Single Regeneration Budget or Capital Challenge and schemes promoted by development agencies, inner city partnerships etc;

- estate-based schemes (eg under the Estates Renewal Challenge Fund) and schemes for the Large Scale Voluntary Transfer of local authority stock.

Authorities should consider the scope for economies of scale where work on regeneration initiatives and private sector renewal can be coordinated. There may also be wider economic, social and environmental benefits from securing the renewal of private housing in parallel with other schemes.

1.5.2   **The views of residents**, which should be taken into account both generally when an authority's strategic approach is being developed, and wherever proposals for the renovation of particular areas are being considered. The public consultation process for housing investment strategies should cover the authority's broad strategies for private sector renewal. Where the renovation of particular areas is being considered, the advice on including residents in the decision-making process for declaring renewal areas contained in the Department's Guidance Manual on Neighbourhood Renewal Assessment is applicable.

1.5.3   **Community care policies**, which recognise the benefits of people being able to stay in their own homes wherever possible. With the increasing support for care in the community, housing, social services and health authorities are likely to share a number of common objectives. This emphasises the importance of close consultation in the preparation of housing strategies and relevant community care plans to ensure that programmes complement one another.

1.5.4   **Planning and land use policies**, especially those set out in local structure and unitary development plans, and in Planning Policy Guidance Note PPG3 on housing development and PPG13 on transport which emphasise the importance of regenerating urban areas. Development within existing towns can be more sustainable than on greenfield sites; it often makes the best use of infrastructure and reduces the need to travel. All available options should be considered, including clearance and redevelopment, and the conversion to housing use of redundant commercial and industrial buildings, as well as the renovation of the existing stock. Authorities should also bear in mind the advantages that often accrue from allowing mixed residential and other uses within a locality.

1.5.5 **Environmental and energy efficiency policies**, including the reports required by the Home Energy Conservation Act 1995. DOE Circular 2/96 gives guidance on the implementation of this Act. To supplement this, the Department intends to issue revised and updated strategic guidance on energy efficiency in housing which will include advice relating to privately owned housing as well as to authorities' own stock. More generally, private sector renewal activities are an important part of the wider policies set out in Local Agenda 21, the Town and Country Quality Initiative and similar policies for meeting housing need in an environmentally sustainable way.

1.5.6 **Policies to tackle crime and anti-social behaviour**. Measures to reduce crime, developed in close consultation with local residents, housing associations where they are significant stockholders, and the police, are beneficial in all areas and essential for rebuilding and sustaining long-term confidence in rundown areas. DOE circular 5/94 gives advice to local authorities, developers and designers about planning considerations relating to crime prevention. The development of mediator services can also play a key role.

1.6 A renewal strategy will not be effective without leadership to champion the strategy and coordinate all the organisations concerned, or without the efforts of qualified, dedicated staff. In preparing their strategies, authorities should ensure that the staff charged with implementation are properly trained for the task. They should also ensure that organisational frameworks are such as to enable an effective and coordinated implementation of their strategies. Team working, quality systems and stated service standards are important pre-requisites.

Chapter 2: Developing Renewal Strategies – General Principles

2.1 OVER-ARCHING PRINCIPLES

2.1.1   A primary justification for public expenditure on the repair and renewal of privately owned housing is to help those in real need who are unable to help themselves. But renewal strategies should also aim to secure the greatest possible wider economic and social benefits that can be obtained from housing improvement and regeneration.

2.1.2   In promoting private sector renewal local authorities act as both

- **enablers**: by encouraging, supporting and assisting others' activity on the renewal of private sector housing and the planning and land use process; and

- **direct actors**: through grants, group repair schemes, renewal areas, regeneration schemes, clearance and enforcement activity.

Renewal strategies should cover both these roles. This will require an open approach to the assessment of priorities, involving residents and the full range of local housing interests.

2.1.3   The following factors should be taken into account in developing strategies.

2.2 Owners' and landlords' responsibilities

2.2.1   Private housing is a private asset. Owners are responsible for its repair and maintenance. Many owners can afford to repair and maintain their properties to an acceptable standard. An effective strategy should aim to encourage owners to keep their properties in good order by making them aware of the importance and longer-term cost benefits of doing so. This may involve:

- advice on sound maintenance practices;

- the provision, where appropriate, of professional, technical and administrative assistance to enable owners and tenants to carry out repair and maintenance works (eg using the powers available under section 169 of the Local Government and Housing Act 1989) – *see also Chapter 4, paragraph 4.9;*

- the direct provision or funding of home improvement agencies;

- assistance through housing advice centres;

- providing lists of local building services and contractors who have successfully completed grant work;

- encouraging local building materials suppliers to offer advice;

- working with financial institutions to ensure that owners are made aware of the need to keep their properties in good repair and that loan finance is available, if necessary, to help them do so.

2.2.2   Action to assist owners' repair activity helps ensure that the bulk of resources can be directed towards helping those in real need. Timely preventative action by owners also helps avoid properties deteriorating to the point where public investment is required, and in areas where public investment has been targeted in the past, acts to protect that investment. – *see also paragraphs 2.5 and 2.6 below.*

2.3 **Involving the wider community**

2.3.1   The views of residents should be taken into account both in the development of private sector renewal strategies generally; and whenever proposals for the renovation of particular areas are being considered. Advice on including residents in the decision making process for declaring renewal areas is contained in the Department's guidance manual on Neighbourhood Renewal Assessment – *see paragraph 3.9.2 of Chapter 3.*

2.3.2   In addition, partnership approaches can often generate additional activity and unlock additional resources. Local authorities should consult and involve a wide range of interests in developing, implementing and monitoring strategies, including:

- **housing providers**: eg private landlords, housing associations, rural housing trusts;

- **community organisations**: eg social services authorities, voluntary organisations, residents' associations;

- **local and national businesses**: eg builders, mortgage lenders, building materials suppliers, employers and retailers.

The role and nature of each organisation's contribution will depend on its particular interests and character and the objectives and focus of particular strategies.

2.4 **Value for money and the best use of resources**

2.4.1   Strategies should deliver value for money and make the best use of available resources, including local authority staff and the local community. Ways of achieving this will vary according to the particular private sector renewal problems that authorities face and the additional private investment that public investment can stimulate. However, all strategies should be based on an assessment of possible options for tackling identified problems and of the likely available resources and local priorities.

2.4.2   Authorities should be positive in looking at ways of drawing in private finance which can make public resources go further. Private finance may manifest itself in a variety of ways ranging from investment by owners in their own homes to the possibility of investment by housing associations (see below) and by financial institutions in vehicles such as local housing companies. Authorities should actively explore the scope for establishing effective partnerships with local businesses and other private sector organisations in their areas.

2.5 **Preventing decline**

2.5.1   Authorities should focus particularly on areas or individual properties which might be slipping into decline. This requires effective mechanisms to identify such areas and may require the injection of resources or support both to prevent dwellings deteriorating to a point at which intervention would be required and to maintain the local environment.

2.6 **Sustaining renewal**

2.6.1   When investing in areas or individual dwellings authorities should promote the use of materials which will reduce the need for future maintenance. Households should be encouraged to develop awareness and skills which will enable them to look after their own dwellings. Areas should be monitored to identify early signs that they may again be beginning to deteriorate.

2.7 Housing association rehabilitation and development

2.7.1   Housing associations can play an important role in complementing local authority private sector renewal activity. Authorities should consult the Housing Corporation, housing associations and other registered social landlords (as introduced by the Housing Act 1996) working in their areas when developing their strategies. To maximise the role of housing associations and other registered social landlords, local authorities should:

- clearly define how such bodies can contribute to housing renewal and regeneration by setting priorities in terms of the size, type, special needs and location of housing association developments or acquisitions of existing properties;

- make their policies in this regard clear when consulting the Housing Corporation and associations, and establishing the local contribution of housing associations and other registered social landlords to the housing renewal strategy;

- consult with the Housing Corporation before establishing partnership initiatives with housing associations;

- consider the provision of local authority social housing grant for new build or rehabilitation schemes which complement the authority's renewal strategy.

2.7.2   Authorities should also consider identifying the opportunities for initiatives such as do it yourself shared ownership, low cost home ownership and short life empty property schemes. Housing associations can play an important role in assuming the management of properties and through on-going maintenance and programmes such as HAMA plus.

2.8 Enforcement

2.8.1   Although strategies which encourage the cooperation of individuals in making their own properties fit may be preferable in ensuring long term sustainability, authorities need to bear in mind the need to include clear policies on the role to be played by fitness enforcement action in dealing with properties that are unfit and in serious disrepair. This may be particularly important in the case of HMOs and the private rented sector – *see Chapter 6* – where some of the worst housing conditions are to be found. Enforcement policies should enable the circumstances and views of tenants, landlords and owners to be considered. Enforcement should generally be viewed as a last resort, and the need for it minimised by engaging owners and landlords in a long-term constructive dialogue. Further guidance on fitness enforcement is given in the code of guidance for dealing with unfit premises in *Annex B*.

2.9 PRE-REQUISITES FOR EFFECTIVE STRATEGIES

2.9.1   An effective strategy requires a clear framework to enable the development of aims and objectives which can be translated into the policies, targets and output measures that form the core of a strategy. Authorities should:

- ensure that there is good leadership to champion a strategy and that staff charged with implementation are sufficient in number and properly trained;

- adopt a corporate approach with effective consultation and decision-making processes;

- be clear about aims, and determine objectives and targets for dealing with identified private sector housing needs and conditions in their areas – an important part of this will involve assessing alternative approaches and deciding best courses of action; and

- monitor and review action taken in accordance with strategies to ensure that targets are being met and that strategies can be adjusted to meet changing circumstances.

2.9.2   The following processes are likely to be important elements in the development of effective strategies.

2.10   Consideration of overall approach to the private sector stock

2.10.1   Authorities should determine:

- what role they consider private housing plays in meeting the overall housing needs of their areas; the extent to which that role is already being played;

- how this has been achieved and the scope for further development, including the potential role and input from residents;

- the role of private sector renewal in relation to wider area regeneration, community care and environmental policies.

In considering these points authorities should reflect the balance of their priorities for action – and therefore the resources they are prepared to make available – between the private and public sector housing in their areas.

2.11   Involving key interests – a corporate approach

2.11.1   **A corporate approach to strategy development is essential**. Local authorities need to

- identify the responsibilities and input of all their staff involved in private sector renewal;

- establish arrangements for coordinating their own efforts and those of other public and voluntary agencies such as health authorities, social services and voluntary organisations providing services or advice; and

- consult and involve relevant housing providers, community organisations and local and national businesses mentioned in *paragraph 2.3.2.*

This highlights the need – as emphasised in *paragraph 1.6 of Chapter 1* – for good leadership and for clear assignment of responsibilities.

2.12   Assessing the condition, location and occupation of the stock

2.12.1   Section 605 of the Housing Act 1985, as amended by paragraph 85 of schedule 9 to the Local Government and Housing Act 1989, requires authorities to consider the condition of housing in their areas at least once a year. The requirement does not neccessarily imply an annual physical inspection of all housing. The primary purpose of the annual consideration is for the authority to maintain an awareness of the state of the stock in its area and how this changes as a result of its action and wider activity. Of equal importance will be the consideration of local housing market conditions, the housing need in relation to the available supply; and the extent to which private sector interest in regeneration and in particular renewal and improvement can be stimulated and maintained. Regard should also be had to housing conditions in areas or estates that were largely in local authority ownership prior to the right to buy legislation.

2.13 Local house condition surveys

2.13.1   Information on the condition of the stock, its location and occupation is essential for the development of effective private sector renewal strategies. One means of obtaining such information is through local house condition surveys. Many local authorities have already undertaken such surveys. A local house condition survey will not by itself deliver an effective strategy. But it can provide a basis for determining:

- the nature and extent of problems in the private sector stock;

- the levels of investment required to tackle them;

- priorities for action; and

- the effectiveness of decisions already taken and expenditure already committed.

2.13.2   Local house condition surveys are costly. Before they are carried out authorities need to be clear as to their purpose, how they plan to use the information and how it is to be updated. Unless an authority is clear in these matters they will not be able to specify the scale and scope of the survey. They should consider whether stock surveys can be combined with other information gathering exercises – eg local needs surveys. Comprehensive guidance on the carrying out of local house condition surveys has been issued by the Department : *Local House Condition Surveys – Guidance Manual, DOE, HMSO, London 1993.*

2.13.3   Survey information can be updated in a number of ways. Examples are:

- repeating stock surveys at intervals;

- carrying out selected revisits to sampled dwellings to monitor how condition is changing;

- using information from other records – eg grants and enforcement to estimate likely change in condition.

The Department plans to update its Stock Survey Guidance Manual to provide further advice on how surveys can be updated.

2.14 Other sources of information

2.14.1   Other sources of information will be also be useful in developing a strategy. Census statistics on the general characteristics of the population may serve to indicate those areas which need further investigation. A general knowledge of the distribution, age and type of housing within a district will help to identify those areas which might merit a more thorough investigation. Here local estate agents, letting agents, landlords and property developers should be able to offer an insight.

2.14.2   Other information may be available from records of enforcement action or grant applications; from complaints about private sector housing; from local authority and housing association waiting lists and management and maintenance records; from overall vacancy rates and numbers of right to buy properties; or in documents associated with the preparation of development plans and with planning applications. Social services departments, housing associations and organisations such as Age Concern, home improvement agencies and the fuel and water utilities may also be able to offer helpful information.

2.15 Setting aims, objectives and targets

2.15.1 Local authorities should determine their own aims, objectives and targets in light of their individual circumstances and in response to relevant policy directions from central Government – eg as conveyed through the Housing Investment Programme process. The aims, objectives and targets should reflect an authority's assessment of housing needs and conditions and the available resources. Aims, objectives and targets and the timetable for achieving them, should be clearly defined, challenging, but realistic.

2.16 Contributions to other programmes

2.16.1 Local authorities need to identify the contribution – actual and potential – that private sector renewal can make to other programmes – eg regeneration, planning, local employment initiatives, community care strategies, etc – and ensure where appropriate that there is synergy between programmes.

2.17 Publication and promotion

2.17.1 Draft strategies will generally be public documents and authorities should consider making them available in libraries etc. Once authorities have determined their strategies, they should consider the need to publish and promote them, either generally or to the particular local interest groups who may be affected.

2.18 Monitoring, evaluation and feedback

2.18.1 Local authorities need to review their private sector renewal strategies on a regular basis to ensure they are developing and delivering in accordance with agreed aims, objectives and targets. Whereas long term aims and objectives may not change substantially from one year to another, more immediate programmes and targets will need to be assessed continuously. The views of residents and others involved in housing provision and services in the area should be sought regularly about how strategies are being delivered and how they can be further developed and improved.

2.18.2 In order to review their strategies authorities need to have in place effective monitoring arrangements and output measures which enable them to evaluate whether they are achieving their objectives. The Department proposes to issue supplementary guidance to its Neighbourhood Renewal Assessment guidance manual (*see paragraph 3.9.2 of Chapter 3*) which will cover monitoring arrangements.

2.19 FUNDAMENTAL ISSUES TO CONSIDER

2.19.1 The statutory duty on local authorities to review housing needs and conditions in their areas provides a basis for considering solutions for addressing identified problems. Local authorities have wide discretion in their choice of solutions and in the aims, objectives and targets they set for working towards those solutions.

2.19.2 When considering how best to support the improvement of conditions in the private sector stock, authorities need, in particular, to consider :

- the strategy or strategies most appropriate for tackling the particular problems identified in their areas (*see paragraph 1.4 of Chapter 1*);

- the quality and effectiveness of those strategies both for tackling problems and for maximising resource allocations from central government and levering in resources from other sources (*paragraphs 2.4.1 and 2.4.2 above*) – eg through challenge and partnership funding, matching EU funding (eg for environmental works such as energy efficiency) and through housing associations and private sector interests such as landlords and lending institutions;

and, within the framework of their strategies, they should consider :

- which areas, client groups and property types and elements require more active intervention;

- the best means of dealing with priority areas (eg through area based approaches and/or a more active approach to specific problems such as houses in multiple occupation);

- the interrelationship between the objectives of the housing strategy and the community care plan (*see also paragraph 1.5.3 of Chapter 1*);

- how to deal with condition problems which are dispersed by setting out criteria on which action on such dwellings will be taken, including giving discretionary grants;

- the likely take up of disabled facilities grants, the management of such grants and the possible need for discretionary grant-assisted improvement work to properties where DFGs are approved.

- the role and use of fitness enforcement action – as mentioned in *paragraph 2.8.1 above* – having regard to the statutory guidance set out in *Annex B*, and bearing in mind that enforcement action should generally be a last resort;

- local participation (*paragraph 2.3 above*): in particular the role to be played by other housing, social services and community care providers and home improvement agencies;

- procedures that provide for the effective stewardship of grant resources and which provide for accountability to local residents, and to central government where exchequer contributions are paid;

- deployment of available resources – both staff and financial;

- effective measures to safeguard against abuses and fraud in the system;

- mechanisms for monitoring the implementation of strategies and the process of review.

KEY POINTS:

Strategies – general principles:

- ensure there is leadership, team working and qualified, dedicated staff to champion the strategy.

- adopt a corporate development and implementation approach.

- identify problems that need to be tackled.

- identify who should be involved and consulted, and how.

- consider all options and identify the best approach or approaches for tackling problems.

- agree aims, objectives, targets and output measures and prioritise against available resources.

- draw up a clear implementation plan.

- develop effective monitoring procedures.

- regularly review performance against targets and priorities.

- consider publication and promotion of the strategy.

Chapter 3: Strategies into practice – tackling identified problems: Area based approaches

3.1 Strategies for dealing with identified problems

3.1.1 A key role of a private sector renewal strategy is to set out a framework for addressing problems identified from a consideration of the condition of the stock and housing needs in a local authority's area. As mentioned in *Chapter 2* a clear understanding of stock condition, housing needs and the operation of the local housing market is important:

- to establish the nature and extent of problems;

- as a basis for deciding the most effective approaches for tackling those problems;

- in deciding priorities and targets for action; and

- in evaluating the effectiveness of past expenditure.

3.2 Types of strategy

3.2.1 Private sector renewal strategies need to be flexible in order to address the range of problems a local authority might identify in its area. The main strategy types are identified in *Chapter 1* – that is area based; based on property type; based on meeting particular kinds of property condition; issue based; client based; or a combination of these.

3.2.2 Area based strategies are likely to be particularly appropriate where there are geographical concentrations of unfitness and disrepair or in turning round neighbourhoods which are at risk from being sucked into a spiral of decline and for which concentrated area action might provide an effective solution. Small scale area renewal or group repair approaches are also appropriate for tackling disrepair and unfitness in rural village communities.

3.2.3 An area based approach can offer many benefits. These include the opportunity:

- to improve the housing, general amenities and mixed uses in an area in which poor housing is likely to be combined with social and environmental problems;

- for the local authority to develop effective partnerships with residents and other private and public sector interests;

- to bid for and bring to bear challenge fund resources to enhance action in the area;

- to stimulate private investment alongside the use of public resources by giving residents, and others such as developers, housing associations and financial institutions, greater confidence in the future of an area;

- to provide a local strategic framework for the use of group repair, renewal, clearance or targeted renovation.

3.2.4 The problems in a local authority's district may however suggest a need for non-area based approaches as an alternative or complement to area based approaches. Non-area based approaches aimed at property types or particular groups of people or issues may be appropriate:

- where a local authority considers priority should be given to the repair of types of property – for example houses in multiple occupation; blocks of flats; pre-1919 houses;

- in dealing with particular types of property condition – for example by securing the repair of empty properties and encouraging the role of the private rented sector;

- in helping meet community care objectives by enabling elderly households or disabled people to stay in their homes through the provision of grant assistance;

- where there are particular environmental problems of local concern such as high radon levels or lead water supply pipes and grant assistance can help;

- where a targeted approach is considered necessary – for example in rural areas where unfit properties are more likely to be isolated from one another, or in renewal areas where it is not possible to tackle the whole area at once.

3.3 The tools for tackling identified problems

3.3.1   There are a range of tools and instruments available to enable local authorities to tackle identified problems and put their private sector renewal strategies into practice. Those relevant to area based strategies are described below; those for individual properties and special needs in *Chapters 4-7*.

3.4 Area based approaches

3.4.1   The need to meet the demand for mandatory grants has meant that, prior to the 1996 Act, local authorities have not always been able to pursue their priority objectives. The new private sector renewal framework introduced by that Act provides authorities with greater flexibility to develop strategic approaches and to tackle identified problems through local area based initiatives.

3.4.2   Along with other approaches, area based action is seen by the Government as playing an important role in improving the condition of the private housing stock. The Secretary of State is keen to see local authorities use the increased flexibility provided by the 1996 Act to pursue area based approaches wherever these are seen to provide the most satisfactory course of action for improving private sector housing conditions and targeting resources.

3.4.3   The main instruments available for putting area based strategies into practice are renewal areas, group repair schemes and area clearance. This part of the guidance concentrates on providing strategic advice on each of these instruments and their various components. The detailed rules and powers associated with each are contained in the relevant annexes.

3.4.4   Many of the advantages of renewal areas may be capable of being realised in respect of smaller area-based schemes without the need for formal declaration. Authorities may wish to adapt the guidance on renewal areas accordingly, to suit their local circumstances. Authorities may also decide to use individual renovation grants or home repair assistance as strategic tools in an area-based approach.

3.5 Renewal areas

3.5.1   Renewal areas, which normally last for ten years, provide authorities with real scope to:

- improve the housing and general amenities of an area in which social and environmental problems are combined with poor housing;

- develop effective partnerships with residents and private sector interests;

- bring about a wide based regeneration, including the scope for mixed-use development;

- secure maximum impact by increasing community and hence market confidence in the future of an area and, through this, help to reverse the process of decline.

If left unchecked, decline can quickly affect a whole neighbourhood leading to a downward spiral of degeneration as residents lose pride in their homes and the wider environment and perhaps even leave the area.

3.5.2   Declaration of a renewal area therefore provides an important signal to residents and local businesses that:

- the problems of an area have been recognised; and that

- public resources are being committed to help tackle them.

Declaration of a renewal area gives authorities the powers to carry out environmental works as well as increasing the amount of public sector support for renewal works such as group repair. The financial implications are discussed further in *Chapter 8*. While renewal areas provide a means of concentrating public resources to maximum effect it is important that efforts are made to try and stimulate private investment by residents and others such as developers, housing associations and lending institutions.

3.5.3   A decision to declare a renewal area should only be taken:

- after full consideration of the options and likely benefits;

- with the active involvement of all those in the area whose interests are likely to be affected;

- taking account of the other social and economic issues within an area.

If long term confidence is to be generated and investment safeguarded a comprehensive approach is essential.

3.6   Resources

3.6.1   A successful area renewal programme will require careful planning and a substantial commitment of resources. This will limit the scope for authorities to undertake activities elsewhere in their areas. Authorities will be expected to maximise the contribution of the private sector and it will therefore be essential to ensure the co-operation of both developers and the lending institutions. Authorities should consider their priorities for targeting Housing Corporation Investment on renewal areas and should consult the Housing Corporation where the authority anticipates investment through the Corporation's Approved Development Programme. Authorities will need to explain that, in committing resources to the renewal area, investment elsewhere will be reduced. It is essential that declared areas are given priority in allocating resources; and in setting an authority's Housing Investment Programme allocation, their renewal area programme will be taken into account.

3.7   Conditions for declaration

3.7.1   For a renewal area to be declared, the following conditions must be fulfilled:

- **the area must contain at least 300 dwellings** (including houses in multiple occupation);

- **at least 75% should be privately owned** (that is, owned by anyone other than a local authority, new town corporation, urban development corporation, housing action trust or the Development Board for Rural Wales);

- **at least 75% of the dwellings must require works for the one or more of the purposes mentioned in sections 12, 17, 27 or 60 of the 1996 Act** (NB the properties do not have to be statutorily unfit);

- **at least 30% of the households in the area** (NB this includes public sector households) **must appear to the authority to be eligible for Council Tax Benefit, Disability Working Allowance, Earnings Top Up, Family Credit, Housing Benefit, Income Support or Job Seeker's Allowance**; and

- **the area should be coherent** and not fragmented or include land designated for the establishment of a housing action trust.

3.7.2   The reasons for these statutory conditions are explained in *Annex C2*. The Secretary of State has power to vary these requirements – see below.

3.8   Before declaring a renewal area

3.8.1   Before declaring a renewal area, an authority must prepare a report in accordance with the provisions of section 89(1) and (3) of the 1989 Act. This is a report from a suitably qualified person (who may be an officer of the authority) showing:

- the **living conditions** in the area concerned;

- the **ways in which those conditions may be improved** (whether by the declaration of a renewal area or otherwise);

- the **powers available** to the authority if the area is declared to be a renewal area (see *Annex C4*);

- the **authority's detailed proposals for the exercise of those powers;**

- the **cost** of those proposals; and

- the **financial resources available**, or likely to be available, to the authority (from whatever source) for implementing those proposals.

The report must contain a recommendation, with reasons, as to whether a renewal area should be declared.

3.9   Neighbourhood Renewal Assessment

3.9.1   In order to comply with the requirement to prepare such a report, the Secretary of State continues to recommend authorities to carry out a comprehensive appraisal using the method known as **Neighbourhood Renewal Assessment (NRA)**. The NRA (which builds on the statutory framework in Part VII of the 1989 Act) is an aid to decision-making comprising a series of logical steps which, when taken together, provide a thorough and systematic appraisal method for considering alternative courses of action for an area. It recommends:

- **strong leadership and a corporate approach**. Renewal areas are not just about housing. They should aim to effect the comprehensive revitalisation of an area bringing improvement to homes, shops, other commercial premises, the local environment and infrastructure and community opportunities. Authorities therefore need to consider the full range of disciplines that should be included in the team which undertakes the assessment and coordinates subsequent implementation, and the extent to which the process should be completed in-house;

- **identifying aims and objectives** at an early stage. These need to be flexible and may need to be changed in the light of consultation;

- **taking an overview of conditions throughout the authority's area** to identify neighbourhoods for which concentrated renewal area action might be the most satisfactory course of action;

- **community involvement** in the generation of options. Authorities must in any event comply with the statutory publicity and consultation requirements (section 89(5) of the Local Government and Housing Act 1989) set out in the direction at *Annex C1*. But these are an absolute minimum. The Secretary of State attaches great importance to the consultation process, and authorities should always consider whether further consultation might be necessary. The success of a renewal area will depend on the good will and participation of residents and other interests. Every effort should therefore be made to meet their concerns;

- **gathering survey information** to inform option development and appraisal;

- **deciding priorities:** this may not always mean tackling the worst areas first. In terms of improving market confidence and maximising private sector inputs it may sometimes be better to concentrate on turning round those areas which have yet to be fully drawn into the spiral of decline;

- **taking full account** of any statutory planning framework and other policy objectives already established for the area;

- **a rigorous method of option appraisal**. This involves two elements:

  - **an economic assessment,** looking at the present value of costs (public and private) over a 30 year period; and

  - **a socio-environmental assessment** which looks at non-quantifiable benefits weighted according to the importance which the authority attaches to them.

The conclusions are brought together in the report: it is for the authority to balance costs against benefits and decide what action, if any, to take.

3.9.2   Although it is for local authorities to decide the extent to which they use NRA, they must have regard to the guidance in *Annex C3* in reaching that decision. Further guidance on a framework within which local authorities can operate NRA was published in 1992 : *Neighbourhood Renewal Assessments – Guidance Manual, DOE, HMSO, 1992*. It is planned to supplement this in due course drawing from recently published research : *Neighbourhood Renewal Assessment and Renewal Areas DOE, HMSO, 1996*.

3.10   Defining the Renewal Area

3.10.1   Once the authority have reached a preliminary decision that the problems in an area could best be met by declaring it to be a Renewal Area, they need to **decide the area to be declared.** In defining the preliminary boundaries, the widest possible view should be taken to maximise opportunities for synergy with other objectives. Final boundaries may be narrower than those originally drawn and will depend on the results of the NRA process. Authorities should:

- consider the **relationship** between properties which form the potential area and all adjoining land uses;

- in particular, examine the **redevelopment opportunities** which areas of vacant, under used or derelict land in the vicinity may offer and consider the advantages of incorporating such sites;

- bear in mind the potential for **complementing action** being taken on their own, or housing association, stock;

- consider the possible **synergy with other social and environmental initiatives** within or adjacent to the potential renewal area;

- examine the scope for levering-in **private sector finance** and long-term investment;

- ensure that the **statutory conditions** for a renewal area are met: see *Annex C2* and below.

3.10.2   Some of these issues may have already been addressed as part of the NRA process. Once the proposed boundaries have been set, the authority should show them on a map.

3.11 **Pre-declaration publicity and consultation**

3.11.1   Before coming to a final view, the authority must (see paragraph 2 of *Annex C1* for details):

- **publish a notice of their intentions** in at least two newspapers;

- **display** similar notices on conspicuous sites throughout the area;

- **deliver** statements to each address in the area containing the same information, together with a summary of the report explaining why they propose to make the declaration;

- **consider all representations;** and

- **give written reasons** for not accepting a point made.

3.12 **Declaring the Renewal Area**

3.12.1   If the renewal area does not meet the statutory conditions specified by the Secretary of State in directions (*see paragraph 3 of Annex C1*), the authority may apply for a **special direction** waiving or modifying the conditions. Such directions will only be given in exceptional circumstances – see *paragraphs 2 to 5 of Annex C2*.

3.12.2   Once the authority are satisfied, in the light of the report and any representations, that the unsatisfactory living conditions in the area can most effectively be dealt with by declaring the area to be a renewal area (and that the area meets the conditions specified in the Secretary of State's general or special directions), then they may pass a resolution to that effect. The resolution:

- has effect from the day on which it is passed; and

- is a local land charge.

The finalised renewal area must again be shown on a map.

3.13 **Post-declaration publicity and consultation**

3.13.1   After declaration, the authority must (see section 91 of the 1989 Act for details):

- **publish notice of the resolution** in at least two newspapers;

- **send a copy of the map, resolution and report** to the Secretary of State at the appropriate Government Office, along with **a statement of the numbers of dwellings and houses in multiple occupation and hostels in the area** on the day it was declared and **a statement containing any other information** relating to the declaration or the authority's proposals for the area that the Secretary of State may require;

- **use their best endeavour** to ensure that the resolution is brought to the attention of owners or occupiers of property in the area, and that those people know who to contact with any inquiries or views about the action which is to be taken;

- **secure an advice and information service** for those who wish to carry out any works to housing in the area. Authorities need to consider the most appropriate way of meeting this requirement in relation to the particular needs of each renewal area. Such a service should assist householders to identify and implement major schemes of works to their properties and stress the importance of undertaking on-going maintenance programmes once works have been completed. Section 169 of the 1989 Act enables authorities to provide or fund such services, and authorities may wish to establish a home improvement agency in the renewal area or to make use of an existing agency for this purpose.

3.14 **Implementation**

3.14.1   The report required before declaration of the renewal area should have set out a comprehensive strategy for the regeneration of the area in its widest context and carried with it a commitment to implementation from residents, private sector interests and other public agencies. Authorities need to maintain this commitment and impetus. This will often be best achieved by having:

- a **clear implementation strategy** setting out who is responsible for delivering the renewal area; what contributions are to be made from other departments in the authority and what resources are available and when. It should set out how an early impact in the area is to be achieved. This is important if programme momentum is to be sustained and community confidence retained.

- a **project manager** and coordinator; and/or

- a **small management team** dedicated to securing implementation of the chosen strategy;

- a **management committee** through which elected members and officers can keep in touch with the wide range of interests (public and private) represented and deal with problems and new issues as they arise;

- a **community based approach** – this is an essential ingredient for success;

- **effective corporate co-ordination** and implementation of other schemes in the area such as litter collection, grounds maintenance, etc to demonstrate to residents the local authority's commitment to the area.

- **effective and close co-ordination** with other relevant agencies e.g. housing associations.

3.15 **Monitoring and review**

3.15.1   Over the normal 10 year life of a renewal area authorities need to establish a programme of monitoring and review. Critical to this process is the setting up of **performance measures** based on the objectives of the area. Monitoring should evaluate whether :

- the objectives remain relevant to the current situation;
- the objectives are being met;
- the renewal area is having any side effects which need to be addressed;
- the renewal strategy is being implemented efficiently and according to programme.

3.15.2   Effective monitoring requires the collection of relevant information and must be able to demonstrate the impact of the resources expended. This process need not be over-elaborate. It is unlikely that a complete resurvey of an area will be needed more than once or twice in the life of a renewal area. But the strategy for a renewal area must be flexible enough to respond to changes where monitoring (quantitative and qualitative) indicates these are necessary, and in order to accommodate changes in authorities' internal corporate strategies.

3.15.3   The authority must publish progress reports on the action they are taking in the renewal area at intervals of no more than two years. Again, this should be by publication in two local newspapers; display on conspicuous sites; and direct delivery to each address (see *paragraph 5 of Annex C1 for details*). The information must cover:

- the **further action** the authority propose to take in relation to the area;
- the **action they have already taken;** and
- the **assistance** available for carrying out works in the area.

3.16 **Cessation or withdrawal from renewal areas**

3.16.1   An authority may resolve to exclude land from a renewal area or bring a renewal area to an end within the 10 year period. Before doing so, they must comply with the Secretary of State's directions as to publicity and consultation under section 95(2) of the 1989 Act (*see paragraph 6 of Annex C1*). After passing the resolution, they must also take the steps required by section 95(3) to (5) of that Act.

3.16.2   Authorities need to consider at an early stage the best means of withdrawing from areas (whether during or after the 10 year period). This is partly to safeguard the work already carried out. Authorities should consider ways of continuing the involvement of residents and encouraging them to continue maintaining their properties. One way is through the promotion of education measures to show residents how best to maintain their homes – for example by exhibitions, home logbooks and leaflets giving best practice advice on regular maintenance.

3.17 **Statutory rules and conditions**

3.17.1   The statutory rules governing the declaration of renewal areas are set out in Part VII of the 1989 Act and in the subordinate legislation made under those provisions set out in *Annex C1*. This covers:

- pre-declaration consultation and publicity requirements (section 89(5) of the 1989 Act);

- conditions for declaration of a renewal area (section 90(1)) – the rationale for these is explained in *Annex C2*;

- the requirement for submission of a statement of numbers of dwellings, HMOs and hostels following declaration (section 91(2));

- post-declaration publication of information requirements (section 92(2));

- consultation and publicity requirements prior to exclusion of land from, or termination of, a renewal area (section 95(2));

- the requirement to submit a copy of a map showing land excluded from a renewal area (section 95(3));

- the general determination of expenditure eligible for contributions from the Secretary of State (section 96(2));

- the conditions imposed on payment of contributions (section 96(3));

- the determination of information to accompany applications for payment of contributions at an increased rate (section 96(4)) – see also *Annex C2*.

Annex C2 also explains the procedure for applying for:

- special directions specifying different conditions for a renewal area (section 99); and

- the considerations the Secretary of State will take into account in deciding whether to give such directions or approvals.

KEY POINTS:

Renewal areas:
Before declaration

- carry out comprehensive appraisal of proposed area.

- use NRA process to help.

- identify resources for development and 10 year programme.

- comply with publicity and consultation requirements – s.89 1989 Act.

- prepare report – s.89 1989 Act.

- check whether S of S approval required for declaration.

After declaration

- comply with information and advice service requirement – s.91 1989 Act.

- prepare an implementation plan.

- monitor and review renewal area action.

- devise at an early stage a strategy for withdrawal at end of programme of action.

- coordinate renewal area action with other LA schemes in the area.

3.18 Group repair schemes

3.18.1   Group repair schemes seek to achieve renovation of whole blocks or terraces of housing drawing in a mixture of public sector funding and contributions from owners. They are a valuable tool for use in an area based strategy – both within and outside renewal areas.

3.18.2   The 1996 Act introduces changes to the provisions governing group repair. These are designed to provide local authorities with greater flexibility. The key changes (discussed in more detail in *Annex D1*) are :

- **the extension** of group repair to purpose-built flats (particularly with a view to including those known as 'Tyneside flats');

- **removal of the requirement** that all the buildings in a scheme have to be contiguous and adjacent to one another;

- **relaxation of the requirement** for the primary building to comprise at least 4 houses;

- **new conditions** requiring the balance of the cost of works to be paid if the property is sold or no longer occupied by the person participating in the scheme;

- **discretion** for local authorities to waive payment of the balance of cost – eg in cases where recovery in full would cause hardship;

- **power to vary schemes** after approval – eg to include late participants;

- **the extension** of group repair to deal with structural instability (whether or not associated with disrepair).

3.18.3   *Annex D1* gives **detailed general guidance** on the group repair provisions in the 1996 Act and the detailed eligibility criteria set out in the **Group Repair (Qualifying Buildings) Regulations 1996**. It also explains the **general approvals** criteria and gives guidance on applications to the appropriate Government Office for special approval for schemes or variations falling outside the terms of the general approvals. The terms of **the general approval** for schemes are set out in the **Group Repair Schemes (England) General Approvals 1996** which are reproduced at *Annex D2*.

3.18.4   The Secretary of State is keen to see local authorities make full use of the increased flexibility they now have for undertaking group repair schemes. The object remains that of securing the external fabric of a group of properties so that they are in reasonable repair and structurally stable on completion of the works. By tackling groups of adjoining properties, group repair can:

- **provide effective action** on external disrepair and provide for coordinated treatment of problems not possible with individual renovation grant action;

- **create the impetus for owners to invest** in keeping the inside of their properties in good order and in the subsequent maintenance of the exterior;

- **combine visual impact and financial assistance** to make residents feel more positive about their neighbourhood;

- **create confidence in the area.**

3.19 Selection of schemes

3.19.1   Authorities need to satisfy themselves that group repair represents the most satisfactory course of action for securing the condition of a specific group or terrace of housing. Group repair schemes should focus on houses or flats which are in sufficiently poor condition to warrant intervention, but good enough to justify investment. They are therefore likely to be most appropriate in areas where generally low income levels have prevented residents from investing adequately in the maintenance and repair of their properties.

3.19.2   The Secretary of State continues to attach importance to authorities **carrying out a thorough appraisal of each potential group repair scheme**, where appropriate, in order to satisfy themselves that schemes provide value for money and are the most satisfactory course of action. In particular, authorities will normally be expected to undertake a cost-benefit appraisal of the options available having regard to advice set out in *Annex D3*.

3.19.3   Value for money may not always be the overriding consideration and authorities should take account of other factors, including:

- proposals for dealing with **other problems** already identified in the area;

- the overall **condition** of the properties, their **layout** and **density**;

- the **need** for the particular type of housing in the area;

- the **likelihood** of the properties being improved without group repair action, including the scope for housing association involvement;

- **alternative uses** for the site;

- the **views** of residents;

- the **social and demographic characteristics** of residents;

- the effect of **alternative courses of action** on the community;

- **visual impact** of the scheme on the wider street environment.

3.19.4   Properties being considered for inclusion in a group repair scheme should not normally have had significant grant aided work carried out on them. Where poor conditions persist in the face of substantial previous grant investment, authorities should consider carefully whether further renovation, including group repair, will provide the most satisfactory course of action.

3.20   Preparation of schemes

3.20.1   Local authorities remain responsible for initiating group repair schemes. This includes the necessary arrangements for execution and payment of works and for collecting contributions from participants. **No scheme can go ahead until all participants have signified their agreement to take part**. Authorities therefore need to ensure that while a scheme is worked up all the residents likely to be affected are fully consulted. Effective consultation will make it easier to secure the agreement and cooperation of residents and enable their wishes to be taken into account wherever possible. It will also ensure they appreciate the extent of the proposed works and understand the arrangements for the payment of contributions where these are required.

3.21   Implementation

3.21.1   Once a decision has been taken to proceed with a group repair scheme, authorities will need to set up the works on behalf of the participants and arrange and monitor the contract. Authorities should maintain close contact with participants while the works are being carried out and consider best ways of encouraging participants to prepare for their on-going maintenance responsibilities, through such means as the provision of advice and information, providing advice contact points and continuing liaison.

KEY POINTS:

Group Repair Schemes:

- provide a valuable strategic tool for improving the exterior appearance of properties both within and outside renewal areas.

- enhanced flexibility in 1996 Act arrangements includes extension of schemes to cover flats and structural instability problems.

- need to consult residents and seek their consent to works.

- must carry out appraisal of schemes and other options to ensure group repair is the most satisfactory course of action.

- seek any necessary S of S approval to proceed.

- coordinate works and monitor contract.

- keep participants in the picture.

3.22 CLEARANCE AREAS

3.22.1   Replacement of worn-out housing is an important dimension of housing strategies. Authorities need to consider the extent to which demolition – as part of clearance area activity or otherwise – should form part of an effective strategy for tackling private sector renewal problems in their areas. Automatic preference should not be given to renovation especially in the face of assessments which indicate that the economic and other interests of an area are best served by clearance.

3.22.2   Local authorities should consider renovation and clearance on an even handed basis and pursue clearance in cases where it is considered to provide the most satisfactory course of action. They should not reject the possibility that demolition and rebuilding in conjunction with the private sector and housing associations may sometimes offer the most effective means of meeting local housing needs. It is imperative that the housing needs of those who might be dispersed by clearance action is considered from the outset. **The factors to which local authorities should have regard in deciding whether clearance is the most satisfactory course of action are set out in *paragraph 39 of Annex B.***

3.23 Relocation Grants

3.23.1   The system introduced under the 1989 Act of market value compensation for owners and disturbance payments, supplemented by Exchequer slum clearance subsidy, remains unchanged. But Part IV of the 1996 Act provides local authorities with the power to give relocation grants to help overcome the problems experienced by local authorities and low income home owners faced with the clearance of unfit housing. Their introduction follows a pilot study commissioned by the Department in conjunction with Birmingham City Council. Although clearance sometimes offers the best solution for dealing with unfit properties, it is often resisted by residents for fear that it will break up the local community. The grants are designed to bridge the "affordability gap" between compensation payments and the cost of buying more suitable properties in the locality or another designated area. The study showed that the availability of grants could help reduce resistance to clearance and allow people to remain home owners when they might otherwise have to be rehoused by the local authority.

3.23.2 The Secretary of State hopes that local authorities will look closely at the scope for giving relocation grants in cases where clearance is considered to be the most satisfactory course of action and where they consider that the giving of grants would facilitate that activity and be an effective use of their private sector renewal resources. The case for considering relocation grants is likely to be strongest in areas where:

- there are significant demands for retention of home ownership;

- there are demands for local rehousing and the retention of community ties;

- low incomes and unemployment make levels of market value compensation inadequate to allow for the purchase of an improved property;

- there are shortages of housing to rent from social landlords – of an appropriate size and type – available in the locality.

3.23.3 Sections 131 to 140 of the 1996 Act are not expected to come into force before April 1997. They will enable local authorities to give relocation grants in respect of clearance areas declared after the provisions come into force. Regulations providing for this will be laid in 1997 and be accompanied by further guidance on the use and operation of the grants.

3.24 Before declaring a clearance area

3.24.1 Authorities need to take a range of factors into account in deciding whether to declare a clearance area, including:

- **alternative options** for the area and their cost;

- **sustainability** of the area in providing long term satisfactory housing;

- the proportion of unfit and fit properties and the **general layout** of the area;

- the **views** of local residents (see the section on consultation below);

- arrangements for **rehousing**;

- the **after-use** of the area proposed for clearance with particular reference to its ability to attract private sector resources, whether or not these are linked to housing association investment.

3.24.2 In considering the after-use of a cleared site, authorities should consider the possibilities for promoting **mixed-use development**, such as a combination of residential uses with leisure or commercial uses, especially where the land is close to town or city centres. This can bring a number of benefits:

- increased **vitality and attractiveness** to visitors and tourists;

- **enhanced quality** of the local environment;

- a strengthened **economic base**;

- improved **take-up** of vacant or derelict sites;

- improved **security**;

- **reduced travel** requirements;

- **training and employment** opportunities.

3.24.3 Where a proposed clearance area is within a renewal area, the work undertaken prior to declaration of the renewal area should have identified those areas potentially suitable for clearance. Authorities will need to decide whether this work provides sufficient detailed information to support declaration of a clearance area. One deciding factor will be the time that has elapsed since declaration of the renewal area.

3.24.4   The **prime responsibility of authorities** is to consider the desirability of clearance in the context of proposals for the wider neighbourhood, whether within a renewal area or not. Authorities **must satisfy themselves** that clearance is the most satisfactory course of action having regard to the code of guidance for dealing with unfit premises in *Annex B*.

3.25 Compulsory purchase

3.25.1   Section 290 of the Housing Act 1985 enables local authorities to acquire properties in clearance areas, either compulsorily or by agreement, in order to undertake or secure clearance. Authorities may also acquire added lands surrounding a clearance area where there is justification for doing so and the proposed after-use cannot otherwise be achieved.

3.25.2   Further guidance on authorities' acquisition powers is given in *Annex E1*. The Annex also provides guidance on the compensation provisions for owners of properties in clearance areas; right of way extinguishment orders; and valuations of land. The current slum clearance subsidy determination is reproduced in *Annex E2*.

3.26 Consultation

3.26.1   Before declaring a clearance area local authorities are required to consult those who would be directly affected (section 289 of the Housing Act 1985 as amended by paragraph 25 of schedule 9 to the 1989 Act). This requires:

- serving a **notice of intention** to declare a clearance area on every person who has an interest in any building or flat in the proposed area;

- taking **reasonable steps** to bring proposals to the attention of the occupants of residential buildings in the proposed area – eg through explanatory leaflets and local meetings;

- deciding whether it is necessary to **inform** the occupiers of non-residential buildings about the proposals;

- placing **advertisements** in a minimum of two local newspapers circulating in the area;

- inviting **representations** from those consulted, allowing at least a period of 28 days for any representations to be made;

- considering the desirability of **recording** the action taken under section 289(2B) of the 1985 Act in a formal council report as a safeguard against any subsequent challenge about the validity of the declared area.

More generally, the clearance area process needs to be managed in a sensitive manner.

3.26.2   Where in a proposed area there are a significant number of individuals from ethnic minority groups for whom English is not their first language, authorities should consider the need to communicate with them in their own language.

3.26.3   Any representations received **are required** to be taken into account before reaching a decision on whether to proceed with a clearance area. This requirement emphasises the importance of authorities providing those consulted with information about:

- **the alternative courses of action open to the authority;**

- the perceived benefits of clearance;
- the redevelopment proposals; and
- the arrangements for compensation and rehousing.

Authorities will be aware that any proposal to declare a clearance area will **blight** that area and authorities will need to consider how best to mitigate this and to handle complaints from those affected.

3.27 After consultation

3.27.1 Following consultation an authority may proceed to declare a clearance area with or without the exclusion of any particular properties. If the exclusion of properties results in the area originally proposed being divided into two non-contiguous areas, separate clearance areas **must** be declared. Authorities should also consider taking alternative fitness enforcement action on any unfit properties excluded from those originally proposed for clearance or if a decision is taken not to declare a clearance area.

3.28 After declaration

3.28.1 Section 289(5) of the Housing Act 1985 provides that following the declaration of a clearance area authorities must send a copy of the resolution and other documents to the Secretary of State. The documents, which should be sent to the relevant Government Office for the Region, are listed in *Annex E1*. Again it is important that authorities manage the post declaration aspects of clearance area action in a sensitive manner.

KEY POINTS:

Clearance Areas:
Before declaration

- consider case for clearance on equal basis with renovation.
- consider scope for giving relocation grants.
- consider need to compulsorily acquire properties and surrounding lands.
- consult those directly affected – s. 289 1985 Act as amended by 1989 Act.
- take representations into account before reaching decision.

After consultation

- proceed to declare area if most satisfactory course of action.
- decide on the exclusion of any properties.
- decide on the basis of exclusions the need to declare separate areas.
- be open, keep people informed.

After declaration

- manage clearance process in a sensitive manner.
- provide relevant documents to Government Office for the Region.

Chapter 4: Strategies into practice – individual properties

4.0.1   The purpose of dealing with individual properties may be property based or people based or a mixture of both. For example, authorities may simply want to focus their attention on the worst condition properties in their areas or they may combine this objective with giving priority to such dwellings occupied by elderly households, additionally authorities may want to deal with condition problems – for example, radon specific problems. Mechanisms for delivery will cover both statutory and non statutory action. Such proactive approaches should not be new to local authorities. Most authorities find that where they are willing to make an additional commitment to initiate a particular strategy the benefits provide ample justification.

4.1   Dealing with individual condition problems

4.1.1   Authorities should have a clear strategy for how they propose to deal with individual condition problems. The strategy should set out clearly which types of properties, in what circumstances and occupied by which households will receive priority and what mechanisms are to be used to deliver that action in what circumstances. The strategy should be both proactive and responsive. This chapter gives guidance on the proactive aspects ie. the policies by which authorities should seek to improve the quality of housing in their area. *Chapter 5* gives guidance on the responsive aspects ie. those which relate to how the authority will deal with cases where individuals apply to the authority for grant or other assistance rather than the authority initiating the action.

4.2   Dealing with empty properties in the private sector

4.2.1   It is inevitable that there will be a number of dwellings vacant at any given time to allow the housing market to function effectively, facilitating residential mobility and the improvement or redevelopment of the stock. However, local authorities should seek to identify the most effective means of bringing long term empty private housing back into use. Bringing empty homes back into use can serve the dual purpose of meeting particular housing needs in an area and improving the condition of some of the worst housing.

4.2.2   Many vacant dwellings which need action to bring them back into use originate in the private rented sector and will require the active involvement of private landlords. Guidance related to the private rented sector is given in *Chapter 6*. More generally authorities should:

- focus policy on problematic vacants, ie those which remain vacant for a long period of time and are often in poor or deteriorating condition. Authorities will need to identify and monitor such vacants.

- promote measures to encourage owners to bring dwellings back into use, highlighting the problems of long term vacancy. There is often scope for bringing property back into use quickly and temporarily especially in the private rented sector, by giving advice and practical assistance.

- direct help to owners and landlords where the empty property is in a poor condition, by considering grants or loans. Housing associations and other landlords can assist by acquisition and improvement, or by short term leasing schemes.

- make greater use of the full range of legal powers available to local authorities under housing and environmental health legislation against owners who deliberately neglect their property leaving it empty and allowing it to fall into a derelict state. Compulsory purchase (or the threat of compulsory acquisition) is a possible option.

- involve the wider community in identifying long term vacant dwellings and make good use of local publicity.

4.3 Promoting energy efficiency

4.3.1   Local authorities should actively seek to integrate an energy efficiency policy into their housing strategies and operational plans, and work with other local organisations, such as house improvement agencies, in promoting energy efficiency. This should complement any activity under the Home Energy Efficiency Scheme.

4.3.2   Energy efficiency in housing enables people to enjoy warmer, more comfortable and healthier homes which are cheaper to heat. Landlords benefit from reduced management and maintenance costs. There is also the contribution that energy efficient housing can make towards reducing carbon dioxide emissions and therefore helping to safeguard the future environment.

4.3.3   Local authorities with their knowledge of their local areas are well placed to promote energy efficiency across all housing sectors. The Home Energy Conservation Act 1995 requires local authorities to address the energy efficiency of all residential accommodation, not just their own stock, by preparing an energy conservation report identifying measures which will lead to a significant improvement in the energy efficiency of residential accommodation in their area. Guidance to local authorities about the Act has been issued in DOE circular 2/96. Effective action which they are able to take includes:

- making an assessment of the energy efficiency of the housing stock in their areas as a basis for setting and agreeing energy efficiency aims, objectives and targets – some assessment will be necessary for the energy conservation report;

- drawing up plans for informing and involving residents in the planning and agreement of energy efficiency strategies;

- acting as focal points for energy efficiency promotion and education in partnership with local businesses, voluntary and community groups, schools and colleges and directly with residents;

- acting as providers of energy efficiency information and advice to residents on matters such as financial assistance, energy efficiency works, available products and likely costs, contractors to carry out works and other organisations who can provide advice;

- actively exploring the scope for levering in private sector finance to help facilitate energy efficiency.

4.3.4   Authorities should also consider particular means of promoting and improving energy efficiency in relation to private sector housing such as setting specific targets for energy efficiency in relation to private sector housing, reassessing their approach to integrating energy efficiency into private sector renewal programmes and evaluating their criteria for allocating renovation grants and other private sector renewal resources for energy efficiency work.

4.4 Using sustainable materials

4.4.1   In developing a renewal strategy authorities should actively seek to integrate a policy of environmental awareness where possible, for example, by maximising the use of sustainable and low maintenance materials. In addition authorities should have regard to the ability of households to maintain their property. With this in mind low maintenance materials should be specified in order to minimise the need for future maintenance activity and prolong the life of the building.

4.5 Anti-crime measures

4.5.1   In developing renovation strategies based on local need, the adoption of anti-crime measures as part of an authority's strategy for a particular area may be appropriate. So, for example, if an authority is implementing a scheme to replace old windows they may wish to consider providing window locks as well as catches. Authorities may be able to use or assist in making more widely known the "Secured by Design Refurbishment" initiative which is promoted by police forces throughout the country. The initiative encourages architects and builders to apply police recommendations for the security of all types of residential refurbishment projects, from single houses to estates, and provides guidance on best practice.

4.6 Guidance on specific problems

4.6.1   In developing a strategy for dealing with individual properties authorities may need to have regard to more specific matters from time to time. These may include:

- **listed buildings:** particular difficulties may arise with regard to applications in respect of listed buildings since the standards and the works necessary for grade I and II listed dwellings are determined by outside bodies which may make little, if any, financial contribution. Where there are additional costs associated with the improvement and repair of listed buildings authorities will need to consider the implications of these costs. Authorities should ensure that specifications reflect a reasonable balance between cost and aesthetic requirements. Alternative sources of funding, including English Heritage, local preservation trusts and charities, could be approached to cover any additional costs involved in the renovation of such buildings.

- **treatment of curtilages:** the Secretary of State has issued a general consent enabling authorities to determine grant applications for works outside the curtilage of a dwelling or HMO provided that certain conditions are met. The types of work outside the curtilage for which grant may be given are limited to works in respect of utilities provided by public or private sources and works to facilitate access to and from a dwelling by a disabled person. Some of these cases are covered by a general direction, which is set out in *Annex J4*. Where any of the conditions which are not covered by that direction are not met an authority will need to apply to the Department for an individual direction.

- **radon:** the Secretary of State has specified radon remedial works as a purpose for the main grants *(Annex J4)* and in some circumstances it may be appropriate for an authority to provide a grant to help owners with the cost of such works. In considering whether to make an award of grant the authority must satisfy itself that the remedial works for which grant aid is sought are necessary to reduce the radon level below the action level. They must also be satisfied that the works have been carried out satisfactorily before paying grant. Further advice on radon is provided in *paras 47 - 49 of Annex F*.

- **lead water pipes:** there may be a need to provide advice to owners and/or occupiers of properties on how they can establish whether there are lead pipes supplying water to their kitchen taps. Local authorities may wish to make available to householders the leaflet published by the Drinking Water Inspectorate entitled *"Have you got lead pipes?"* which advises householders on how to check whether they have lead pipes and, if so, on the measures they can take should they be concerned about the effects of lead. It may be appropriate for an authority to provide financial assistance, by way of renovation grant or home repair assistance, towards the cost of replacing lead pipes between the water company stop valve and the kitchen tap. Some water companies have schemes for assisting householders with replacement of lead pipes and there may be opportunities for local authorities to assist in making these schemes more widely known.

4.7 Mechanisms for delivery: Main Grants

4.7.1 Where authorities decide to use main grants they should adopt practices designed to improve the quality of housing in their areas and secure the maintenance of high standards. Some measures which authorities might take to help achieve their objectives are:

- **use of schedules:** it is important that authorities set clearly and precisely the schedules of works to ensure that the identified defects and deficiencies are remedied and that the fitness standard is achieved. The schedules should address the content and extent of any preliminaries, the phasing of individual work schedules and the pricing of works.

- **use of competent builders:** work should be carried out by one of the contactors whose estimate accompanied the application or, where only one estimate was required (*see paragraph 72 of Annex F*), the contractor. It is not currently the Secretary of State's intention to make regulations to require authorities to establish and maintain lists of approved contractors to carry out grant-aided works, and to make it a condition of grant that the works shall be carried out by a contractor on the list, but authorities may wish to consider the benefits of so doing. More detailed advice is given in the section on contractors issues in *Annex F*.

- **establishment of a home improvement agency:** offers a local authority the opportunity of introducing an agency to take the securing of acceptable standards beyond the administrative duty of the local authority.

4.7.2 An important question will be which grant is the most appropriate. Four main grants are available as before – renovation grant, common parts grant, disabled facilities grant and HMO grant. Details of these grants and the purposes for which they may be used are set out in *Chapter 5 and Annexes F, G and I*. The framework for administering the four types of grant is broadly the same but there are important distinctions. Authorities will need to consider which grant is the most appropriate in each particular case.

4.7.3 Help is also available for small scale works under home repair assistance. In deciding whether to award home repair assistance or a main grant, authorities will need to consider issues such as whether the applicant qualifies and the life and age of the property concerned. Urgent minor repairs might be justified where property is due for demolition in the future or as an interim measure where major renovation work is required. Home repair assistance could also be used for non priority cases or areas as a holding operation. Authorities might also target assistance according to the specific needs of its own area, eg relating it to the needs of elderly residents. Guidance on home repair assistance is given in *Annex H*.

4.8 Mechanisms for delivery: Application of fitness standard and role of enforcement (*details in Annexes A and B*)

4.8.1 The standard of fitness for human habitation is set out in section 604 of the 1985 Act as amended by paragraph 83 of Schedule 9 to the 1989 Act.

4.8.2   Local authorities' function of enforcing the statutory housing fitness standard will continue. Where under the provisions of section 606 of the 1985 Act a local authority has recently inspected and found a property to be fit no further inspection to identify whether unfit should be necessary. But where a property is found to be unfit authorities must decide the most satisfactory course of action having regard to the guidance set out in *Annex B*. Authorities should bear in mind that there is no obligation to give a thirty year life although that may be appropriate in some cases. Often a shorter period may be more appropriate.

4.8.3   If an authority decides that repair is the most satisfactory action they will need to decide whether a grant should be awarded to help with the work and this is now at an authority's discretion. They will need to consider how the circumstances fit in with their strategic priorities for dealing with individual dwellings. If a grant is awarded the authority must be satisfied that the repaired property will meet the required fitness standard on completion of the works. Where an authority decides not to award a grant they may wish to offer advice on possible alternative action.

4.9   Mechanisms for delivery: promoting good maintenance

4.9.1   A key element of a renewal strategy is the development of an effective strategy for encouraging repair and maintenance by home owners. The promotion of good maintenance as a preventive measure and as a means of maintaining renovated dwellings in good repair should be the key objective of local authority activity. Not maintaining a home can often be for a complex range of reasons eg high crime in the area, poor environment, low level of community activity. Any effective strategy for improvements in the private sector will therefore need to take account such issues. In developing an effective strategy authorities should take account of the initiatives which already exist. These include:

- **handy person services** : a free/low cost service on request of client or by referral, providing minor repairs of all types. Schemes are facilitated by local authorities, housing associations, home improvement agencies and independent or charitable organisations.

- **emergency repair service** : nationally available emergency repair services offering two levels of assistance – the provision of accredited builders and trades persons and a 24 hour emergency repair service. Provided by private companies and funded by charges to clients.

- **subscription-based maintenance services** : run by local building companies and includes exterior survey and maintenance plan, with free call out in emergencies and fee charged for materials and labour. Where these services are not being provided local authorities might wish to take steps to encourage builders to do so.

- **money advice** : Any increase in the amount of home maintenance activity has the potential to involve owners spending their own money. Therefore money advice relating to loans, benefits, savings, etc should be an important part of any maintenance strategy, particularly for owners on low income.

- **advice and information** : provision of leaflets and displays in offices on repair and maintenance issues, and verbal advice on repair and maintenance problems and solutions. More extensive advice to grant recipients when work is completed is provided by some authorities and other specialist advice on security and energy efficiency is also sometimes available. Schemes are provided by local authorities and home improvement agencies.

- **home maintenance surveys** : house maintenance survey provided with written report on short and long term repair and maintenance requirements and estimated costs. Free schemes or schemes making a charge are operated by local authorities and home improvement agencies.

- **tool loans** : local authority or community-based schemes which arrange for short term loan of tools, including specialist or expensive items such as cement mixers, scaffolding, ladders and hand power tools.

- **home maintenance training** : local authority funded courses and seminars focusing on maintenance awareness or on specific maintenance skills. Providing young people and schools with information and opportunities for project based involvement could be helpful.

- **volunteering schemes** : it may be possible to help elderly, disabled and other vulnerable residents by encouraging other residents within the community to offer voluntary help. This could be encouraged through a local maintenance strategy.

4.9.2   The main providers of home maintenance schemes in addition to local authorities are the private sector and home improvement agencies. Authorities should explore the scope for acting in partnership with those providers or enabling them to expand their activities in the authority's area. In pursuing this objective it may be helpful to liaise with Care and Repair, the national co-ordinating body for agencies, who will offer independent advice as to possible models of provision.

4.9.3   A successful maintenance strategy may depend on specific targeting of activity. The groups who tend to be least aware of the problems with their homes are older people, those with mental health problems, and those on low incomes and it is those groups who are largely the clients of existing maintenance schemes (except the commercial emergency repair services). Ethnic minority groups may also be a potential target for some authorities.

4.10   Mechanisms for delivery: Powers of authority in default

4.10.1   If an authority wishes work to be carried out to an empty building it can do so without requiring an application to be made by paying for the cost of the works under the provisions of Part VI of the 1985 Act. Similarly, if a successful applicant finds they are unable to pay their contribution towards the cost of the works, it is open to the authority to fund this amount at its own expense in default and seek repayment at a later date. This would entail placing a charge on the applicant's dwelling. However, authorities should do so only in exceptional circumstances, bearing in mind that it is undesirable to increase applicants' debt liability. Works in default procedures can be long and complicated and authorities should give careful thought before commencing such works.

4.11   Mechanisms for delivery: Home Improvement and Other Agencies

4.11.1   Agencies, both those run by local authorities in-house and those run by other organisations, have a significant contribution to make for both the applicant and the authority. There are specific gains to be made for particular client groups, for example, the elderly, where the agency is experienced in their dealings with that group. Guidance on the role of agencies in assisting elderly and disabled people seeking grants and/or help with works or adaptations is given in *Chapter 7 and Annex I*, and in the delivery of home repair assistance in *Annex H* and can also be obtained from Care and Repair.

4.11.2   In more general terms, advantages include:

- support for applicants, many of whom will be disadvantaged and unfamiliar with matters such as administration, employing builders, building standards and often the substantial finance involved;

- defining and enforcing quality standards;

- providing for applicant and contractor the security of knowing that all relevant matters have been dealt with;

- the capacity to plan work programmes and expenditure profiles;

- the promotion of community care policies by enabling people to remain in their homes.

4.11.3   Agencies vary in their complexity and sophistication but will generally include:

- a form of agreement between owner and builder which includes arrangements for payment, determination and mediation and damages;

- an approved contractor list;

- a building works specification;

- arrangements for works supervision and administration;

- a project manager or supervisor;

- a supportive approach to clients needs, including visiting them in their own homes;

- assistance in identifying finance, **including private finance**;

- referral to other appropriate organisations for assistance.

Chapter 5: Stategies into practice – responsive strategies

5.1 **Making grant assistance available**

5.1.1   While there is no longer a mandatory entitlement to grant assistance for the improvement of an unfit property, it is the intention of the Government that local authorities should still make use of discretionary grants and home repair assistance (grant) for the improvement of private sector housing. The provisions in Chapter I of Part I of the Housing Grants, Construction and Regeneration Act 1996 set out the purposes for which main grants may be available. These are for:

- the improvement or repair of dwellings, houses in multiple occupation (HMO), or the common parts of buildings containing one or more flats and

- the provision of dwellings or houses in multiple occupation by the conversion of a house or other building.

The grants for these purposes are a renovation grant, common parts grant or HMO grant.

5.1.2   Under the provisions of the 1989 Act local authorities were required to approve applications for grant assistance where:

- a property was unfit,

- improvement was the most satisfactory course of action and

- the grant applicant was eligible for assistance.

Part VIII of the 1989 Act did not require authorities to differentiate between applications so long as the application was determined within the specified period. In practice however, many local authorities have found it helpful to develop their own policies for approving applications based on local circumstances. Such policies are often set out in their housing strategy statement.

5.1.3   The move to a mainly discretionary grant regime will highlight the need to have in place a clear strategy within which all grant applications can be considered. The application of the strategy will need to be:

- objective

- fair and reasonable

- open and transparent.

If a local authority chooses to operate an initial enquiry system for those seeking grant aid, it should be made clear to individuals seeking grant assistance what constitutes a valid application, the submission of which to the local authority triggers the six month period for determining the application. The 1996 Act provides for no appeal mechanism where a grant application has been refused or approved with a lesser specification than has been requested by the grant applicant (see paragraph 5.3.1). Where a grant is approved, the authority must specify the amount of the grant and how it is calculated. It is not intended that this be burdensome and it may take the form of a copy of the means test calculation, the agreed (or amended) tender or a list of costings for works where this is more appropriate. However where an application is refused, the authority must notify the applicant of the reasons for refusing grant. Once a grant application has been determined the decision is final with the legislation providing no opportunity to revisit a decision.

5.1.4   It will be a matter for individual authorities to decide the basis of their strategy and the extent to which it is proactive or responsive. This is likely to be governed largely by:

- local house conditions,

- the extent of demand for grants,

- the resources available to an authority,

- the most suitable approach to address the identified needs,

- local priorities,

- wider regeneration and repair initiatives elsewhere in the authority,

- ensuring that where possible there is consistency of approach in delivering the broader strategic aims of the authority and

- demographic and socio-economic factors.

Guidance on the development of effective strategies is given in *Chapters 1 and 2*.

5.1.5   The Department will continue to make available an information leaflet for use by local authorities to publicise and inform applicants about renovation grants. In distributing the leaflet, local authorities will help enquirers if they also provide accompanying information on their private sector renewal policies. Where members of the public contact the Department direct they will be informed of the availability of grants and will be referred to their local authority for information on local policy and possible grant availability.

5.2   Using grant assistance

5.2.1   The Secretary of State would consider that a local authority was failing in its duty as a housing enabler and in its responsibility to consider the condition of the local private sector stock if it did not have some provision for grant assistance. While a local authority's renewal strategy will always be a relevant consideration when deciding when to offer grant assistance it should not override the authority's general duties. Therefore in pursuing its local strategy for the private sector, it is possible that a local authority may turn down a grant application where it does not fall within the ambit of a published strategy or criteria but it may not refuse to **consider** any application (ie it may not turn down an application out of hand) or refuse an application which does not meet its criteria without some mechanism for determining applications which fall outside existing policy.

5.2.2   Any criteria adopted should always include provision to ensure that where a strong case based on need has been established an individual application is considered on its merits, even where it does not fall within the authority's strategic objectives. A local authority may find the use of a points based system helpful when considering applications. Any system should ensure consistency in decision making and provide a clear audit trail with working papers supporting the decision made. It is for each authority to weight their system to reflect local priorities and circumstances where local authority intervention is seen as necessary.

5.2.3   There has always been a judgement to make on whether grant is best targeted towards addressing the immediate needs and personal circumstances of a person living in an unfit property, which may only need relatively small scale works, or on bringing a property up to a standard which will require little further work for a number of decades. Where a local authority is undertaking a strategic approach to renewal of a particular area or a particular type of property, such as an HMO, it is more likely they will wish to look to long term repairs. On the other hand, when grant assistance is for an individual property outside a targeted area a less comprehensive programme of works may be more appropriate.

However where a main grant is given the property must be judged by the local authority to have been made fit on the completion of the works. Where the works are to an HMO prior consultation with the landlord and tenants on the timescale, accessibility and scheme content should help reduce the risk of tensions between all parties.

5.2.4   However a local authority will not always want, or be able to, offer a grant to everyone seeking assistance. Where possible the authority should work with potential applicants to explain the authority's local priorities and how, if at all, the application relates to the policy adopted by the authority. However if the application is in respect of an unfit property the authority will need to decide what action they should take in response to their statutory obligation to deal with properties they identify as unfit – *see also paragraph 4.8.2 of Chapter 4*. Guidance on local authorities fitness enforcement duties, and the options open to them on deciding the "most satisfactory course of action" for dealing with unfit property, is given in *Annex B*.

5.2.5   The 1996 Act introduces a new fitness enforcement option: the deferred action notice. The option is intended among other things to assist authorities where they recognise that a property is unfit, but not in a condition, area, or owned by a priority applicant that the authority is targeting and therefore unlikely to secure grant assistance in the short term. *Annex B* provides further guidance on deferred action notices. In managing their enforcement duties local authorities will be expected to use the deferred action notice option sensibly and in relation to the degree of formal enforcement action they are already taking. It is not intended that authorities should use the option as a means of seeking out unfit properties within their area if they have no intention of bringing the owners within a wider renewal initiative.

5.3   Publishing criteria and open decision making

5.3.1   A local authority will need to have clear criteria against which to consider individual applications. The criteria should be agreed by the appropriate Council Committee and feature within an authority's housing strategy and implementation plan. It is recommended that grant criteria are published and readily accessible to enquirers and grant applicants. This will help to ensure that applicants do not undertake unnecessary preparation work and incur costs where there is little likelihood of grant being available. If a local authority is clear at the outset of an enquiry that approval is unlikely when judged against the local authority's published criteria this should be drawn to the attention of the grant applicant. A local authority will wish to consider the merit of having in place an **internal** referral mechanism which would operate before a decision is made. The referral would be to an officer independent of the officer who is to make the grant decision. In difficult cases, such a referral should help to ensure that the decision is made on a sound and informed basis; and the fact that such a referral has taken place should reassure the grant applicant.

5.3.2   If it is unlikely that grant will be forthcoming, authorities should consider using their powers under section 169 of the 1989 Act to provide the enquirer with practical advice or assistance. Such help might include advice:

- on how to remedy unfitness problems;
- on ways that the works may be financed;
- on how to engage a suitable builder and
- on agency services which might be able to assist.

5.4   Grants available for individual properties

5.4.1   The range of grants available fulfils broadly similar purposes to the grants introduced under the 1989 Act. The principal difference is the move away from the obligation on the local authority to give grant assistance. The only mandatory grant retained is disabled facilities grant. *Annex F* gives general guidance on the operation of the main grants.

5.5   Discretionary Renovation Grants

- The new discretionary renovation grant provisions in section 12 of the 1996 Act replace the mandatory and discretionary renovation grants available under section 112, 113 and 115 of the 1989 Act. Grant is available to bring a property up to the fitness standard, to comply with a statutory notice under sections 189 or 190 of the Housing Act 1985 or for other works to a property additional to those required by enactment. These include works to provide adequate thermal insulation, fire precaution works (not required by an enactment) and to provide satisfactory internal arrangements. While no overall standard is prescribed for the grant assisted works, the works should be completed in a competent manner so that a property will be fit on their completion (section 13(5)). *See Annex G1.*

5.6   Mandatory and Discretionary Disabled Facilities Grants

- These are specifically intended to help disabled people. Mandatory grant is available for a broad range of essential adaptations and discretionary grant for works beyond the essential to make the dwelling suitable for the accommodation, welfare or employment of the disabled person. *See Chapter 7 and Annex I.*

5.7   Common Parts Grants

- A grant available for purposes similar to a renovation grant but for those parts of a building which comprise the common parts, as defined in section 58 of the 1996 Act. These include the structure and exterior of the building and the common facilities provided whether in the building or elsewhere. People who have a duty or a power to carry out or contribute to the cost of the works may apply. These may be the landlord and/or occupiers of one or more flats in the building. *See Annex G2.*

5.8   HMO Grants

- A grant for the improvement or repair of an HMO. Works can be to make the house suitable for the number of occupants (including fire safety works), to make the property comply with the fitness standard or to go beyond fitness such as works to improve thermal efficiency. *See Annex G3.*

5.9   Home Repair Assistance

- This builds on the former Minor Works Assistance. It is a discretionary form of assistance of either grant or materials available for the repair, improvement or adaptation of a house, mobile home or houseboat. Full eligibility is set out in section 76 and 77 of the 1996 Act. All elderly, infirm and disabled people, irrespective of income, and those on income related benefits are eligible, so long as they meet the other qualifying criteria. The assistance has fixed cash and time limits but where the applicant is eligible the assistance will meet 100% of the costs. *See Annex H.*

5.10 **Discretionary Main Grant for Conversions**

- A discretionary renovation or HMO grant may be given to convert a house or other building into a single or multiple dwellings, to extend into adjacent property where it helps meet an identified housing need by providing a larger or additional dwelling(s)or to convert a property into a house, flats or an HMO.

5.11 **Prior Qualifying Period**

5.11.1   The 1996 Act introduces a new prior qualifying period for renovation grants (ie not common parts grant, HMO grant, disabled facilities grant or, subject to the Secretary of State's power in section 10(5) of the 1996 Act, grants to landlords) to owner occupiers and tenants with a repairing obligation. It is currently set at 3 years, although this can be varied by the Secretary of State. It is the Department's intention that local authorities should ensure that the norm is that the condition is rigorously applied as grant assistance should primarily be for those who are already living in unfit property and unable to meet the cost of improvement. However local authorities do have discretion to disapply the condition where they consider there are **good** reasons why grant should be given even though the 3 year prior qualifying period cannot be met. Such circumstances might include:

- bringing empty property back into use;

- seeking to attract people to return to an area;

- the strategic importance of the property within the locality;

- the cost-effectiveness of giving grant assistance against the alternatives – eg. through rehousing or closure;

- assisting first time buyers where this is a particular local priority or a special initiative.

There is no prior qualifying period for:

- applications for conversion of a property;

- applications in renewal areas;

- applications for works to provide for means of escape in case of fire.

5.12 **Grant conditions and recovery**

5.12.1   There are a number of changes to the conditions that apply to grants once they have been approved. These are generally covered in sections 44 to 55 of the 1996 Act. The key change is the increase from 3 years to 5 years of the period in which grant is repayable if the property is disposed of. In addition there is no longer a taper with the full grant being recoverable at any point during the 5 year period. The grant condition period of 5 years also applies to other conditions ranging from intended occupancy through to conditions attached by local authorities to ensure wider benefits from the payment of grant.

- The new 5 year repayment period applies to all grants paid to owner occupiers and landlords except disabled facilities grants and home repair assistance. There are in place a wide range of relevant disposals that are exempt disposals (set out in section 54 of the Act). In addition local authorities have discretion in certain circumstances not to recover grant where there is a relevant disposal which is not an exempt disposal– ie. moving to be cared for or to care for a sick relative (a wider category than previously found in the section 121(7) of the 1989 Act). In addition there is a power for the Secretary of State to consider applications from local authorities to waive recovery of grant (sections 45 – 47 of the Act). It is not anticipated that there should be many such requests, and any which are submitted should be supported will a full justification and endorsed by the authority. However there is a general consent covering disposals arising from the need to move following acceptance of employment (where the disponor or his partner would otherwise become unemployed) and where a mortgagor exercises their power of sale (and the mortgage was entered into before the application for grant was made). For these cases local authorities will have the discretion to decide whether or not it is appropriate to recover grant (*see Annex J4*).

- There are a number of alterations related to change of circumstance of the applicant during the grant works. These include grant recovery where an applicant ceases to be a person entitled to grant before payment of grant (section 40); procedures for assessment of grant where there are changes in circumstance affecting the disabled occupant (section 41); cases in which grants may be recalculated, withheld or repaid (section 42); repayment where the applicant was found not to be entitled to grant (section 43) and possible courses of action where the grant applicant dies once works have commenced (section 56).

- Where an applicant has breached the owner occupation condition or letting condition a local authority has a duty to recover grant. However authorities will now have the power to waive recovery of grant or recover less where this is considered to be appropriate. The considerations that are relevant in considering whether to waive recovery in part or whole are likely to differ from case to case (sections 48-50).

- A new provision is included to allow local authorities to recover grant where the works for which grant are paid are the subject of an insurance or legal claim against another person. It is likely that works subject to such claims are those that a local authority would of necessity need to respond to quickly. This provision is intended to allow local authorities to recover all or part of the costs where another person may be liable and may eventually make payment to cover all or part of the cost (section 51). The Secretary of State has given a general consent enabling a local authority to impose such a condition requiring the applicant to take reasonable steps to pursue any relevant claim to which section 51 of the Act applies and to repay the grant, so far as is appropriate, out of the proceeds of such a claim. (*see Annex J 4*).

- Local authorities will be able to make the availability of grants payable under Chapter I of Part I of the Act subject to compliance with local conditions applied under section 52. There is a general consent at *Annex J4* which covers, among other things, notice of relevant disposal (whether or not the relevant disposal is exempt), nomination rights, property repair, insurance and recovery of specialised equipment – eg DFG adaptation equipment. The Department is keen to ensure that grant applicants are not discriminated against through unreasonable grant conditions and will require any application from an authority for an individual specific consent to be accompanied by a full justification.

- The conditions under which a local authority may waive renovation grant repayment have been relaxed further in relation to moving into care and moving to care for a sick relative. In addition the relevant disposals which are exempt from grant recovery have been extended to include disposals made as a result of orders made in proceedings relating to divorce, inheritance or children (section54(1)(c) and 54(3)), leasehold enfranchisement and a number of other disposals (section 54(1)(g) to (l)). The current exempt disposals between family members are still permitted. However for renovation grants the grant conditions will now remain in force in respect of the new owners (section 45(6)), preventing onward sale by the new owner free of the requirement to repay grant. This is similarly the case for breach of the owner occupation conditions (section 48(6)). It is considered that this will prevent an abuse that had been practised under the 1989 Act provisions.

5.13 Newly eligible applicants

5.13.1   Under the 1989 Act applicants were only eligible for assistance if they could satisfy the condition relating to their interest in the property (section 104). While this remains generally the case under the 1996 Act , the actual eligibility criteria are set out in the context of each grant and where necessary tenancy type. Further guidance on the eligibility criteria is given in *Annex F.*

5.13.2   The 1989 Act offered no assistance to mobile home owners, house boat owners and those who occupied their property under a trust for life or more than five years. However it is now recognised that occupants in these categories could be in need of assistance. Therefore the new home repair assistance will cover both these properties and tenancy arrangements. However a 3 year prior qualifying period will usually apply in respect of such applications reflecting the need for confirmation of long term parking, mooring, or residency arrangements. (see section 78(2)).

5.14 Fire Precaution Works

5.14.1   The purposes of renovation grants, common parts grants, HMO grants and home repair assistance have been extended to cover works to provide means of escape in case of fire and other fire precaution works.

5.15 Contractors Issues

5.15.1   At the outset of any grant assisted works it will be advisable for the local authority to make clear the nature of their involvement in seeing works completed. Grant applicants should be left in no doubt that it is they, and not the local authority, who are the clients in terms of managing the timetable and standard of the contract works. Where a local authority, home improvement agency or other party has been specifically engaged to provide an agency service for the grant applicant then they will fulfil the role as client's agent.

5.15.2   Greater powers have been provided to help local authorities in the processing of grant payments. Where a grant applicant has agreed that any payment may be made direct to the contractor this agreement can no longer be withdrawn at a later stage. A local authority may also notify a grant applicant of their intention to pay grant direct to the contractor. However this places a duty on the local authority to ensure that all parties are satisfied with the general standard of the work and that the contractor has not unfairly used his knowledge of payment direct from the local authority to undertake substandard work. Where the local authority is concerned about the standard of work they may choose to withhold payment or make payment to the grant applicant. Where payment is to be made direct to the grant applicant section 39(1)(b) provides for payment to be in a form made payable to the contractor.

5.15.3   Further guidance on contractors issues is given in *paragraphs 72 – 82 of Annex F.*

Chapter 6: Strategies into practice – private rented sector issues

6.0.1   Some of the poorest housing is privately rented and effective strategies for private sector renewal need to address problems identified among the private rented stock – particularly in relation to fitness and safety and in helping to bring empty properties back into use. Authorities' strategies should take into account, encourage and support the contribution that a healthy private rented sector can make in meeting local housing demand.

6.0.2   Local authorities have a **strategic and enabling role** with regard to the private rented sector. This may involve support to private landlords and tenants by helping people to find privately rented homes; promoting safety; and improving standards. It may also involve ensuring that the private rented sector contributes effectively to meeting demands for good quality accommodation in their areas. Provision of advice to landlords; the discretion to give renovation grants to landlords and tenants with repairing obligations; the effective administration of housing benefit; and the exercise of enforcement powers where necessary (*see paragraph 6.1.3 below*) are all part of this role. Authorities' policies towards the private rented sector need to be balanced as between the interests of landlords and tenants – for example in considering responsible management by landlords and in engendering tenant confidence.

6.0.3   The Housing Act 1996 (section 179) contains provisions to strengthen duties on local authorities to ensure that proper housing advice services are available in their areas. Together with the relaxation in the rules to make it easier for local authorities to provide rent guarantees (brought about through a general consent made in 1995 under sections 24 and 25 of the Local Government Act 1988), this means that authorities should in future work in closer partnership with private landlords.

6.0.4   This chapter focuses on those private rented sector issues that are likely to impact most on local authorities' private sector renewal activities.

6.1   Involving private landlords, tenants and others

6.1.1   Private landlords are a diverse group and if an authority wants to tackle condition problems within the private rented sector in its area it will need to recognise the different types of landlords – including management companies, universities and other partnerships – and understand their motivations and reasons for providing private rented accommodation. Different groups of landlords may need to be dealt with in different ways. Most private lettings are owned by landlords who do not let property as a full time occupation. The majority of landlords are not aware that local authorities can provide assistance in helping them improve the properties they own, and those that are aware of the grant system may lack information on what it can provide. Landlords owning only one or two properties are likely to need more practical help, support and guidance than portfolio landlords. But local authorities also need to work closely and constructively with portfolio landlords and particularly with those who have a large number of properties in one area and as such play an important role as accommodation providers in the area.

6.1.2   In involving private landlords local authorities may also find it helpful to refer to two publications arising out of DOE commissioned research – "*In from the Cold – Working with the Private Landlord*" (*DOE, June 1995 – see bibliography for availability*) and "*Private Landlords in England*" (*HMSO, 1996*). Involvement should not be confined solely to landlords. The role that tenants, and voluntary organisations representing them, can play and the contribution they can make also needs to be taken into account.

6.1.3   It is important that authorities deal with landlords and tenants consistently and fairly when identifying the work which they require to be carried out. While enforcement will have a role to play in a strategic approach it should generally be viewed as a last resort. Guidance on the enforcement actions and options open to authorities – including the power to charge for enforcement action; pre-formal enforcement action procedures; and the deferred action notice option introduced by the 1996 Act – is given in the code of guidance for dealing with unfit premises in *Annex B*.

6.1.4   Effective strategic work in the private rented sector requires good information on, and communication with, landlords and tenants. A survey of landlords is one way of obtaining information. Links with tenants and voluntary organisations representing them will be another important source of information. But whatever information gathering process is used it is important to understand what role locally the private rented sector is playing in order to consider where to encourage change and investment. This will then allow a dialogue with providers which can lead to an effective landlords' forum. A forum established without such understanding and without contact with many providers is unlikely to be effective. An effective landlords' forum can:

- be the vehicle by which a private rented sector strategy is developed;

- provide a regular means of consultation;

- improve and develop services to landlords and tenants;

- promote and encourage participation in schemes to renovate the private rented sector.

6.2   **Houses in Multiple Occupation**

6.2.1   The majority of houses in multiple occupation (HMOs) are in the private rented sector where they provide an important source of rented accommodation for low income households. However, some of the worst private sector housing conditions can be found in HMOs including disrepair, inadequate basic amenities and means of escape from fire, and the living arrangements in HMOs place increased demands on the management of such properties.

6.2.2   Provisions in Part II of the Housing Act 1996 are directed towards improving health and safety standards in HMOs, by giving landlords clearer responsibilities and local authorities stronger powers to take action. The provisions which are expected to come into force during 1997 will:

- **place a new duty on HMO landlords** to ensure that their properties are safe – based on advice in an HMO Code Of Practice – or risk prosecution with a fine up to £5,000 (provision for this will not be commenced until after the new Code of Practice has been finalised – *see paragraph 6.2.4 below*) ;

- **provide for a revised HMO registration scheme** which allows local authorities to adopt one of two model registration schemes. A scheme with control provisions will enable an authority to refuse to register any property where conditions are substandard. Authorities will be able, with the Secretary of State's agreement, to depart from the model schemes and in particular to adopt registration schemes with special control provisions allowing them to close down HMOs if they cause a nuisance or annoyance to the neighbourhood. They will also be able to prevent new HMOs from opening if they would be detrimental to an area;

- **allow authorities to charge HMO landlords** registration fees, and fees for re-registration after five years, to help them meet the costs of HMO enforcement activity. The maximum fine for not complying with a registration scheme containing control provisions will be increased to £5,000;

- **allow authorities to recover from HMO landlords** the reasonable administrative expenses – up to a maximum amount to be prescribed by order – they incur in serving an enforcement notice under section 352 of the Housing Act 1985 to make an HMO fit for the number of occupants;

- **extend local authorities' mandatory duty to ensure there are adequate means of escape from fire in larger HMOs** to include the provision of other fire safety precautions. The duty will be extended through secondary legislation, following further consultation over its scope; and

- **protect HMO landlords from being forced to undertake works twice** because standards have been revised. Local authorities will be unable to serve a second HMO enforcement notice, requiring works to be carried out to make a property fit for the number of occupants, within a five year period in respect of the same requirement unless they consider that there has been a change of circumstances in relation to the premises.

6.2.3   Some local authorities have developed strategies for tackling HMOs in response to earlier guidance from the Department in circular 12/93 (*HMOs – Guidance to local housing authorities on managing the stock in their area*). The circular provides comprehensive guidance on developing and implementing strategies specifically for HMOs, including guidance on:

- identifying and locating HMOs;

- the interface of planning policies with those for HMOs;

- risk assessment to identify priorities for scarce resources;

- enforcement action on HMOs.

Authorities should also take account of the findings of research commissioned by the Department to identify and evaluate good practice in developing and implementing strategies for dealing with HMOs – *Houses in multiple occupation : establishing effective local authority strategies – DOE 1996 – see bibliography for availability.*

6.2.4   Under powers in section 77 of the Housing Act 1996 the Secretary of State has power to approve Codes of Practice in relation to any policy issue on HMOs. A Code of Practice is planned for 1997 aimed primarily at updating the standards of fitness for HMOs currently set out in DOE circular 12/92 (*Houses in Multiple Occupation : Guidance to local housing authorities on standards of fitness under section 352 of the Housing Act 1985*).

6.3   **Role of renovation grants**

6.3.1   Guidance on renovation grants is given in *Chapter 5 and Annexes F to H*. This should be read in place of the guidance on grants in section 5 of circular 12/93. The majority of landlords are able to fund repairs to the properties they own but some have difficulties with wider improvements. Grants can be a way of encouraging the landlord to invest, resulting in higher standards achieved than would otherwise have been realised.

6.3.2   It will be for authorities to decide on the level and proportion of grant they wish to make available to private landlords – *see also paragraph 6.5.2*. In considering grant assistance to landlords, authorities will need to consider the balance between the landlord investment such assistance might stimulate, and the scope for matching funding through the resources which landlords are able to bring to bear to improve their properties. The generally higher levels of unfitness in the private rented sector are likely to mean that improvement costs will be higher. A factor to consider may therefore be the financial equation between work costs and reasonable rents and whether grant assistance would help in achieving viable improvement.

6.4 Empty housing

6.4.1   Across England over 4% of housing is vacant, about 800,000 homes. Around 700,000 of these are in the private sector. But the total number of vacant dwellings in the private sector exaggerates the problem. Research has identified two types of vacancy:

- **"transitional vacants"** – that is, those properties which are re-occupied relatively quickly and are necessary for the mobility of the housing market; and

- **"problematic vacants"** – that is, those properties which are inactive in the housing market, often in poor condition and empty for a long time.

6.4.2   There are about 250,000 problematic vacants in the private sector. It is these which require concerted action in order to bring them back into use more quickly – see *Chapter 4*. While the majority of empty property may not be in the private rented sector, research has shown that properties which had been privately rented were more likely to become vacant and to remain empty for a longer period than those which had been owner occupied. There is also more scope for bringing property back into use temporarily through the private rented sector.

6.4.3   In targeting action and assistance to help bring empty properties back into use, local authorities need to consider carefully the balance between empty property that has previously been let in the private rented sector – and the need here to safeguard against the risk of properties being left to fall into disrepair and become vacant in the knowledge that assistance may be available – and assistance to bring previously unlet empty property into the private rented sector. Further guidance on points to consider in grant-aiding the renovation of empty property is given in *Annex F*.

6.4.4   Local authorities are recommended to develop effective empty property strategies for their areas as an important element of their overall local housing strategies and housing investment programmes. The Department is supporting the Empty Homes Agency which has been established to provide authorities with detailed guidance on the development of empty property strategies and examples of best practice. Many authorities are working closely with the Agency. The Agency can be contacted at 195-197 Victoria Street, London SW1E 5NE (tel: 0171 828 6288).

6.5 Role of private sector renewal

6.5.1   Local authorities should consider ways in which private sector renewal mechanisms might be employed to help tackle the problem of empty housing in their areas, especially in the private rented sector. Private sector renewal mechanisms are likely to play a particularly important role in empty property strategies for tackling "problematic vacants" since these properties are most likely to be in a poor or deteriorating condition. But there does need to be a clear correlation with housing needs in the particular area.

6.5.2   Private sector mechanisms might be used:

- **through discretionary renovation grants to landlords.** These:

  can help speed up the reuse of empty property in unfit or poor condition where lack of resources on the part of landlords is a significant barrier;

may prove a more flexible and direct means for bringing empty properties back into use than, for example, Housing Associations as Managing Agents (HAMA) plus or short life grants; authorities should additionally consider the desirability of seeking nomination rights and other conditions attached to grant; the attachment of conditions to grant aid can provide an effective way of increasing its strategic effectiveness;

- **through grant-aided initiatives linked to leasing and management schemes.** For example, bringing empty property back into use through a local authority or housing association intermediary who leases or manages the property with associated funding to repair or convert for reuse;

- **through housing investment trusts,** which offer a new way of bringing in private finance to secure the provision of private rented property, and joint venture partnerships;

- **through effective use of enforcement and other powers available to authorities under housing and environmental health legislation** – particularly where non-enforcement avenues have been tried and failed. Compulsory purchase (or threat of compulsory purchase) is an option which may need to be considered.

- **in combination with other measures** directed towards bringing empty properties back into use, converting properties into residential use, or as a last resort to acquire, demolish and redevelop.

Chapter 7: Strategies into practice – community care and special needs

7.1 Policy on housing for disabled people

7.1.1   It is a main aim of the Government's policy for housing and community care that, wherever possible, care and support should be provided to people in their existing homes. Suitably designed or adapted housing along with appropriate health and social care services will be key components in enabling frail elderly and disabled people to remain living in their own homes as comfortably and as independently as possible.

7.1.2   As part of this policy, it is important that local authorities encourage private sector developers **to build housing accessible to disabled people.** But, the adaptation, where needed, of existing dwellings occupied by elderly and disabled people who have special needs, is also important to the success of community care. The availability of financial help towards such works is therefore part of the wider provision of support given to those who need it.

7.1.3   As part of their role in preparing plans for the provision of community care services in their areas, social services authorities are required to consult local housing authorities in so far as these plans affect or are affected by the availability of suitable housing in their area. In assessing individuals' need for community care services, social services authorities must involve housing authorities if there appears to be a housing need. This need includes adaptations, repairs or improvements to allow people to stay in their existing homes.

7.1.4   In most cases this package of services will be based on a person's existing home. However, in some cases alternative accommodation may be the only available option.

7.2 Private sector housing renewal strategies

7.2.1   Private sector housing renewal strategies developed in the context of the Housing Investment Programme, will need to take account of the wider pattern of increasing demand for disabled facilities grants (DFGs) across the local authority area arising from community care plans as well as the likely demand for individual grants. This will include disabled people requiring help with adaptations which may be additional to any wider services of care and support given to elderly and disabled people under community care. In planning its strategy therefore, an authority should be looking to work up clear and identifiable proposals within its overall strategy for private housing renewal, for dealing with demand across the local authority area, including proposals for prioritising between competing demand for grant at the local level. The strategy should reflect the separate funding for private sector renewal and disabled facilities grant.

7.2.2   Housing authorities and social services authorities should co-operate fully in the planning and assessment procedures, bringing in other providers of housing in the public and voluntary sectors where they can make a valuable contribution to meeting need. Such close co-operation and liaison will ensure that there is consistency between housing strategies and community care plans. Where appropriate, consultation should include neighbouring authorities or regional bodies so that a strategic pattern of provision can be established across a wide area. Guidance on the role of housing authorities and social services departments in implementing community care policy is given in DOE Circular 10/92 (Department of Health Circular LAC(92)12).

7.3 Financial help with adaptations

7.3.1 For those such as frail elderly or disabled people who live in homes in need of improvement or adaptations because of their special needs and who also need help in meeting the costs of the required works, Government financial assistance should be available at a level reflecting assessed need. Through the help provided by housing and social services authorities, many people are able to remain in their homes in comfort and remaining independent, where this is their wish and where it is reasonable and practicable for them to do so.

7.4 Help with adaptations through social services departments and housing associations

7.4.1 The existing statutory duties of social services departments under Section 2(1)(e) of Chronically Sick and Disabled Persons Act 1970 to provide assistance to disabled people needing home adaptations and other facilities designed to secure the greater safety, comfort and convenience of a disabled person, remain. Such help is normally available in the form of financial assistance, including loans, to assist with equipment in the home but, under these powers, social services authorities have a duty to assist disabled people who, because of their particular circumstances, cannot afford the assessed contribution towards the cost of works for which a DFG has been approved by the housing authority. Resources are also available to fund adaptation work either from housing associations or from the Housing Corporation where the adaptation is required for a property in that sector and local authorities may wish, where appropriate, to ensure that this option is considered.

7.5 Disabled facilities grants

7.5.1 Where people need adaptations so that they may gain better access to and move around their home freely or use the essential facilities within the home so that they can manage as independently as possible, help is available from housing authorities through **disabled facilities grants (DFGs)**. *Annex I* provides guidance on the operation of disabled facilities grants. Since they were introduced in 1990 as part of the house renovation grant system under Part VIII of the Local Government and Housing Act 1989, DFGs have made a valuable contribution in meeting these special needs particularly in the context of the Government's policies for Care in the Community.

7.5.2 The prominent purpose for which **mandatory** disabled facilities grant is given is that of **access and provision: this includes access into and around the dwelling, to essential facilities and amenities within the dwelling and the provision of certain facilities within the dwelling, such as a making the building safe, where this is the only or most suitable option**. The purposes for which **discretionary** disabled facilities grants are available are for works **to make the dwelling suitable for the accommodation, welfare or employment of the disabled person. Discretionary grant is also available where a local authority decides to meet the cost of works which are mandatory in nature but in excess of the grant limit for mandatory asssitance.** Detailed guidance on the eligible works qualifying for mandatory and discretionary grant is given in *Annex I*.

7.5.3 The means testing of all applicants for DFG ensures that the available resources are effectively targeted on those in the greatest need of help in paying for adaptations and that those who are better able to contribute to the cost of works should do so. The means test for DFGs differs from that applied to applicants for renovation grants in that it is applied only to the disabled occupant and their spouse or partner and not to other members of the household. The disabled occupant may or may not be the applicant. In the case of adaptations for a disabled child, the test will take into account the resources of the parents (or relevant person where the child does not live with his parents). Guidance on the workings of the means test and details of the prescribed application forms for disabled facilities grant is given in *Annex J2*.

7.5.4   Local authorities have discretion to notify the grant applicant that payment of their mandatory disabled facilities grant will not be made until a date not more than 12 months following the date of the application (section 36 of the 1996 Act). This should enable authorities to manage their resources better between financial years by prioritising cases. However, this power should be used only in exceptional circumstances and not where the applicant would suffer undue hardship. There is no expectation that the contractor would complete the work in advance of the date the grant has been scheduled for payment. The 12 month period for completion of grant assisted works is not affected although the date from which this runs will be the date in the notification of the authority's decision. Guidance on the particular circumstances where authorities may consider the use of the delayed payment option is given in *Annex I*.

7.6   Funding of adaptations

7.6.1   Under arrangements agreed between the Secretaries of State for Health and the Environment, help with equipment which can be easily installed and removed with little or no modification to the dwelling, is normally the responsibility of the social services authority under its responsibilities under the 1970 Act with larger adaptations requiring structural modification of a dwelling normally coming within the scope of a disabled facilities grant. However, it is for housing authorities and social services authorities between them to decide how the particular adaptation needs of a disabled person should be funded. In taking such decisions authorities should not forget that **the needs of the disabled occupant are paramount within the framework of what can be offered.**

7.6.2   Close cooperation between the respective authorities is vital to ensure that those requiring help in paying for works for essential adaptations to meet their special needs, are given the most efficient and effective support.

7.7   Co-operation and collaboration between housing and social services authorities

7.7.1   Section 24(3) of the 1996 Act imposes a duty on local housing authorities to consult social services authorities in coming to their view on whether the proposed works for which an application for a disabled facilities grant has been made, are **"necessary"** and **"appropriate"** to meet the needs of the disabled occupant. However, housing authorities themselves must decide whether those works are **"reasonable"** and **"practicable"** having regard to the age and condition of the building.

7.7.2   Within their statutory responsibilities, housing and social services authorities are expected to co-operate fully in carrying out the assessments under section 24(3) for the purposes of meeting the needs of disabled people in their area. In many areas, efficient and effective systems of consultation between the respective authorities have been developed locally in meeting these statutory responsibilities. This not only enables people needing help to receive the best possible service but also ensures that there are common practices for consultation with all those involved. It also ensures that there is wide consistency across the area covered by individual social services authorities.

7.7.3   Detailed guidance on the procedures for collaboration between the respective authorities and on the referral and assessment procedures of those seeking help through a DFG, is given in *Annex I*. It also provides examples of good practice which authorities might wish to consider in implementing the DFG provisions.

7.8   Role of home repair assistance

7.8.1   Authorities should consider making full use of home repair assistance (HRA) in providing help with the costs of small works of improvement or adaptation to a dwelling for applicants who meet the eligibility criteria. In particular authorities should make use of the discretionary assistance in cases where small but essential works to a property, including a mobile home, will enable the applicant to remain living there or to enable an elderly or disabled person to move into a household to be cared for. In such cases a mainstream renovation grant or DFG might be considered excessive especially where the costs can be contained within the limits for HRA prescribed in the Disabled Facilities Grants and Home Repair Assistance (Maximum Amounts) Order 1996.

7.8.2   Advice on the circumstances in which home repair assistance might be given for small works of repair or adaptation for an elderly or disabled occupant is given in *Annex H* which also contains guidance on the operation of home repair assistance.

7.9   Role of home improvement agencies/other agency services

7.9.1   Home improvement agencies (HIAs), often known as "Care and Repair" or "Staying Put" agencies, provide a valuable contribution in assisting vulnerable groups, mainly elderly people, people on low incomes and those with **disabilities**, to carry out repairs, improvements and adaptations to their homes. This makes a significant contribution to the effective delivery of the Government's housing and community care policies by enabling people to remain living for longer in their own homes, within their own communities. Agencies have been set up by a variety of organisations, often housing associations and charitable groups: some also operate independently. Many local authorities have set up their own arrangements to perform a similar service for those seeking grant from the authority. Local authorities can approach Care & Repair, the national co-ordinating body for home improvement agencies, for independent advice on establishing and running home improvement agency services.

7.9.2   HIAs provide a comprehensive home improvement service, helping their clients through the administrative process of deciding what works are needed, advise on and help organise finance for works including grants, organising the building work and seeing that the works are completed satisfactorily. This helps to alleviate the worry and disruption many people face in arranging the works and in applying for grants. HIAs may charge a fee for these services and, where they do, so grant may be given towards these costs (see service charges SI–Housing Renewal Grants (Services and Charges Order 1996).

KEY POINTS:

- housing strategies to include provision for adaptation needs.
- DFG contributes to community care.
- close liaison and co-operation between housing and social services is essential in meeting need.
- home repair assistance is a quick means of giving help with adaptations.
- HIAs provide valuable service to elderly and disabled people seeking grants and/or help with works or **adaptations**.

Chapter 8: Financial matters

8.1 Exchequer Contributions

Parts I and IV of the Housing Grants, Construction and Regeneration Act 1996 and Part VIII of the Local Government and Housing Act 1989

8.1.1 Section 92 of the 1996 Act allows the Secretary of State to pay contributions towards local authorities' expenditure incurred under Part I of the Act and by virtue of The Housing Grants, Construction and Regeneration Act 1996 (Commencement No. 2 and Revocation, Savings, Supplementary and Transitional Provisions) Order 1996 contributions can be paid in respect of expenditure under Part VIII of the Local Government and Housing Act 1989. Section 139 of the 1996 Act allows contributions to be paid in respect of relocation grants under Part IV of the Act. The present contribution rate is 60% towards most types of expenditure. The Secretary of State reserves the right from time to time to determine a different rate or rates of contribution.

8.1.2 Expenditure for these purposes includes:

- the amounts paid in grants;

- expenditure incurred by local authorities in relation to works carried out in group repair schemes;

- expenditure incurred by authorities in carrying out duties on behalf of the grant applicant, which would otherwise be the applicant's responsibility (but not in carrying out their statutory duties);

- Home Improvement Agencies' costs attributable to grant works under Part I of the 1996 Act.

8.1.3 Expenditure which does not attract contribution includes:

- local authorities' administrative costs relating to grants or group repair schemes, where these form part of the authorities' duties in administering the scheme. The costs incurred in administering the grant system are already taken into account in calculating the other services block of the Revenue Support Grant (RSG).

- contributions towards expenditure incurred by the local authority as an unassisted participant in a group repair scheme.

8.2 Relocation Grants

8.2.1 *Paragraphs 3.23.1 to 3.23.3 of Chapter 3* provide general information about relocation grants. Regulations to provide for these grants will be made in the new year and be accompanied by detailed guidance on the use of relocation grants and the financial provisions relating to them.

8.3 Contributions towards other private sector renewal expenditure

8.3.1 *Slum clearance*

8.3.2 Where local authorities make a loss on expenditure relating to their slum clearance functions, the Secretary of State will pay a contribution of 60% of the authorities' net loss. Where authorities incur a surplus in any financial year, they are required to repay to the Secretary of State an amount equal to 60% of the surplus.

8.3.3   The grant determination is at *Annex E2* and payments will be made as described in *paragraphs 8.11.1 to 8.12.6.*

8.4   Environmental works

8.4.1   The Secretary of State may pay a contribution of 50% towards expenditure incurred by authorities in carrying out environmental improvement works in a renewal area declared under Part VII of the Local Government and Housing Act 1989. Details of the payments and conditions applying are given in the determination at *Annex C1.*

8.5   Improvement for sale

8.5.1   The Local Authorities Improvement for Sale scheme (LAIFS) allows authorities to bring dwellings which are in need of substantial repair and improvement back into use. It can include both houses and flats and applies to properties already owned by the authority and to those purchased specifically for the scheme.

- Exchequer contribution is payable towards any net loss incurred by an authority in carrying out a LAIFS scheme.

- Details of the scheme and subsidy levels are given in DOE circulars 20/80 and 18/81.

8.6   The 1989 Act financial regime

8.6.1   Although the Secretary of State's power to pay contributions is discretionary, under the 1989 Act regime payment will normally be made in all instances where the statutory requirements for the grant have been met. The system is as follows:

- contributions are paid as Specified Capital Grant(SCG);

- payment is based on authorities' actual expenditure, rather than on the amount allocated to authorities for the year in their Housing Investment Programmes (HIP);

- Supplementary Credit Approvals (SCAs) are issued up to the level of authorities' HIP allocation, where needed, to compensate for the statutory requirement to reduce relevant credit approvals to match the amount of SCG received.

8.6.2   This system will remain for all expenditure until the end of March 1997 and, beyond that date, for all expenditure in relation to mandatory and discretionary disabled facilities grants.

8.6.3   Claiming procedures are described in *paragraphs 8.11.1 to 8.12.6.*

8.7   The 1996 Act financial regime

8.7.1   Except for disabled facilities grants, the payment of contributions (including those for slum clearance) will change from 1 April 1997. From that date:

- contributions will be paid as a Specific Grant to be known as private sector renewal support grant (ie a cash grant with **no** requirement attached to make matching reductions in credit approvals) ;

- this grant will be payable where the statutory requirements for the grant have been met but only up to the amount allocated to each authority for the year as part of their HIP allocation;

- No SCAs will be needed as there will be no requirement to make a matching reduction in credit approvals.

Application to the Secretary of State for a higher rate of contribution in respect of renewal areas

8.7.2   A case for a higher rate of contribution may be made in respect of renewal areas:

- where the local authority considers that the standard rate of contribution will be inadequate, bearing in mind the action they propose to take and the area;

- before declaration of the renewal area;

- where accompanied by:

(a)   a full justification of why the higher rate of contribution is necessary;

(b)   detailed costings and specifications of the proposed works; and

(c)   a map on which the proposed renewal area is defined and the report referred to in section 89 of the 1989 Act.

(*See "Directions, Specifications , Determinations, Requirements and Conditions Imposed Under Part VII of the Local Government and Housing Act 1989" at Annex C1*)

Each application will be considered on its merits. A higher rate of contribution will only be given where the Secretary of State is satisfied that the particular renewal area merits exceptional treatment. Grant assisted expenditure would still have to remain within the HIP allocation cash limit.

Cases in which contributions are not payable towards expenditure which would normally be eligible

8.7.3   The Secretary of State will not normally pay contributions towards:

- expenditure on disabled facilities grants for an authority's own tenants;

- any grant expenditure which does not accord with the grants legislation;

- any expenditure in excess of the notified allocation.

Disabled facilities grants for local authority tenants

8.7.4   Although local authority short term tenants are not eligible to apply for most grants under the Act, they may apply for disabled facilities grants, in the same way as any other tenant.

8.7.5   However, in the case of their own tenants, local authorities will be expected to finance expenditure by the following means:

- from their own capital receipts;

- by means of direct contributions from revenue;

- to the extent that credit approvals are used, there will be a pound for pound increase in the amount charged to the Housing Revenue Account (HRA) (or a reduction in the amount debited from the Account);

- provided that the local authority's ceiling for credit approvals eligible for HRA subsidy, as shown in the subsidy determination, is not exceeded, the net additional cost will be reflected in the calculation of HRA subsidy payable to the authority.

8.8 **Record of contributions**

8.8.1   The payment of Exchequer contributions will be subject to such conditions as to records, certificates, audit or otherwise as the Secretary of State, with Treasury consent, may impose.

8.8.2   The relevant conditions are set out in the grant determination at Annex J3.

8.9 **Claiming Procedures**

8.9.1   Payments will be made in advance, in ten instalments (May – February), based on authorities' first and second advance claims for housing subsidy (the FH claim forms). Payments made will be adjusted as necessary on receipt of the authorities' final advance and audited claims.

8.9.2   Entitlement to Exchequer subsidy is conditional upon submission of an audited final claim. The Secretary of State reserves the right to suspend or abate on-account payments in respect of any particular claim where the conditions of payment of contribution have not been met and he considers it reasonable to do so.

8.9.3   Supplementary credit approvals (SCAs) are also issued to authorities under the 1989 Act; they will continue to be issued for all types of grant expenditure up to an authority's guideline allocation until the end of the 1996/97 and for expenditure on DFGs in subsequent years. These compensate for the reduction in relevant credit approvals authorities are required to make on receipt of specified capital grant(SCG).

8.9.4   SCAs are issued in two tranches:

- the first tranche is issued by Government Offices at the beginning of the financial year. This tranche will be half the amount of the authority's guideline HIP allocation or half the first advance claim for SCG. The second tranche is issued towards the end of the calendar year, following receipt of authorities' second advance claims and final claims for the previous year.

- SCAs issued are tied to authorities' entitlement to SCG, taking account of payments in advance for the current financial year and any repayment due in respect of advance payments for previous years;

- entitlement to SCAs will be limited to the authorities' HIP allocations, although any SCA entitlement surrendered by authorities not likely to use their full entitlement will be redistributed by the Government Offices to authorities with a need for additional SCAs;

- where an authority does not receive sufficient SCA to cover the required reduction in credit approvals, the reduction must be made from other relevant credit approvals and, if the authority cannot meet the requirement in the year in which it receives the SCG, the requirement will carry over as a debt against the first available credit approvals in the following year. For debt-free authorities, the requirement will carry forward indefinitely but, should the authority have a need for credit approvals at any time in the future, the debt will have first claim against any credit approvals received;

- this requirement will not affect the credit ceilings of authorities who are debt-free or compromise their debt-free status. Procedures under section 57 of the Local Government and Housing Act 1989 are distinct from "use" of a credit approval as set out under section 56, which is what increases the credit ceiling;

8.10 Procedures for payment of private sector renewal support grant.

8.10.1   From 1 April 1997, payment in relation to all eligible expenditure, except mandatory and discretionary disabled facilities grants, will be paid as specific grant and will be cash limited.

8.10.2   Payment will be made on account, as at present, based on authorities' first and second advance claims for the year and adjusted to take account of the advance final and audited claims for the year.

8.10.3   Where an authority's advance final or audited final claim shows that there has been an overclaim of on-account payments for that year, an adjustment will be made to reduce the next payment due to the authority to effect recovery.

8.10.4   Where the final claims show an underpayment of specific grant for that year, any additional payment made to the authority will have to be accommodated within that year's grant ceiling. Where an authority has surrendered part of its grant entitlement the additional payment will only be paid up to the level of the revised ceiling. In any other case, no additional payment can be made.

8.10.5   Where an authority's expenditure is such that the Exchequer contribution would exceed the authority's specific grant allocation for the year, unless specific grant surrendered by other authorities is available for redistribution by the Government Office, the authority will have to meet the full cost of the expenditure. No further contribution will be available.

8.10.6   Grant determinations giving further details of payments and conditions are at *Annex J3*.

8.11 Repayment of Grant

8.11.1   Where there has been a breach of the grant conditions, except in certain circumstances prescribed in the legislation, authorities are required to demand repayment of grant from the grant recipient. This applies to grants approved under the 1996 Act or under the Local Government and Housing Act 1989.

8.11.2   On recovery of the grant, authorities are required to repay the Exchequer contribution (according to the percentage payable at the time the contribution was claimed). This will usually be 60%, the contribution rate introduced in 1993.

8.11.3   The total amount recovered during the year should be entered in the authority's final FH claim form for the year and will be deducted from payments made to the authority.

8.12 Residual payments in relation to grants approved under Part XV of the Housing Act 1985

8.12.1 Contributions will continue to be paid in respect of completed grants under this Part of the 1985 Act but the method of claiming will depend on the date of approval of the grant.

- For grants approved on or after 15 June 1989, Exchequer contribution should be claimed as a capital grant payment on authorities' FH claim forms.

- For grants approved before this date, claims should be submitted on claim form FED 0867A. These forms are available from the Department of the Environment, Housing Renewal Policy Division. A guidance note on claiming Exchequer subsidy, giving the address from which application forms may be obtained, is at *Annex J7*. Payment will be made as a commuted sum, based on notional loan charges over a twenty year period.

- Grant recoveries, where grant was approved before 15 June 1989, should also be entered on form FED 0867A. A repayment of part of the commuted sum paid to the authority will be required, based on the amount recovered and the number of years and months still outstanding of the twenty year loan period at the time of the grant recovery.

Annexes

Annex A

HOUSING FITNESS STANDARD

1.INTRODUCTION

1.1.   This annex gives guidance on the housing fitness standard which is set out in section 604 of the 1985 Act as amended by paragraph 83 of Schedule 9 to the 1989 Act. It aims to assist local housing authorities in determining whether a dwelling house is or is not unfit in accordance with the standard.

1.2.   This guidance is advisory: local housing authorities are asked to have regard to it when applying the standard but must form their opinion in the light of all relevant circumstances. Statutory guidance on the action to take in dealing with unfit premises is given in *Annex B*.

1.3.   In this annex, unless the context requires otherwise: 'the standard' means the housing fitness standard; and 'the authority' means the local housing authority.

1.4.   The guidance in this annex, as issued in 1996, reproduces with some minor up-dating revisions the guidance in Annex A to DOE circular 6/90.

1.5.   The Government has announced that it will launch a review of the fitness standard before the end of 1996. The review will be carried out in consultation with the local authority associations and other bodies such as the Chartered Institute of Environmental Health, and is expected to be completed within about 18 months. If appropriate, a revision of this guidance will be published in the light of the conclusions from the review.

2.   THE FITNESS STANDARD

STATUTORY STANDARD – Housing Act 1985 as amended by Local Government and Housing Act 1989

"Fitness for human habitation.

604.   (1) Subject to subsection (2) below, a dwelling-house is fit for human habitation for the purposes of this Act unless, in the opinion of the local housing authority, it fails to meet one or more of the requirements in paragraphs (a) to (i) below and, by reason of that failure, is not reasonably suitable for occupation,–

    (a)   it is structurally stable;

    (b)   it is free from serious disrepair;

    (c)   it is free from dampness prejudicial to the health of the occupants (if any);

    (d)   it has adequate provision for lighting, heating and ventilation;

    (e)   it has an adequate piped supply of wholesome water;

    (f)   there are satisfactory facilities in the dwelling-house for the preparation and cooking of food, including a sink with a satisfactory supply of hot and cold water;

    (g)   it has a suitably located water-closet for the exclusive use of the occupants (if any);

(h) it has, for the exclusive use of the occupants (if any), a suitably located fixed bath or shower and wash-hand basin each of which is provided with a satisfactory supply of hot and cold water; and

(i) it has an effective system for the draining of foul, waste and surface water.

and any reference to a dwelling-house being unfit for human habitation shall be construed accordingly.

(2)   Whether or not a dwelling-house which is a flat satisfies the requirements in subsection (1), it is unfit for human habitation for the purposes of this Act if, in the opinion of the local housing authority, the building or a part of the building outside the flat fails to meet one or more of the requirements in paragraphs (a) to (e) below and, by reason of that failure, the flat is not reasonably suitable for occupation,–

(a) the building or part is structurally stable;

(b) it is free from serious disrepair;

(c) it is free from dampness;

(d) it has adequate provision for ventilation; and

(e) it has an effective system for the draining of foul, waste and surface water.

(3)   Subsection (1) applies in relation to a house in multiple occupation with the substitution of a reference to the house for any reference to a dwelling-house.

(4)   Subsection (2) applies in relation to a flat in multiple occupation with the substitution for any reference to a dwelling-house which is a flat of a reference to the flat in multiple occupation.

(5)   The Secretary of State may by order amend the provisions of subsection (1) or subsection (2) in such manner and to such extent as he considers appropriate; and any such order–

(a) may contain such transitional and supplementary provisions as the Secretary of State considers expedient; and

(b) shall be made by statutory instrument which shall be subject to annulment in pursuance of a resolution of either House of Parliament."

Background Note

(i)   In deciding whether a dwelling-house is or is not unfit for human habitation, discomfort, inconvenience and inefficiency may be relevant factors but the primary concern should lie in safeguarding the health and safety of any occupants.

(ii)   The extent to which a building presents a risk to health and safety is governed by the nature of the defects present. However, the probability of accidents or damage to health may be increased either by the severity or extent of those defects. The location of defects may also be a material factor, as in some cases, may the persistence or duration of defects.

(iii)   As a matter of general principle, the fitness standard should be related to the physical characteristics and condition of the dwelling-house and not to the particular current occupants or way that the house or flat is currently occupied. Thus, fitness under section 604 does not mean that the dwelling-house is necessarily 'fit' for the present type or number of occupants. For example, it may be fit, but wholly unsuitable for a particular disabled person or be statutorily overcrowded and have unlit and unventilated spaces currently used as bedrooms.

(iv)   That said, to be fit for human habitation a dwelling-house must by definition, be reasonably suitable for occupation effectively for all household sizes and types of potential occupant who might reasonably be expected to occupy such property. Of the latter, the elderly and young children tend to spend the greatest time in and around the home children are typically the most vulnerable to health and safety risks, not only because of their greater susceptibility, but because they tend to spend the greatest time in and around the home.

Fitness standard - guidance note

2.1   A dwelling-house is unfit for human habitation if, in the authority's view, it fails to meet any one of the requirements specified in subsection 604(1) or, where it is a flat, it so fails to meet subsection 604(1) or the building or a part of the building outside the flat fails to meet any one of the requirements in subsection 604(2), and because of the failure to meet that particular requirement, it is not reasonably suitable for occupation.

2.2   In deciding whether a dwelling-house is or is not unfit, the authority should determine for each of the statutory requirements in turn, whether or not the dwelling-house is reasonably suitable for occupation because of a failure of that particular matter. In reaching this decision, the authority is asked to have regard to the general guidance note below and, specifically, to the note on each particular requirement. However, in addressing each requirement, the list of items for consideration and the advice given in respect of defects mentioned under each section are not exclusive and all other relevant items will need to be considered.

2.3   The order of sections reflects the general need to maintain a conventional inspection procedure, notwithstanding the determination of each requirement individually. Defective items are frequently inter-related and the consideration of, for example, repair and the cause or reason for any disrepair may assist in identifying a failure to meet other requirements, particularly structural stability and dampness. Consequently, a thorough internal and external inspection of the whole dwelling-house and building should normally be undertaken, before determining which of the individual requirements meet or fail the standard.

2.4   In assessing fitness for human habitation, consideration should be given to the condition of all rooms and spaces in the dwelling-house and of all parts of the fabric of the building and of the fixtures which, were the accommodation rented, would normally be provided by a landlord.

2.5   For the purposes of subsection 604(1), a dwelling-house is defined as including "any yard, garden, outhouses and appurtenances belonging to it or usually enjoyed with it... " Although it is not expected that the poor condition of outbuildings, of boundary walls and of the surfaces of yards and paths will normally be sufficient, in the absence of defects in the house itself, to render it unfit, the condition of these items should also be taken into account in assessing the unfitness of the dwelling-house, particularly with regard to the matters of repair, stability and drainage. Where the boundaries to the dwelling-house are unclear, for example, on farms and small-holdings, only the adjacent outbuildings used for domestic purposes should normally be considered – subject to paragraph 2.7 below.

2.6   For the purposes of 604(2), section 183 of the Housing Act 1985 (by virtue of section 623(2) of that Act) will have effect to determine whether a dwelling-house is a flat. In determining whether a dwelling-house which is a flat is or is not unfit, the parts of the building outside the flat must satisfy subsection (2) in addition to the flat itself satisfying subsection (1). Thus, the condition of the structural elements and of the external envelope (roof, walls, etc) of the building and of the hall, stairway, access ways and other common areas, may fall to be considered in addition to that of the particular flat, but only with regard to the matters of repair, stability, dampness, ventilation and drainage. Moreover, these matters should only be considered to the extent that they affect the particular flat in question. Consequently, the failures which fall to be addressed are generally those in the parts of the building directly affecting the flat concerned, for example, those in the particular structure or part of the building accommodating the flat and/or its primary means of access.

2.7   All buildings which include commercial premises, whether this be a small front room shop or a large shop or suite of offices below a top floor flat may be approached in the same way as a block of flats, the non-residential parts of the building being considered under subsection 604(2) to the extent that they affect the particular dwelling-house.

2.8   Houses in multiple occupation (HMOs) come within section 604 by virtue of subsection (3). The section 604 standard may be applied to HMOs by considering the whole house including any kitchen and bathroom facilities as 'the dwelling-house', irrespective of any sub-division into household spaces which are not fully self-contained. Flats in multiple occupation come within section 604 by virtue of subsection (4), and may be similarly considered. Thus, for example, provided at least one W.C. is present and not shared with the occupants of another separate dwelling-house, such a house or flat may be deemed to have this amenity "for the exclusive use of the occupants", notwithstanding that it is shared by the different households within that house or flat.

2.9   Fitness for human habitation under section 604 does not mean that the house or **flat is fit for** multiple occupation, and for this subsequent determination, guidance on section 352 of the Housing Act 1985 as amended by the Local Government and Housing Act 1989 is given in *circular 12/92*.

2.10   Underground rooms are particularly prone to defects, for example, of repair, dampness, inadequate lighting and ventilation and specific advice is given where appropriate (Dampness 5.4, Ventilation 6.6, Lighting 8.6 and Drainage 12.4 & 12.9). However, whether or not potentially unfit as a separate household space in an HMO or already forming a self-contained flat, underground rooms may, for the purpose of section 604, be assessed essentially on the same criteria as all other rooms and spaces in a dwelling-house. As with all rooms and spaces, they should be considered with regard to their intended use in the context of the whole house or flat. Thus, although largely dependent on the particular matter in question, the weight given to some defects may vary with the intended use of the room or space in which they occur. (Ventilation 6.8, Lighting 8.9)

2.11   For the purposes of this guidance, "habitable room" may be taken to comprise a room such as a living room, study, dining room or bedroom intended for sitting and sedentary work, eating or sleeping. It should include all such rooms in a basement and attic accessed by fixed stairs and naturally lit, which in an older house may have formed the servants quarters, and any kitchen providing space for sitting or eating over and above that required for the preparation and cooking of food. Conversely, "habitable room" may be taken to exclude a purely working kitchen, for example, of the galley type, a utility room, bathroom or toilet, stairs, hall, landing and other circulation space, and small box room or storeroom intended only for storage, as well as any cellar room, attic space or extension not intended for or subsequently converted to a room for sitting, eating or sleeping.

2.12   Subject to the location of defects, a dwelling-house or building may fail to meet a particular requirement, either due to the severity of a defect or by reason of the extent of defects. However, it is only unfit if, because of that failure, it is not reasonably suitable for occupation.

2.13   In this respect, a dwelling-house would not normally be expected to be unfit for human habitation where it fails a particular requirement merely because of a minor defect. Such defect might include: a loose or broken socket in an otherwise sound electrical system; an isolated area of damp caused by a raised flower bed covering the damp proof course in an otherwise dry house; temporarily boarded-up windows or screwed up window openings; the odd missing or broken window pane in an otherwise reasonably wind and weatherproof dwelling; slipped or blocked gutters in an otherwise adequate drainage system; and other comparable defects. Nonetheless, the location, duration or consequence of even an apparently minor failure to meet a requirement may be such as to lead an authority to conclude that a dwelling-house is not reasonably suitable for occupation.

2.14   Although allowance should be made for any temporary failure to meet a requirement due to ongoing improvement or repair work, the fitness standard may be relevant where the failure is a consequence of the non-completion or poor quality of building work and a reasonable time for the completion or re-execution of such work has elapsed.

2.15   Generally, the decorative condition of a dwelling-house or building may be overlooked. Although exterior painting may be necessary for weather protection, lack of it does not by itself render a dwelling-house unsuitable for occupation, albeit it may lead to relevant items of disrepair. Similarly, the internal decoration is normally unimportant in this context. Obviously, in this respect, caution may be needed in some occupied properties where the excellent state of decoration and furnishings may give a misleading impression of the dwelling's condition, especially when compared with vacant, particularly long-term vacant, properties in poor decorative condition, unfurnished and harbouring dirt and litter.

2.16   Subject to the re-instatement of the odd fixture or fitting which may have been removed by the outgoing occupants or owners or subsequently broken through vandalism, a vacant dwelling should be judged on its fitness for human habitation on the assumption that it will be occupied in its existing condition. In this respect, the criteria used in judging a vacant dwelling should be generally no different from that of an occupied dwelling.

2.17   In all cases, an authority should decide whether a dwelling-house is or is not unfit on the basis of its current condition, having regard to the findings of a recent inspection and any other information laid before it.

3.   REPAIR

STATUTORY REQUIREMENT
"it is free from serious disrepair"
[Housing Act 1985, s.604(1)(b) and (2)(b)]

Background Note

(i)   While most of the requirements in the fitness standard are concerned with the suitability and adequacy of the design and installation of the building elements and fixtures, disrepair is generally concerned with their subsequent deterioration.

(ii)   Although not usually so critical or extensive as to affect the structural stability of the building, disrepair may lead to parts of the fabric being so insecure as to seriously prejudice the safety of the occupants. For example externally, a variety of heavy or sharp-edged building elements or parts may be liable to fall from chimneys, roofs, walls or windows during normal weather conditions as a consequence of severe disrepair.

(iii)   Internally, the main risks are less from falling elements than from serious disrepair further increasing the risk of the occupants or visitors falling, falls generally being the main type of accident in the home. For example, staircases, banisters, internal steps, timber and solid floors may all become dangerous as a consequence of rotting or broken timber or spalling or loose screeds and floor tiles. There is also a danger of cuts from insecure or broken glazing in windows, doors and partitions.

(iv)   The disrepair of fixtures can also be seriously prejudicial to safety either directly or by constituting a fire hazard. As well as causing deaths directly through electrocution, bad wiring results in numerous house fires each year. Old and neglected wiring, particularly the rubber-covered cable used up to the 1950's, is more like-

ly to be faulty and cause fires. The disrepair of gas-fired boilers, space and water heaters may also cause a fire hazard or may lead to the emission of toxic gases and vapours, the latter resulting in many accidental deaths in the home each year.

(v)   As well as a risk to safety, extensive disrepair of the fabric and fixtures, particularly in a kitchen and bathroom, may also be prejudicial to health by preventing the walls, floors, other surfaces and fixtures from being effectively cleansed.

(vi)   Finally, disrepair can result in a failure to meet other requirements. For example, severely leaking roofs, eaves, foul or surface water drainage or plumbing may lead to dampness prejudicial to health and/or the rotting of the structural fabric to an extent which threatens stability.

References

3.0   In assessing the severity and extent of disrepair, regard may be had to the following standards and regulations for new building work and the maintenance and repair of existing work, but failure to meet these would not, in itself, necessarily constitute grounds for unfitness.

   (1)   BS 5262: 1991 *Code of practice for external renderings.*

   (2)   BS 5492: 1990 *Code of practice for internal plastering.*

   (3)   BS 5534: *Code of practice for slating& tiling,* Part 1: 1978 (1990) *Design.*

   (4)   BS 6270: *Code of practice for cleaning and surface repair of buildings,* Part 1: 1982 *Natural stone, cast stone and clay & calcium silicate brick masonry,* Part 2: 1985 *Concrete and precast concrete masonry.*

   (5)   BS 7671: 1992 *Requirements for electrical installations.* Institution of Electrical Engineers (IEE), *16th edition.*

Repair – guidance note

3.1   A dwelling-house is unfit for human habitation if, in the authority's view, it is in serious disrepair or, where it is a flat, it or the building or a part of the building outside the flat are in serious disrepair, and for that reason it is not reasonably suitable for occupation.

3.2   In deciding whether a dwelling-house is or is not unfit, the authority should consider whether the dwelling-house or building is currently free from items of disrepair which either individually or due to their combined effect are so severe and/or extensive that they present a risk to health and safety, or cause serious inconvenience to any occupants.

3.3   In reaching a decision, the authority should have regard, amongst other things, to the extent to which by reason of the disrepair:

   (a)   the fabric is liable to failure, dislodgement or spalling or is otherwise prejudicial to safety;

   (b)   the fabric prohibits normal usage of the dwelling-house, increases the risk of falls or is otherwise prejudicial to health or safety;

   (c)   the fixtures and internal surfaces are incapable of being cleansed;

   (d)   the condition increases the risk of electrocution, toxic fumes, explosion or fire; and

   (e)   the condition increases the risk of water penetration or is otherwise prejudicial to the structural fabric.

3.4   Serious disrepair may be due to the severity of one item of disrepair or be due to the combined effect of two or more items. A multiplicity of items, none of which, by themselves, would be sufficiently serious to provide grounds for unfitness, may well constitute serious disrepair when combined.

3.5   To be satisfactory, any element of the dwelling-house or building should function in the manner in which it was intended. Externally, chimney pots and bricks, slates and tiles, bargeboards, gutters, downpipes, stacks, parapets, window heads and sills, casements and sashes, glazing, balcony elements and other elements of the building, should be generally secure so as to withstand normal weather conditions and normal usage. While the odd slipped slate would not normally be expected to constitute serious disrepair, severe nail sickness affecting a major portion of the roof might do so. Similarly, stone, brick and concrete walling, lintels and sills etc should be safe from severe spalling. (Fitness Standard 2.5)

3.6   Perished pointing and open jointed masonry may be of major concern, if so severe as to affect the integrity of the brickwork or stonework or to cause penetrating damp prejudicial to health. Similarly, the latter may be caused by rendering which is spalling, unbonded or seriously cracked. The rotting of windows and door frames might also constitute grounds for unfitness, if so severe as to render the windows unsafe or if causing the serious deterioration of the structural fabric and/or dampness prejudicial to health. (Fitness Standard 2. 15)

3.7   Internally, staircases, floor boarding etc should be sufficiently secure, free of rot and insect infestation to generally withstand normal domestic loads. Floors and steps, banisters, doors and windows should not be so distorted, rotten, infested or broken as to endanger the safety of any occupants. While the odd loose, rotten or broken floor board or loose or missing floor tile would not be expected to constitute serious disrepair, the extent or critical location of such defects could constitute grounds for unfitness.

3.8   For reasons of hygiene, walls, floors, ceilings and other surfaces as well as fixtures and facilities, particularly in the kitchen and bathroom, should not be in such extensive disrepair as to prevent these surfaces and facilities from being properly cleaned. (Fitness Standard 2. 15, Food Preparation 10.6, Water Closet etc 11.5)

3.9   Electrical wiring should not be so old and in such disrepair as to cause a major risk of electrocution or fire. However, failure to meet the current IEE regulations, for example, by old electrical wiring would not by itself normally constitute grounds for unfitness, unless the authority properly considers the installation to be dangerous and in need of immediate replacement. Gas pipes, boilers, space and water heaters and flues should not be broken or in such disrepair as to seriously increase the risk of fire, explosion or the emission of toxic fumes. (Fitness Standard 2. 13, References 3.0 (5))

3.10   The water supply, foul, waste or surface water drainage systems should not be in such disrepair as to cause persistent leakage, blockage or broken seals which either directly or through problems of dampness presents a risk to the health of any occupants. (Water Supply 9.4, Drainage 12.6)

3.11   Any disrepair of the fabric or fixtures should not be so serious as to cause, through persistent water penetration, rotting, warping, rusting or in any other way, the serious deterioration of the structural fabric such as to prejudice the integrity and stability of the building. This is particularly important in the case of dwellings of steel framed or timber framed constitution.

3.12   Where the dwelling-house is a flat, the building or a part of the building outside the flat should not be in such disrepair as to put the health and safety of any occupants of the flat at risk, for example, when gaining access to the flat or using the common facilities. While some forms of disrepair may be less critical in common areas than in the dwelling-house itself, others such as an unsafe or missing balustrade on a common stairway or access balcony could, depending on the circumstances of the case be sufficient to make a flat unfit.

4   STRUCTURAL STABILITY

STATUTORY REQUIREMENT
"is structurally stable"

[Housing Act 1985, s.604 (1)(a) and (2)(a)]

Background Note

(i)   The purpose of maintaining structural stability is not only to avoid safety hazards of a catastrophic nature such as death and injury due to collapse but, by preventing severe settlement cracks, to avoid health hazards, such as those resulting from cracked sewers, fractured damp-proof courses and water and wind penetration.

(ii)   Structural instability in dwellings may originate either as a result of faults in the design (e.g. faults in the original specification); and/or faults of construction (e.g. resulting from poor materials or poor workmanship on site); and/or faults during use (e.g. caused by overloading, modifications weakening the structure or the deterioration of the fabric); or as the result of subsidence.

(iii)   In domestic buildings, deterioration of materials, original design faults, inappropriate improvements and subsidence have probably contributed to the greatest number of collapses. In traditional housing, some of the more common causes of instability are settlement due to inadequate foundations, ground subsidence or shrinkage, slipped arches and lintels over openings, wall-tie failure, wall and roof spread and the distortion of chimneys resulting from sulphate attack. Internally, a major problem in the older stock is the loss of the bearing of floor joists due to rotting caused by rising or penetrating damp.

(iv)   In buildings above two storeys – often, but not exclusively, of non-traditional construction – there have also been cases of cladding becoming detached or spalling off. These failures are often the result of faulty design or workmanship related to fixing details, but may also be the result of inadequate maintenance or incorrect repair.

References

4.0   In assessing the severity and extent of defects in respect of structural stability, regard may be had to the following regulations, standards and code of practice for new building work, but failure to meet those would not, in itself, necessarily constitute grounds for unfitness.

(1)   Building Regulations, 1991, Manual and Approved Documents A1 *Structure*, A2 *Loading and ground movement.*

(2)   BS 5268: *Structural use of timber*, Part 2: 1991 *Code of practice for permissible stress design, materials and workmanship*, Part 3: 1985 *Code of practice for trussed rafter roofs*, Part 5: 1989 *Code of practice for the preservative treatment of structural timber*, Part 6: 1988 *Code of practice for timber framed walls.*

(3)   BS 5628: *Code of practice for use of masonry*, Part 1: 1992 *Structural use of unreinforced masonry*, Part 2: 1985 *Structural use of reinforced and prestressed masonry.*

(4)   BS 6399: *Loading for buildings*, Part 1: 1996 *Code of practice for dead and imposed loads*, Part 2: 1995 *Code of practice for wind loads*, Part 3: 1988 *Code of practice for imposed roof loads.*

Structural stability - guidance note

4.1   A dwelling-house is unfit for human habitation if, in the authority's view, it is structurally unstable or, where it is a flat, it or the building or a part of the building outside the flat are structurally unstable, and for that reason it is not reasonably suitable for occupation.

4.2   In deciding whether a dwelling-house is or is not unfit, the authority should consider whether the dwelling-house or building is currently able to withstand the combined dead, imposed and wind loads to which it is likely to be subjected in the ordinary course of events and when used for the purposes for which it is intended, and normal ground movement of the sub-soil caused by swelling, shrinkage or freezing; and is free from ongoing movement and the probability of movement which constitutes a threat to any occupants.

4.3   In reaching a decision, the authority should have regard, amongst other things, to:

(a)   the stability, distortion or spreading of roof structures, chimneys or parapets;

(b)   the stability, distortion and cracking of walls and continuity of wall-ties;

(c)   the structural adequacy and bearing of floors, stairs, ceilings and balconies;

(d)   the distortion, integrity and movement of foundations or footings; and

(e)   the integrity of any structural frames and wall panels.

4.4   Structural stability is concerned with the basic integrity of the building, that is the stability of the basic structure or major parts of the structure down to such elements as chimneys, parapets, window arches and lintels. The stability of non-structural elements or of small parts of the structure which do not threaten the building's basic integrity, such as isolated areas of spalling brickwork, slipped copings or rotten floor boards, may be considered more relevant to the repair requirements. (Fitness Standard 2.5, Repair 3.5, 3.6 & 3.7)

4.5   In assessing whether the dwelling-house, the building or part thereof is capable of withstanding normally combined dead, imposed and wind loads and normal ground movement, where appropriate, regard may be had to the extent to which the structure falls below the provisions set out in current regulations, standards and codes of practice. (References 4.0(1) to (4)).

4.6   In most cases, it should be possible to determine this requirement outright. However, assessment of ongoing movement may sometimes require the monitoring of the building over a period of time with 'tell-tales'. If the stability of the building is in doubt, it is suggested that an assessment be carried out by a specialist building professional who, in the case of non-traditional or high-rise housing, should be a structural engineer.

4.7   Past settlement or movement of a building, even though it may have left cracks and/or floors and walls out of level, is not expected to make a dwelling-house unfit on the grounds of stability, if the building still remains stable and there is no probability of further movement. However, even where the original movement has ceased, the building may be unstable if the structure has already been weakened to the point where it is no longer capable of withstanding normal loads or normal ground movement. Even if structurally stable, a dwelling-house may be in serious disrepair on account of such previous movement, for example, because of open structural cracks through external walls or severely sloping floors. (Repair 3.7).

5. DAMPNESS

STATUTORY REQUIREMENT
"it is free from dampness prejudicial to the health of the occupants (if any)"

[Housing Act 1985, s.604(1)(c) and (2)(c)]

Background Note

(i)   *Wet surfaces caused by condensation or rising or penetrating damp, encourage the formation of moulds, and the proliferation of moulds and mites in conditions of high relative humidity is associated with ill health. It has been estimated that some 15 to 20% of the population suffer some form of allergic disease, rhinitis and asthma being the most common, and a proportion of these can be attributed to mite and mould allergy. A number of recent studies also conclude that damp and mouldy housing has both direct and indirect effects on physical and mental health.*

(ii)   *Dampness in clothing and bedding may, by the process of cooling through evaporation, also prejudice the maintenance of body temperatures, particularly in young children and the elderly.*

(iii)   *Such problems can be minimised by not allowing the relative humidity in the dwelling to rise above 70%, except for short periods, and by avoiding condensation where possible. However, relative humidity below 40`% is also undesirable in view of the possibility of increasing the incidence of respiratory discomfort and infection.*

(iv)   *Dampness can also be prejudicial to health and safety through its action on the building fabric. It has the effect of lowering the ambient temperature, both by reducing the insulating capacity of external walls and by using up heat in the process of evaporation. Consequently, a marginal heating system can be rendered inadequate by persistent dampness.*

(v)   *The presence of excess moisture can also lead to instability and disrepair through the decay of building materials, for example, the corrosion of metal ties, fixings and reinforcement, perished plasterwork, swelling and warping of timber etc. Such moisture may be the result of interstitial condensation or of penetrating or rising damp. In the latter, dissolved salts in ground water carried through the structure by capillary action, may be deposited by tie process of evaporation on wall surfaces; if hygroscopic, these salts will attract moisture from the air, even at low relative humidities, and cause the wall to become permanently damp and to deteriorate through frost and other damage. In underground rooms dampness may also be transmitted through hydrostatic action.*

(vi)   *Moisture levels in timber in excess of 22% will also encourage the germination and growth of wood rotting fungi, and may result in the rotting of structural members.*

References

5.0   In assessing the severity and extent of defects in respect of dampness, regard may be had to the following regulations, standards and code of practice for new building work, but failure to meet these would not, in itself, necessarily constitute grounds for unfitness.

(1)   Building Regulations, 1991 Manual and Approved Document C4 *Resistance to weather and ground moisture.*

(2)   BS 5250: 1989 *Code of practice: the control of condensation in buildings.*

(3)   BS 5628: *Code of practice for use of masonry,* Part 3: 1985 *Materials and components, design and workmanship.*

(4)   BS 8200: 1985 *Code of practice for the design of non-loadbearing external vertical enclosures of buildings.*

(5) CP 102: 1973(sections 2 and 3 only) *Code of practice for protection of buildings against water from the ground*.

(6) BS 8102 : 1990 *Code of practice for protection of structures against water from the ground*.

(7) BS 8215 : 1992 *Code of practice for design of dpc in masonry construction*.

(8) Thermal Insulation: Avoiding Risks : *BRE report (second edition) 1994, BR 262*.

Dampness - guidance note

5.1 A dwelling-house is unfit for human habitation if, in the authority's view, it suffers from dampness prejudicial to the health of any occupant or, where it is a flat, it or the building or a part of the building outside the flat suffer from dampness, and for that reason it is not reasonably suitable for occupation.

5.2 In deciding whether a dwelling-house is or is not unfit, the authority should consider whether the dwelling-house or building is free from the occurrence of rising and penetrating damp, and from persistent condensation and mould growth. It should consider whether the dampness is attributable to the physical characteristics or condition of the building and whether, either directly or through its action on the structural fabric, it may be prejudicial to the health of any occupants.

5.3 In reaching a decision, the authority should have regard, amongst other things, to the extent and persistence of:

(a) rising damp in walls and floors;

(b) penetrating damp through roofs, walls or other parts of the building;

(c) interstitial condensation in the building fabric (where detectable);

(d) surface condensation; and

(e) any mould growth and mildews.

5.4 Dampness in a dwelling can arise from any one of three principal causes: capillary attraction of ground water into the structure in contact with the ground, i.e. rising damp in the floor slab and walls; penetration of the fabric or its joints by rainwater or meltwater from standing snow; and condensation. As well as being prone to rising damp, underground rooms are also liable to dampness caused by hydrostatic action.

5.5 Rising and penetrating damp can generally be attributed to design, inadequate construction or disrepair, and any dampness so caused, if sufficiently serious, may constitute unfitness. The absence or disrepair of a damp-proof course would not, by itself, normally constitute grounds for unfitness, unless it is the cause of rising damp prejudicial to health. (Fitness Standard 2.13)

5.6 Dampness from condensation should only be considered as constituting unfitness, if it is persistent and primarily attributable to the design, construction, modification, standard of amenities or state of repair of the dwelling. However, a dwelling should be able to withstand a degree of moisture generation appropriate to its size, without resulting in such condensation as to be prejudicial to the health of any occupants. (Ventilation 6.2, Heating 7.2)

5.7 The extent, location, frequency and persistence of any dampness, of whatever cause, will be particularly important in determining whether this is prejudicial to health. For example, a small patch of damp caused by defective pointing around a window reveal or door jamb or by a defective rainwater pipe is due to disrepair rather than inherent dampness. But, the premises should be free from the latter both during and following periods of reasonably severe and prolonged inclement weather. In this respect, obviously the authority should take care not to be misled by temporarily adequate conditions, or to make false assumptions on the cause of dampness, when inspecting during a prolonged dry spell.

6. VENTILATION

STATUTORY REQUIREMENT
"it has adequate provision for ventilation"
[Housing Act 1985, s. 604(1)(d) and (2)(d)]

Background Note

(i)   Ventilation is essential for the removal of pollutants which are directly or indirectly injurious to health. These pollutants may be generated within the building; by the occupants' cooking, bathing, smoking etc., by fuel combustion, by off-gassing from furniture and fittings, and by the materials and moisture used in the building process; or may be generated outside the building.

(ii)   The principal domestic pollutants are:

(a)   metabolic products, such as water vapour, carbon dioxide and body odour, which are not health problems in themselves but may be indicative of other problems;

(b)   combustion products, such as carbon monoxide and nitrogen dioxide, which may be produced by defective domestic heating and cooking appliances. Without adequate ventilation, the former can accumulate in concentrations sufficient to cause death, while the latter is thought to contribute to respiratory infections;

(c)   organic compounds such as wood preservatives and formaldehyde used in particle board and foamed insulation, the latter of which can cause irritation; and

(d)   particulate material, which may be non-viable as in asbestos, or viable, for example, mites, moulds, yeasts and fungi, and which are an established health risk.

(iii)   Of these, the most acute risk comes from carbon monoxide poisoning generated by incomplete combustion in unflued stoves and portable heaters and open flued combustion equipment. There are also serious long term risks from asbestos fibres and possibly tobacco smoke and formaldehyde and wood preservatives, while nitrogen dioxide and the micro-organisms moulds etc, can contribute to long term respiratory diseases. In addition high concentrations of water vapour may result in condensation, leading to mould growth and the other health issues discussed under dampness.

References

6.0   In assessing the severity and extent of defects in respect of ventilation, regard may be had to the following regulations and standards for new building work, but failure to meet these would not, in itself, necessarily constitute grounds for unfitness.

(1)   Building Regulations, 1995, Manual & Approved Documents Fl *Means of ventilation*, F2 *Condensation*.

(2)   BS 5250: 1989 *Code of practice: the control of condensation in buildings*.

(3)   BS 5440: *Code of practice for installation of flues and ventilation of gas appliances of rated input not exceeding 60 kilowatts*, Part 1: 1990, Specification for installation of flues, Part 2: 1989 specification for installation of ventilation of gas appliances.

(4)   BS 5720: 1979 *Code of practice for mechanical ventilation and air conditioning in buildings*.

(5)   BS 5925: 1991 *Code of practice for the design of buildings: ventilation principles and designing for natural ventilation*.

Ventilation - guidance note

6.1   A dwelling-house is unfit for human habitation if, in the authority's view, it has inadequate provision for ventilation or, where it is a flat, it or the building or a part of the building outside the flat have inadequate provision for ventilation, and for that reason it is not reasonably suitable for occupation.

6.2   In deciding whether a dwelling-house is or is not unfit, the authority should consider whether the dwelling-house or building currently has means of ventilation which under normal conditions are capable of restricting the accumulation of such moisture (which could lead to serious condensation and mould growth, despite adequate heating) and pollutants, originating within the building or curtilage, as would otherwise become a hazard to the health of any occupants.

6.3   In reaching a decision, the authority should have regard, amongst other things, to:

(a)   the size and location of the openable parts of windows and doors;

(b)   the size and location of louvres or other ventilators;

(c)   the position of window openings, doors and ventilators in relation to external obstructions;

(d)   the efficiency of any mechanical ventilation; and

(e)   the type and level of ventilation to unflued and (non-balanced) flued combustion appliances.

6.4   Room ventilation may be achieved by means of ventilation openings direct to the external air, such as the openable parts of a window, a louvre, progressively openable ventilator or an external door, or by means of a mechanical system. In the case of natural ventilation, the ventilator should be capable of being opened to such an extent that fresh air will readily circulate to all parts of the room. However, to control the amount of ventilation and avoid prejudicing security, some part of the ventilation should normally be provided by means other than by just an external side-hung door. (Fitness Standard 2.13)

6.5   As a general guide, the total size of ventilation openings in a habitable room and naturally ventilated kitchen, bathroom or w.c. compartment should not be less than 1/20th of the floor area. In living rooms and kitchens, some part of the opening should normally be at least 1.75m above floor level. (Fitness Standard 2.11)

6.6   Where the free circulation of air may be restricted, such as in a room in a habitable basement, the floor of which is more than 0.9 metres below the surface of the adjacent street or ground, natural ventilation should be direct to the external air. In such situations, there should normally be an unobstructed space immediately outside the window opening which extends the entire width of the window or more and has a depth of not less than 0.6 metres measured from the external wall or not less than 0.3 metres in the case of a bay window with side lights. It is also to be expected that the average height of such rooms from floor to ceiling should be sufficient to encourage the free convection of air within the room. (Fitness Standard 2.10, Lighting 8.6)

6.7   Generally, ventilation by mechanical means should provide at least 1 air change per hour in habitable rooms and kitchens and preferably 3 per hour in bathrooms and w.c. compartments. (Repair 3.9)

6.8   Rooms which fail the criteria in paragraphs 6.5 to 6.7 above may be defective in ventilation. However, in deciding whether the dwelling-house is or is not thereby reasonably suitable for occupation, the severity and extent of the problem should be considered. Thus, a dwelling having defective ventilation in the main living room or kitchen, or in the majority of other habitable rooms might be deemed unfit whereas, for example, a marginal defect in a relatively minor room would not by itself normally be expected to constitute sufficient grounds for unfitness.

6.9   The ventilation of non-habitable spaces in the building, such as cellars, sub-floor spaces, lofts and other roof spaces should not be so inadequate as to cause severe condensation which is prejudicial to the structural fabric. However, it is not expected that inadequate ventilation of such spaces would normally be sufficient, by itself, to render a dwelling-house unfit.

6.10   Fixed heat producing combustion appliances (including cookers) taking air from the interior of the dwelling should have provision for adequate ventilation to ensure complete combustion of fuels and the full discharge of the products of combustion.

6.11   While satisfying provision for ventilation, the level of any permanent ventilation should not be so great as to cause excessive heat loss. (Heating 7.7).

7.   HEATING

STATUTORY REQUIREMENT
"it has adequate provision for heating"
[Housing Act 1985, s.604(1)(d)]

Background Note

(i)   Why adequate provision for heating is important in terms of health is well documented in reports such as, Mant DC and Muir Gray JA "Building regulations and health, BRE, 1986, on which the following extracts are based.

(ii)   According to the 'Mant Report', the most common causes of death in winter are stroke, heart disease, bronchitis, pneumonia hypothermia and accidents, and the mortality rates for these diseases all increase when the ambient temperature declines. In this respect, the evidence for a causal relationship is greatly strengthened by experimental evidence of a biological link between the underlying pathology of these diseases and low temperatures.

(iii)   Hypothermia depends on the core temperature of the body. The elderly appear able to maintain a core temperature when the air temperature is 12 deg C or above, but a significant fall has been shown to occur after two hours at a temperature of 9 dec C. Below 12 deg C there is also an increased strain on the cardiovascular system and these changes increase the risk of myocardial infarction and stroke.

(iv)   Between 12 and 15 deg C, there is evidence to suggest that there persists a potential, albeit less acute, risk to health. There also remains an indirect risk in the high incidence of condensation and mould growth which is associated with low temperatures as well as with poor ventilation. Above 16 deg C there is no longer a significant health risk but discomfort is generally felt when the temperature falls below 18 deg C, particularly when sitting or engaged in sedentary occupations.

(v)   The implication from the above review is that the provision of heating in a main living room should be such as to enable a temperature of 18 deg C to be generally achieved when the outside temperature is 1 deg C (the design temperature for heating systems) so as to prevent both severe discomfort and the maintenance of the 16 deg C health threshold on the, not uncommon, occasions when the outside temperature falls below I deg C.

(vi)   In addition, provisions for heating to achieve an equivalent temperature of 16 deg C in other habitable rooms would generally help to avoid serious condensation and mould growth in bedrooms and elsewhere, and allow a background temperature above 12 deg C during extreme cold weather.

(vii)   Space heaters may also present a safety risk, both in terms of fire and the emission of toxic fumes. Each year, heating appliances cause several thousand domestic fires and result in many deaths, electric heaters leading to half of these fatalities. Because of their greater liability to be overturned, to be located close to furniture and fabrics and to be accidentally covered, portable appliances are a particular risk in this respect, especially in well frequented rooms such as a general living room. Portable unflued combustion heaters as well as being a potential fire risk may, if defective, also present a risk in terms of explosion and carbon monoxide poisoning. (Background note 6 (iii).)

References

7.0   In assessing the severity and extent of defects in respect of heating, regard may be had to the following regulation and standards for building work, but failure to meet these would not, in itself, necessarily constitute grounds for unfitness.

(1)   BS 5449: *Code of practice for central heating for domestic premises*, Part 1: 1977 *Forced circulation hot water systems.*

(2)   BS 5871: 1980 (1983) *Code of practice for installation of gas fires, convection and fire/back boilers (2nd family gases).*

(3)   BS 8211: *Energy efficiency in housing*, Part 1: 1988 *Code of practice for energy efficient refurbishment of housing.*

(4)   BS 8303: 1986 *Code of practice for installation of domestic heating and cooking appliances burning solid mineral fuels.*

(5)   Anderson et al, *BREDEM-BRE Domestic Energy Model background, philosophy and description*, BRE, 1985.

(6)   Thermal insulation: Avoiding risks *BRE Report (second Edition) 1994 BR 262*

Heating - guidance note

7.1   A dwelling-house is unfit for human habitation if in the authority's view it has inadequate provision for heating, and for that reason it is not reasonably suitable for occupation.

7.2   In deciding whether a dwelling-house is or is not unfit, the authority should, consider whether the dwelling-house currently has for heating a main 'living' room, provision for fixed heating capable of efficiently maintaining the room generally at a temperature of 18 deg C or more when the outside temperature is -1 deg C, and for other main habitable rooms, provision for heating capable of maintaining an equivalent temperature of 16 deg C or more. The authority should also have regard to whether the construction and condition of the dwelling-house prevents excessive heat loss and whether the overall level of provision for heating, when combined with adequate ventilation, is sufficient to prevent both condensation and mould growth prejudicial to health.

7.3   In reaching a decision, the authority should have regard, amongst other things, to:

(a)   the presence, type and age of provision for heating in the main 'living' room;

(b)   the presence, type and age of provision for heating elsewhere;

(c)   the capacity of the electrical installation and number and location of outlets;

(d)   the insulating properties of the building fabric; and

(e)   the extent of air leakage through the construction.

7.4   For heating at least one main room intended for general living, there should be provision for fixed heating of sufficient capacity to maintain, after a warming up period, most of the room at a temperature of 18 deg C or more when the outside temperature is -1 deg C. This provision should normally comprise a reasonably efficient and safely designed and installed fixed heating source or, failing this, a safe and fully connected gas point at a working flue, or a safe electrical installation and space suitable for a fixed electric heating appliance. In the latter case, there should be a suitably located (13 amp minimum) outlet which may reasonably be dedicated solely to the appliance. (Fitness Standard 2.16, Repair 3.9)

7.5   For heating each other main habitable room, there should be provision for heating of sufficient capacity to maintain most of the room at a temperature of 16 deg C or more when the outside temperature is -1 deg C. This should normally comprise either a fixed heating source, or a gas point at a working flue, or a safe electric installation suitable for a fixed or portable electric heating appliance. For the latter, there should be a (13 amp minimum) outlet available from an installation of sufficient capacity not to give rise to serious overloading, bearing in mind the size of the dwelling-house and provision in other rooms. (Repair 3.9)

7.6   Generally, the provision may either take the form of a central heating system with, for example, a radiator, underfloor or ceiling element or heating outlet for ducted warm-air, or may take the form of or provide a ready connection for, a direct heating source such as a fire, stove, convector, fan heater, storage heaters etc. Fixed heating may be taken to include those provisions, for example, storage heaters, which regardless of whether actually fixed, are effectively non-portable and stable. (Repair 3.9, Ventilation 6.10)

7.7   The construction of the dwelling and its condition should not be such as to result in excessive heat loss. In this respect, a dwelling is not expected to be fully insulated to modern standards, but should be constructed of materials and in a manner to give an adequate basic level of thermal insulation. Thus, while solid [228mm] walls would normally be considered adequate, a dwelling-house with large areas of 11.5mm brick external wall or constructed of uninsulated or poorly insulated metal or asbestos cement sheeting may well fail in this respect. Similarly, a dwelling-house which is in such condition that it is not generally wind and weatherproof could fail to meet the requirement. (Fitness Standard 2.13, Ventilation 6.11)

7.8   In assessing whether the provision for heating is adequate, the capacity, type and age of the provision should be considered in relation to the size of the room and likely heat loss. For example, while provision only for an open solid fuel fire would not automatically be expected to fail to meet the requirement, it may do so if located in a dwelling-house which, by reason of its characteristics, construction or condition, has a relatively high heat loss. In a similar situation, provision only for a small electric fire may also fail to meet the requirement. In most cases it should be possible to determine this matter outright. However, an objective assessment of any particular situation may be gained by using one of a number of commercially available energy models, based on the Building Research Establishment's domestic energy model BREDEM. (Reference 7.0 (5))

7.9   Overall, the heating provided should be sufficient, when combined with adequate ventilation, to prevent severe or pervasive condensation and mould growth. In this respect, although possibly of adequate capacity, a fixed paraffin appliance, if this were the main provision, may fail to meet this requirement and cause the failure of that relating to dampness because of problems of condensation and mould growth. (Dampness 5.6).

8. LIGHTING

STATUTORY REQUIREMENT
"it has adequate provision for lighting"
[Housing Act 1985, s. 604(1)(d)]

Background Note

(i)   Natural lighting has three important effects on human beings; it influences body rhythms such as sleep patterns, ovulation and hormone secretion; it affects performance, alertness and mood; and exerts a direct physiological effect on skin, including the synthesis of Vitamin D (which is necessary for healthy bones). Consequently, artificial lighting may not be an adequate substitute for natural lighting in many areas of the dwelling.

(ii)   Poor lighting, whether natural or artificial may be a cause of eye strain. Indirectly, both may be a health hazard if they hamper the proper cleaning of the dwelling, particularly in kitchens and bathrooms.

(iii)   Both are a safety hazard because of the connection between poor lighting levels and accidents in the home, particularly on staircases and at changes of level. (Stairs/steps are the feature of the home most frequently involved in fatal accidents.) Because advancing age increases the time taken to adapt to changing lighting levels, providing higher lighting levels on landings etc. without increasing the general level of lighting in the dwelling-house could merely result in increased glare, particularly, for the elderly.

(iv)   In the case of artificial lighting, its ability to minimise accidents will be largely negated if there are not also suitably located light switches.

References

8.0   In assessing the severity and extent of defects in respect of natural and artificial lighting, regard may be had to the following codes of practice and guidance, although failure to meet these would not, in itself, necessarily constitute grounds for unfitness.

(1)· BS8206: *Lighting for buildings*, Part 2: 1992 *Code of practice for daylighting.*

(2)   CIBSE : *Code for interior lighting 1994.*

(3)   Littlefair,P.J., *Site layout planning for daylight and sunlight: a guide to good practice*, BRE Report 209, 1991. Also: *Site layout for sunlight and solar gain*, BRE IP/92, and *Site layout planning for daylight*, BRE IP5/92.

Lighting - guidance note

8.1   A dwelling-house is unfit for human habitation if in the authority's view it has inadequate provision for lighting, and for that reason it is not reasonably suitable for occupation.

8.2   In deciding whether a dwelling-house is or is not unfit, the authority should consider whether the dwelling-house currently has provision for sufficient natural lighting in habitable rooms to enable the normal activities of a household to be carried out, safely and conveniently, without the use of artificial light during normal daytime conditions. It should also consider whether the dwelling-house has provision for sufficient artificial lighting in all habitable rooms, kitchens, bathrooms, w.c. and circulation spaces, to enable the normal activities of a household to be carried out, safely and conveniently and to permit the normal passage of the occupant without increasing the risk of accident.

8.3   In reaching a decision, the authority should have regard, amongst other things, to:

(a)   the size and location of windows;

(b)   the size and proximity of external obstructions;

(c)   the provision and location of light fittings in all rooms;

(d)   the provision, location and type of light switches; and

(e)   the internal arrangement relative to the lighting provisions.

8.4   Habitable rooms should have sufficient natural lighting to enable normal domestic activities to be undertaken without strain during the main hours of daylight without requiring artificial light, unless the day is particularly overcast. However, allowance should be made for particularly dirty or inappropriate glazing, heavy curtaining and any boarding up, for overgrown external foliage or other similar obstructions under the control of the occupant or landlord. (Fitness Standard 2.11)

8.5   The extent of natural lighting will generally depend on the size and height of windows, their location in the room and the size and proximity of external obstructions. As a general guide, the area of glazing in a habitable room should be not less than 1/10th of the floor area, and some part of the window should normally be at least 1.75m above floor level.

8.6   Where there is a continuous solid external obstruction within some 3 metres of the window or windows of a habitable room, for example, as may occur outside a basement, there should normally be a glazed area totaling not less than 1/10th of the floor area of the room, above the points on the window or windows from which a line can be drawn upwards at a vertical angle of 30 degrees with the horizontal to pass the top of the obstruction. For this 'rule of thumb' calculation, a bay window with side lights may be treated as a flat window, equal in area to the sum of the front and side lights and situated at a distance from the face of the wall from which the bay projects equal to half the maximum depth of the projection. (Fitness Standard 2.10)

8.7   All habitable rooms, kitchens, bathrooms and w.c. compartments should have at least one ceiling or suitably located wall lighting outlet with the capacity to enable normal domestic activities to be undertaken without strain after dark. Circulation spaces should also have at least one ceiling or suitably located wall lighting outlet with the capacity of minimising accidents and allowing effective cleaning. With respect to potential accidents, particular care should be given to the location of lighting outlets in relation to stairs and changes of level, especially if there are items of bad arrangement such as steep and winding stairs or trip steps.

8.8   A safe working light fitting is to be generally expected in occupied properties, but in vacant dwellings and rooms a safe working installation, for example terminating at a ceiling rose, may be considered acceptable. Generally, light switches should be present and fixed and should be conveniently located near the entrances to rooms and circulation spaces. Bathrooms should preferably have ceiling pull switches (disregarding any missing cords) or a wall switch outside the room. (Fitness Standard 2.16, Repair 3.9)

8.9   In determining whether a dwelling fails the fitness standard on the grounds of inadequate provision for lighting, the standard of the provision for natural lighting and that for artificial lighting may be considered separately but both in terms of the severity or extent of defects. For example, a dwelling which is severely defective in natural lighting in the main living room or in a majority of other habitable rooms, or in provision for artificial lighting in the kitchen or on the stairs might be deemed unfit. Conversely, defective natural lighting in a minor bedroom, no light fitting in a small box room or a bathroom with a wall switch would not alone be expected to constitute sufficient grounds for a finding of unfitness.

9. WATER SUPPLY

STATUTORY REQUIREMENT
"it has an adequate piped supply of wholesome water"
[Housing Act 1985, s. 604(1)(e)]

Background Note

(i)   Since the beginnings of public health legislation, it has been accepted that some diseases are spread by contaminated water and that the water supply must be wholesome. Under the Water Act 1989, water suppliers have a duty to provide wholesome water as defined by Regulations made under the Act. The Water Supply (Water Quality) Regulations 1989 as amended set minimum quality standards and incorporate those laid down in the European Community Directive on the Quality of Water Intended for Human Consumption. Both public and private supplies are required to comply with the requirements of the Regulations.

(ii)   Ninety nine per cent of the population of England and Wales are supplied from public supplies by water undertakers. The remaining 1 per cent are served from private supplies piped, for example, from streams, wells and boreholes and such supplies are prone to contamination by human or farm sewage or in other ways. It is the Government's intention to make regulations under the Water Act 1989 in order to establish minimum frequencies for the sampling and testing of private supplies by local authorities to ensure that they comply with the requirements of the Water Supply (Water Quality) Regulations 1989, as amended.

(iii)   Even where connected to a main supply, water may become contaminated within the dwelling and its curtilage. The poor siting and disrepair of mains water and drainage pipes may lead to pollution of the former. Water, especially that with a high acidity can dissolve the heavy metals, particularly lead, used for water pipes. Toxic materials can thereby become absorbed in the drinking water and be ingested by occupants.

(iv)   Inadequately covered cold water cisterns can be polluted by the droppings and rotting bodies of birds, small animals and insects.

(v)   An inadequate supply in terms of continuity may present risks to safety as well as health. If he supply is intermittent or has a particularly low rate of flow, it may so fail to replenish the cold water tank as to prejudice the safety of any boiler or water heater. Such a flow might also encourage the use of a supply from a tank, rather than a direct supply, for drinking and the preparation of food.

References

9.0   In assessing the severity and extent of defects in respect of the water supply, regard may be had to the following regulations, byelaws and standard for new building work, but failure to meet these would not, in itself, necessarily constitute grounds for unfitness.

    (1)   The Water Supply (Water Quality) Regulations 1989, as amended.

    (2)   Relevant Water Byelaws (30 etc).

    (3)   BS 6700: 1987 *Specification for design, installation, testing and maintenance of services supplying water for domestic use within buildings and their curtilages.*

Water supply - guidance note

9.1   A dwelling-house is unfit for human habitation if, in the authority's view, it has an inadequate piped supply of wholesome water, and for that reason it is not reasonably suitable for occupation.

9.2   In deciding whether a dwelling-house is or is not unfit, the authority should consider whether the dwelling-house is currently connected to a mains supply or a private supply that is wholesome; has, normally, a continuous and adequate rate of supply, has piping designed, installed and in a condition so as not to contaminate the supply; and has an outlet conveniently located above the kitchen sink.

9.3   In reaching a decision, the authority should have regard, amongst other things, to:

(a)   the presence inside the dwelling of a mains supply or wholesome private supply;

(b)   the siting of this supply relative to the kitchen sink;

(c)   the continuity and rate of flow of the supply;

(d)   the contamination of the supply by the ingress of foul, waste, surface or ground water or otherwise; and

(e)   the contamination of the supply by metals dissolved from the piping.

9.4   Where the quality of supply to the dwelling-house is suspect, bacteriological and chemical testing may be undertaken. The supply to the tap may also need to be tested for contamination emanating in the dwelling or curtilage. for example, from lead piping.

9.5   The water used for drinking and the preparation of food should be drawn from an outlet located inside the dwelling-house. This should comprise a tap, which may be a mixer tap, above the kitchen sink but located to prevent backflow.

9.6   To reduce the risks to health, the drinking water supply should normally come directly from the rising main. However, where a storage cistern supplies drinking water to the kitchen tap, the cistern should have a non-airtight close fitting cover which excludes light and insects, or be otherwise designed to comply with the Water Byelaws. To reduce the risk of organic contamination, it is also preferable if the cold water supply pipe does not run fully and continuously adjacent to hot water pipes or heating appliances, although this defect alone would not normally be expected to result in a finding of unfitness. (References 9.0 (2))

9.7   Under working conditions, the drinking water supply should have a sufficiently continuous and adequate rate of flow to safely replenish water tanks, boilers and hot water cylinders to prevent hazards resulting from overheating. At the kitchen tap, it need not necessarily run full bore but should not be so slow running as to discourage its use for drinking and the preparation of food. Although not required to meet design standards for new installations, the extent to which the flow is inadequate may be assessed having regard to the current British Standard. (Reference 9.0 (3))

10.   FACILITIES FOR THE PREPARATION AND COOKING OF FOOD

STATUTORY REQUIREMENT
"there are satisfactory facilities in the dwelling-house for the preparation and cooking of food, including a sink with a satisfactory supply of hot and cold water"

[Housing Act 1985, s. 604(1)(f)]

Background Note
(i)   The preparation and cooking of food is potentially more dangerous than any other activity which goes on at home. The most frequent home accidents are falls, burns and scalds and a high proportion of such accidents happen while meals are being prepared, served or eaten.

(ii)   Most accidents in the kitchen occur in connection with the cooker, the electrical installation, or out-of-reach storage and can be minimised by a safe layout and adequate circulation space within the kitchen. The location of the cooking appliance in relation to doorways and work surfaces is of particular importance in this respect.

(iii)   Work surfaces of adequate area, depth and height are important in terms of safety in providing space, out of the reach of small children, to receive hot pans and dishes straight from the cooker prior to serving, and in providing similarly safe areas for the operation of potentially dangerous kitchen appliances.

(iv)   As well as reducing the risk of accidents, the design of kitchens can also reduce the risk to health. Many cases of domestic food poisoning arise from the cross contamination of cooked and uncooked foods. This risk is minimised if there is adequate provision for work surfaces for food preparation and if such surfaces and sinks can be readily and properly cleaned.

References

10.0   In assessing the severity and extent of defects in respect of the facilities for the preparation and cooking of food, regard may be had to the following standards and guidance for new building work, but failure to meet these would not, in itself, necessarily constitute grounds for unfitness.

(1)   BS 5482: *Specification for domestic butane and propane gas-burning installations*, Part 1: 1994 Specification for installation at permanent dwellings.

(2)   BS 6172: 1990 *Specification for installation of domestic gas cooking appliances (1st, 2nd and 3rd family gases).*

(3)   BS 8303: 1995 Installation of domestic heating and cooking appliances burning solid mineral fuels:
Part 1 : *Specification for design of installation*
Part 2 : *Specification for installation and commissioning on site*
Part 3 : *Recommendations for installation design and installation.*

(4)   *BRE housing design handbook*, BRE Report 253, 1993.

Food preparation - guidance note

10.1   A dwelling-house is unfit for human habitation if, in the authority's view, it lacks satisfactory facilities for the preparation and cooking of food, and for that reason it is not reasonably suitable for occupation.

10.2   In deciding whether a dwelling-house is or is not unfit, the authority should consider whether the dwelling-house currently has a sink designed and installed so as not to be prejudicial to health and fitted with satisfactory supplies of hot water and cold drinking water. It should consider whether the dwelling-house has provision for an adequate work surface or surfaces for the preparation of food and for the cooking of food, provision for a gas or electric cooker or, failing this, a suitable fixed solid fuel or oil fired cooking appliance; the sink, work surfaces and cooker or cooker space being located within reasonable proximity in a kitchen or kitchen area and sited so as not to be prejudicial to safety.

10.3   In reaching a decision, the authority should have regard, amongst other things, to:

(a)   the presence in the dwelling of a fixed kitchen sink with a drainer and piped hot and cold water, worktop or worktops and cooker points;

(b)   the suitability of the sink and worktops for cleaning;

(c)   the adequacy of the hot water supply;

(d)   the size of the sink, worktops and cooker space; and

(e)   the dimensions and layout of the kitchen or kitchen area.

10.4   It is advised that the kitchen sink should comprise a fixed impervious bowl properly connected through an adequate sized trap to the drains and that there should be at least one drainer (independently or as a combined unit) or second bowl, each of reasonable size.

10.5   The sink should have an adequate piped supply of hot water, which may be from a central source or from a stored and instantaneous unit water heater capable of promoting an adequate supply of hot water. It should also have an adequate supply of cold drinking water, normally piped directly from the rising main. The hot water system should be designed, installed and in a condition so as not to be prejudicial to safety. (Repair 3.9, Ventilation 6.10, Water Supply 9.6)

10.6   For the preparation of food, the kitchen or kitchen area should have a secure fixed work surface or the space for such surfaces, appropriate to the size of the dwelling. The work surface or surfaces and adjacent walls, floors and ceilings should be generally non-porous and reasonably smooth such that they can be cleaned effectively. There should be an adequate number of suitably located electrical power points for the safe use of kitchen appliances. (Fitness Standard 2.16, Repair 3.8 & 3.9)

10.7   For installation of a cooker, the kitchen should have either an electric (30 amp) cooker point, a mains gas point or failing this, a bottled gas installation or a solid fuel or oil fired range permanently connected to a flue. Space or spaces should be available adjacent to the cooker points of sufficient size to take an oven and hob, either in a combined or split level units. Space and points only suitable for a portable worktop cooker or camping stove would not be acceptable as the only cooking provision in the kitchen. (Ventilation 6.10, References 10.0 (1), (2) & (3))

10.8   The dimensions of the kitchen or kitchen area should be sufficient for the safe provision of all the necessary facilities. The location of the cooker space should be safe, particularly in relation to doorways, and there should be sufficient floor space for retrieving items from the oven and for the safe circulation of occupants generally. In short, while a merely inconvenient layout would not be expected to constitute grounds for unfitness, a dangerous layout could. (Reference 10.0 (4))

11.   WATER CLOSET, WASHBASIN AND BATH OR SHOWER

STATUTORY REQUIREMENT
"it has a suitably located watercloset for the exclusive use of the occupants (if any)"

"it has for the exclusive use of the occupants (if any), a suitably located fixed bath or shower and wash-hand basin each of which is provided with a satisfactory supply of hot and cold water"
[Housing Act 1985, s. 604(1)(g) and (l)(h)]

Background Note
(i)   A water closet (w.c.) accessed through the open air even if the access is covered, may be prejudicial to health, particularly for the elderly in winter. It is also more prone to freezing.

(ii)   Research shows that there are significant health risks associated with the use of sanitary conveniences, but that these can be minimised if precautions such as hand washing and cleansing of the sanitary accommodation are properly carried out.

(iii)   Handwashing is the crucial factor in reducing the spread of infection, and the two most important factors in the location of a water closet are the necessity of hand washing and the potential risk of overflow. The risk from direct communication of w.c.s with kitchens derives from the possibility of w.c. users washing their hands in sinks used for food preparation as well as from the airborne contamination of kitchen surfaces.

(iv)   Bathing or showering is required for the efficient cleansing of the body and removal of body odours. It is directly beneficial to health in two main areas, namely skin disease associated with bacteria and lice and the need for bathing for people who are ill.

(v)   The compartmenting within the dwelling-house and location of w.c.s, hand-basins and baths is also important for maintaining basic personal privacy.

(vi)   Both central and unit hot water heaters can be potentially dangerous if not properly designed, installed and maintained, the main risks being the emission of toxic fumes, explosion, scalding and electrocution.

References

11.0   In assessing the severity and extent of defects in respect of the water closet, washbasin, bath or shower and supply of hot and cold water, regard may be had to the following regulations, standards and guidance for new building work, but failure to meet these would not, in itself, necessarily constitute grounds for unfitness.

(1)   Building Regulations, 1991, Building Regulations & Approved Documents G1 *Sanitary conveniences and washing facilities*, G2 *Bathrooms* and G3 *Hot water storage* .

(2)   BS 6465 *Sanitary installations*, Part 1: 1994 *Code of practice for scale of provision, selection and installation of sanitary appliance* and Part 2: 1996 *Code of practice for space requirements for sanitary appliances.*

(3)   BRE *housing design handbook*, BRE Report 253, 1993.

Water closet, etc - guidance note

11.1   A dwelling-house is unfit for human habitation if, in the authority's view, it lacks for the exclusive use of any occupants, a suitably located water closet, a suitably located fixed bath or shower and wash-hand basin each with a satisfactory supply of hot and cold water, and for that reason it is not reasonably suitable for occupation.

11.2   In deciding whether a dwelling-house is or is not unfit, the authority should consider whether the dwelling-house currently has a water closet, for the exclusive use of any occupants, designed, installed and suitably located inside so as to be readily accessible and not prejudicial to health. The authority should also have regard to whether the dwelling-house has a wash-hand basin and fixed bath or shower, for the exclusive use of any occupants, designed, installed and suitably located inside so as to be readily accessible and not prejudicial to health, and fitted with satisfactory supplies of hot and cold water.

11.3   In reaching a decision, the authority should have regard, amongst other things, to:

(a)   the presence in the dwelling of these amenities;

(b)   the capability of the amenities to cleanse (w.c. only) and to be cleansed;

(c)   the adequacy of the hot and cold water supplies;

(d)   the siting of the w.c. in relation to the washbasin and to food preparation and storage areas; and

(e)   the compartmenting and accessibility of the amenity.

11.4   A water closet, wash-hand basin (other than the kitchen sink) and bath or shower should be present and located normally inside the habitable part of the dwelling-house, that is behind the main external doors of the particular house or flat. It is to be expected that in all circumstances they should be capable of being reached under cover without entering the outside air.

11.5   The water closet, washbasin and bath or shower should have a surface which is reasonably smooth and non-absorbent and capable of being cleansed. The flushing apparatus fitted to the w.c. should be capable of cleansing the receptacle effectively. (Fitness Standard 2.16, Repair 3.8)

11.6   The washbasin and bath or shower should each have a piped supply of hot water, which may be from a central source or from a plumbed-in unit water heater capable of maintaining a constant flow of hot water, and a piped supply of cold water. The hot water system should be designed and installed so as not to be prejudicial to safety and both the hot and cold supplies should be adequate for their purpose. (Repair 3.9, Ventilation 6.10)

11.7   The w.c. should be provided in a naturally or artificially ventilated and lit bathroom or separate w.c. compartment, and should not open directly and immediately onto a space intended for the storage or preparation of food. The washbasin should normally be located in or near the room containing the w.c. A bath or shower should be provided in a bathroom or shower room. The w.c., washbasin and bath should be readily accessible at all times without unduly compromising the privacy of the occupants. (Ventilation 6.5 & 6.7, Lighting 8.7).

12.   DRAINAGE OF FOUL, WASTE AND SURFACE WATER

STATUTORY REQUIREMENT
"an effective system for the draining of foul, waste and surface water"
[Housing Act 1985, s. 604(1)(i) and (2)(e)]

Background Note
(i)   *The potential hazard from foul and waste water drainage is considerable, particularly from the parts of the system located above ground, and the basic requirement is that drainage pipes should neither leak nor easily block. Given that this requirement is met, any health risk can be effectively eliminated by the use of water traps and ventilation of stack pipes.*

(ii)   *Except where part of a combined system, the potential health hazard from surface water drainage is less acute. Rainwater down pipes and gutters particularly cast-iron ware can become a safety hazard if not properly fixed and maintained.*

(iii)   *The main concern regarding inadequate or leaking surface water drainage is that it can easily result in penetrating damp and rapidly accelerate the deterioration of structural and other elements of the building fabric, and thus lead to potentially more serious health and safety problems. Inadequate surface water drainage can also lead to the direct flooding of underground rooms and, in winter, result in sheets of ice on yards and paths which are a safety hazard.*

References
12.0   In assessing the severity and extent of defects in respect of the drainage of foul, waste and surface water, regard may be had to the following regulations and standards for new building work, but failure to meet these would not, in itself, necessarily constitute grounds for unfitness.

(1)   Building Regulations, 1991, Building Regulations & Approved Documents H1 *Sanitary pipework and drainage*, H2 *Cesspools and tanks*, and H3 *Rainwater drainage*.

(2)   BS 5572: 1994 *Code of practice for sanitary pipework*.

(3)   BS 6297: 1983 *Code of practice for design and installation of small sewage treatment works and cesspools*.

(4)   BS 6367: 1983 *Code of practice for drainage of roofs and paved areas*.

(5)   BS 8301: 1985 *Code of practice for building drainage*.

Drainage - guidance note

12.1   A dwelling-house is unfit for human habitation if, in the authority's view, it lacks an effective system for the draining of foul, waste and surface water or, where it is a flat, it or the building or a part of the building outside the flat lack such a system, and for that reason it is not reasonably suitable for occupation.

12.2   In deciding whether a dwelling-house is or is not unfit, the authority should consider whether the dwelling-house or building currently has an effective system, both above and below ground, for the draining of foul, waste and surface water, which is designed, installed and in a condition so as not to be prejudicial to the health and safety of any occupants or to the structural fabric.

12.3   In reaching this decision, the authority should have regard, amongst other things, to:

(a)   the coverage and capacity of the system or systems;

(b)   their susceptibility to blockage or leakage;

(c)   the provisions for clearing blockages;

(d)   the seals preventing foul air entering the dwelling and ventilation of the systems (foul & waste water only); and

(e)   the siting, design and installation of any private outfall.

12.4   The capacity of the foul and waste water drainage system as determined by the size and gradient of the pipes, should be large enough to carry at any point the expected flow, as governed by the type, number and grouping of appliances. Foul and waste water pipes, particularly inside the building, for example, those passing through underground and other rooms, should be fully watertight and gastight.

12.5   A water closet should discharge through a trap and branch pipe into a gravity fed discharge stack or drain. However, a macerator and pump small bore drainage system may be considered acceptable if the occupants also have access to a gravity discharged w.c. within the building or curtilage. The sink, washbasin and bath or shower should each discharge through a trap and branch pipe to a discharge stack or, where located on the ground floor, into a gully or direct to a drain.

12.6   All points of discharge into a foul or waste water system should be fitted with a water seal (trap) to prevent foul air from the system entering the dwelling-house under working conditions. To prevent water seals in the traps being lost by pressures which can develop in the system, discharge stacks should be ventilated. To clear any blockages, access points should normally be provided to lengths of pipe which cannot be reached from any other part of the system. (Repair 3.10)

12.7   Foul and waste water should discharge into a suitable outfall such as a public or private sewage system, septic tank, cesspool or settlement tank which has a capacity capable of dealing with the effluent. Cesspools, septic tanks and settlement tanks should be sited so as not to contaminate water supplies and so as to permit satisfactory access for emptying. They should be constructed and in a condition so as to be impervious to leakage or ingress of subsoil water, to have adequate ventilation and to be otherwise non prejudicial to health and safety. The condition of any private outfall outside the curtilage should be considered, whether or not this is shared with other dwellings.

12.8   The capacity of the surface water drainage system as determined by the size and gradient of rainwater gutters and pipes, should be large enough to carry at any point the expected flow, as governed by the area to be drained and an intensity of rainfall typical for the locality. In addition, the gradient of roofs and yards should normally be adequate to ensure proper draining of surface water away from the building. (Fitness Standard 2.13)

12.9 Rainwater pipes should discharge into a drain or gully but may discharge to another gutter or onto another surface or yard if it is well drained. The system should be such as to prevent flooding, particularly of underground and other rooms, and the formation in winter of sheet ice on yards or paths which because of its extent and location presents a serious risk to the safety of any occupants. Where a surface water system would not be expected, for example, on thatched roofs or for small roofs and balconies, the design should be such that rainwater is discharged clear of the building. (Repair 3.10)

12.10 Surface water should normally discharge into a suitable outfall such as a surface water or combined sewer, soak away, a storage container or water course, which is of adequate capacity. Any downpipe which discharges into a combined foul and surface water system should do so through a trap.

Annex B

FITNESS ENFORCEMENT - CODE OF GUIDANCE FOR DEALING WITH UNFIT PREMISES

1.   The guidance in this code is given by the Secretary of State for the Environment under section 604A of the Housing Act 1985 (the 1985 Act) and section 85 of the Housing Grants, Construction and Regeneration Act 1996 (the 1996 Act).

2.   **It is given to all local housing authorities in England and they are required to have regard to it** in deciding for the purposes of sections 189, 264, 265 and 289 of the 1985 Act and sections 81 and 84 of the 1996 Act whether the **"most satisfactory course of action"** in respect of premises that have been identified as unfit for human habitation is:

- **Repair**
  that is the service of a repair notice in accordance with section 189(1) or (1A) of the 1985 Act; or

- **Deferred action**
  that is the service of a deferred action notice in accordance with section 81 of the 1996 Act;

  or the renewal of a deferred action notice in accordance with section 84 of the 1996 Act; or

- **Closure**
  that is the making of a closing order in accordance with subsection (1) or subsection (2) of section 264 of the 1985 Act; or

- **Demolition**
  that is the making of a demolition order in accordance with subsection (1) or subsection (2) of section 265 of the 1985 Act; or

- **Clearance**
  that is the declaration of the area in which the premises are situated to be a clearance area in accordance with section 289 of the 1985 Act.

3.   Under section 97 of the 1996 Act authorities are also required to have regard to guidance given under section 604A of the 1985 Act and section 85 of the 1996 Act in deciding whether completion of the relevant works for which a renovation grant is sought is the most satisfactory course of action. For that purpose authorities are required to treat the guidance in this code on the service of a repair notice as guidance given in respect of the completion of the relevant works.

Power to charge for fitness enforcement

4.   While not formally part of the statutory guidance which forms this code, local authorities attention is drawn to section 87 of the 1996 Act. This provides them with power to make a reasonable charge as a means of recovering certain expenses incurred in:

- serving a repair notice (under sections 189 and 190 of the 1985 Act);

- serving or deciding to renew a deferred action notice;

- making a closing or demolition order.

Subsections (2) to (4) of section 87 specify the expenses which may be recovered. Under subsection (5), the Secretary of State has power to specify by order the maximum amount of any charge. The

Housing (Maximum Charge for Enforcement Action) Order 1996 specifies the maximum amount as £300.

5.   Section 88 of the 1996 Act sets out the powers available to a local authority for recovering any charge they may make under their section 87 powers. In deciding whether to exercise their powers to make a charge and the level of any charge they decide to make, authorities will want to take into account the circumstances of the person or persons against whom enforcement action is being taken.

IDENTIFYING THE NEED FOR ACTION

6.   **The housing fitness standard** (section 604 of the 1985 Act as substituted by paragraph 83 of schedule 9 to the Local Government and Housing Act 1989) sets out the standard for determining whether premises are fit for human habitation. There are a number of ways in which unfit premises might come to the attention of a local authority. These include:

- as a result of a Neighbourhood Renewal Assessment (NRA) carried out with a view to declaring a renewal area;

- as a result of a request for enforcement action to be taken on premises (eg from a tenant or the owner of an adjoining property);

- as a result of an application for renovation grant.

On identifying an unfit property a local authority is statutorily obliged to consider the "most satisfactory course of action" to deal with it.

Pre-formal enforcement action procedures

7.   While formal fitness enforcement action is a necessary and important part of the enforcement process, it should generally be viewed as a last resort. As a matter of good practice where in going about their private sector renewal activities authorities identify premises that while not unfit are likely in their opinion to become so in the future unless remedial action is taken, they should consider the case for drawing this informally to the attention of the owner or landlord as the case may be.

8.   Where an authority has expressed an informal opinion they should be prepared to provide a written explanation if requested by the owner or landlord. Such written explanation should include an explanation of :

- the remedial action which in the authority's opinion is needed and the timescale in which the authority considers such action needs to be taken;

- why the authority considers remedial action needs to be taken and the nature of the enforcement action the authority might be required to take in the future if the premises become unfit, including the right to make representations before, and the right of appeal against such action.

9.   Under section 86 of the 1996 Act, the Secretary of State has exercised his power to specify by order – the Housing (Fitness Enforcement Procedures) Order 1996 – a pre-formal enforcement procedure to be followed by local authorities. This is designed to improve the transparency of the enforcement process through the issuing of a "minded to take action notice"; to help local authorities reach sensible decisions with owners and landlords by giving them the right to make representations; and to help reduce the burden that can arise from having to take formal enforcement action.

10.   Local authorities are required to act in the way specified in the order, but the order provides that they are not **prevented from taking immediate enforcement action in any case where such action appears to them to be necessary**. This broad exemption recognises the need for local authorities to be able to take immediate enforcement action, and that such decisions can only properly be taken by

a local authority in the light of the circumstances of each case. While those circumstances will inevitably vary, examples where immediate action might be warranted include:

- where an authority considers there is imminent risk to the health and safety of the occupants of the premises;

- where an authority has followed pre-formal enforcement procedures with the owner or landlord on previous occasions and considers that to repeat the "minded to take action notice" procedure set out in the Housing (Fitness Enforcement Procedures) Order 1996 would amount to an unreasonable duplication of effort.

Formal action

11.   In deciding the most satisfactory course of action an authority needs to have regard to a wide range of factors. Wherever possible decisions should be made within the context of a local authority's private sector renewal strategy and taking account of the views and circumstances of those directly affected by any decision taken. Part of this will involve making an assessment of the effect of various courses of action in the context of the area in which the unfit premises are situated. The size of the area and the number of properties an authority chooses to take into account for this assessment will depend on the premises concerned and the characteristics of the associated housing stock. In some cases it may be sufficient to assess the immediate vicinity of the premises. In others consideration of several streets or a neighbourhood may be appropriate. There will also be cases where such assessments prove impracticable – eg where the unfitness is so serious that immediate action is required.

12   **Whatever the circumstances, the local authority has to satisfy itself that a fitness enforcement decision represents the most satisfactory course of action. They should also be able to provide reasons for that decision and be able to demonstrate that they have had regard to the guidance in this code in reaching a decision.**

Information requirements and initial assessment

13.   A local authority should obtain sufficient information to enable it to undertake an initial assessment of the alternative courses of action. The Secretary of State recommends the NRA method. This is primarily designed as an aid to deciding strategies for larger scale areas but it can be readily adapted to smaller scale surveys and assessments. It has the advantage that it is based on a series of sequential steps designed to enable local authorities to explore the costs and socio-environmental implications of any course of action.

14.   The NRA method can help authorities to:

- decide the most satisfactory course of action in the prevailing circumstances; and

- explain the chosen course of action to those directly affected; to a county court in the case of an appeal; or to an inspector at any public local inquiry on compulsory purchase orders in a clearance area.

15.   The basic steps for the NRA to be used in the assessment of unfit dwellings are set out in *Annex C3 Appendix 4*. These steps are the same whether they are being used to assess a single unfit dwelling or whether a renewal area is being considered. However the scope and scale of the assessment will differ. Where it is used for a single unfit dwelling most of the information required is likely to be available to the authority and the NRA process becomes a checklist to ensure that all relevant costs and issues have been considered in coming to a decision on the most satisfactory course of action. The scope of the assessment is likely to increase the more properties there are to be considered.

16.   Where the NRA is being used for single unfit premises the neighbourhood to be considered may include:

- a single unfit property;

- a terrace, part of a terrace or block;

- more than one terrace, or other group of dwellings if the unfit premises are in a neighbourhood of properties in similar condition.

17.   The purpose of carrying out a NRA for unfit premises is to ensure that:

- economic, social, and environmental factors are taken into account in determining the most satisfactory course of action;

- the long term consequences of action are considered;

- the action on the unfit premises takes into account the effect of that action on neighbouring premises.

The unfit premises to be assessed may be included within a declared Renewal Area (RA) or within the boundaries of the NRA for a potential RA. Here the neighbourhood will be that of the RA itself and the action on the unfit property will be part of the overall strategy for the area. The assessment of options for the unfit premises will therefore be undertaken in the context of the NRA for the RA.

18.   Although action on the unfit premises is being considered as part of the strategy for the RA, using information obtained as part of the NRA, it is possible that further information will be needed. This may occur as internal inspections will not have been made on all properties in the area. If an external inspection identifies that premises may be unfit then an internal survey must also be undertaken. Full surveys will also be needed on neighbouring properties to establish whether they are unfit as this will influence the most satisfactory course of action.

19.   It should not be anticipated that all unfit premises in a RA will have been identified at the outset. Because not all will have been internally inspected some unfit premises may emerge during the life of the RA. Others may become unfit during the life of the RA. In these circumstances the authority must again consider the most satisfactory course of action for the unfit premises but the choice will be influenced by the overall strategy for the RA. In these circumstances it should be possible to maximise the information already available from the initial NRA for the RA. At most it should only be necessary to fill in gaps in information already assembled.

20.   In developing alternative options for dealing with unfit premises authorities are advised to give equal weight to the socio-environmental factors and the economic appraisal. In undertaking the economic appraisal it is important however to consider both the present and future costs consequences of the options available for dealing with the unfit premises. This can be undertaken through the application of the formula set out in paragraph 30 of *Annex C3 Appendix 4*. Authorities are advised to use the formula as the basis for comparing the financial implications of the alternative courses of action.

21.   The formula produces the total costs incurred over 30 years arising from a given course of action and offsets these against the change in the value of the premises arising from each of the actions taken over the 30 year period. Costs beyond the first year are discounted to present values. Authorities are recommended that they base their costs for year 30 on a further major decision on the future of the dwelling for the following 30 years. The costs included in the formula are total costs rather than those just falling to the public sector. This ensures that decisions are based on an awareness of the overall economics of alternative courses of action and not just on their implications for the public sector.

22.   This assessment related to unfit dwellings will only include the unfit premises whose future is being considered. However, it is likely that decisions taken about these unfit premises will impact on neighbouring dwellings and that associated decisions regarding those neighbouring dwellings will be

affected by the decision for the unfit premises. Where such an impact is likely it will be necessary to work through the economic formula twice – once for the unfit dwellings alone and then again including the other dwellings which may be affected by the decision taken on the unfit premises. This will provide comparisons of the cost implications of each option for the whole group of affected dwellings as well as for the unfit premises alone. This could have an important bearing on the final decision. However the costing used for the whole affected group need not be as detailed as those used for the unfit premises alone.

23.   It is for a local authority to decide on the range of costs to include. It is more important that the range of costs included in each option are consistent rather than ensuring that every conceivable cost has been included. In defining the costs which should be taken into account in comparing alternative courses of action, it is necessary only to include those which differ between alternative courses of action. Costs which are common to each option can be excluded. If there is uncertainty about the scale of the costs it will be necessary to test whether the options are sensitive to alternative assumptions.

RELEVANT FACTORS IN DECIDING THE MOST SATISFACTORY COURSE OF ACTION

24.   The factors a local authority will need to consider in arriving at a decision on the most satisfactory course of action will vary according to the particular circumstances. The most important ones are set out in the paragraphs that follow. The factors do not have any specific weighting, nor do they represent an exhaustive list. Decisions will need to be based on individual circumstances and authorities will need to take into account any other factors they consider relevant. **But an authority needs to be able to demonstrate that they have given consideration to the factors listed in this code alongside any other matters they deem relevant in reaching a decision on the most satisfactory course of action**. Authorities should make a point of clearly explaining decisions to those against whom they take enforcement action. Such practice will be an important factor in helping to avoid frivolous appeals or appeals which might arise from a misunderstanding of the reasons for an authority's decision.

General factors relevant to the fitness enforcement options

25.   The fitness enforcement options open to local authorities are those set out in paragraph 2 of this code – that is repair, deferred action, closure, and demolition, whether or not as part of a declared clearance area. In reaching a decision on whether any of these options represent the most satisfactory course of action a local authority should take the results of the initial assessment and then consider:

- each option within the context of their private sector housing renewal strategy and the resources available for taking the strategy forward;

- the practicality of the options having regard to the physical condition of the premises (eg whether it is practicable to repair or whether the structure is completely outworn) and of any premises onto which they abut (eg within a terrace of houses or a block of flats);

- the life expectancy of the premises if repaired;

- the need to take into account the relationship of the premises with neighbouring properties and the condition of those properties;

- proposals for the future of the area in which the premises are situated, including: whether the premises are within a conservation or renewal area or area which is proposed as a renewal area or whether there are longer term plans for clearance; the need for the particular type of premises both in the short and longer term;

- the owner(s) and occupants of the premises including their circumstances and wishes and any proposals they may have for the future of the premises;

- in the case of rented premises, the management record of the landlord;

- the effect of each option on the community in the area;

- the manner in which each of the options will affect the local environment and overall appearance of the locality.

26.   Factors that are particularly relevant to each of the individual fitness enforcement options are listed in the following paragraphs. In reaching a decision on the most satisfactory course of action a local authority should have regard to these in addition to the general factors listed in paragraph 25 above. Paragraphs 28-33 provide additional background guidance on the deferred action notice option introduced under the 1996 Act.

Decision to serve a repair notice

27.   In deciding whether to serve a repair notice under section 189 of the 1985 Act, a local authority should:

- consider, in the case of those likely to qualify for renovation grant assistance, whether the authority should exercise its discretion to provide such assistance;

- consider the circumstances and wishes of the owner and occupants, including the extent to which they are willing and able to carry out repairs; and the advice and assistance that might be available, or made available, locally to help with that;

- take into account the suitability of the premises for inclusion in a group repair scheme and the extent to which proposals for the preparation of such a scheme have been developed.

Deferred action notice option - background guidance

28.   Section 81 of the 1996 Act enables a local authority to serve a deferred action notice on an unfit property where they are satisfied that this is the most satisfactory course of action. Section 81 also provides that a deferred action notice which has become operative is a local land charge so long as it remains operative.

29.   A deferred action notice must:

- state that the premises are unfit for human habitation;

- specify the works which, in the opinion of the local authority, are required to make the premises fit;

- state the other courses of action which are available to the authority if the premises remain unfit.

The fact that a deferred action notice has been served does not prevent a local authority from taking any other course of action in relation to the premises at any time. They may review a deferred action notice at any time and **must** do so not later than 2 years after a notice becomes operative and at intervals of not more than two years thereafter. A local authority must also inspect the premises for the purposes of reviewing a deferred action notice. Under section 84 of the 1996 Act, the Secretary of State has power to vary the period of review but has no plans to exercise this power at present.

30.   If on review a local authority is satisfied that a deferred action notice remains the most satisfactory course of action they are required (section 84 of the 1996 Act) to renew the notice and serve notice of their decision. There is a right of appeal to the county court against the service or renewal of a deferred action notice (section 83 and section 84(4) of the 1996 Act).

31.   The deferred action notice option has been introduced:

- to assist authorities in the exercise of their fitness enforcement duties having regard to the discretionary renovation grant system introduced under the 1996 Act;

- to provide authorities with additional flexibility to develop and implement strategies for tackling the worst private sector renewal problems identified in their areas, having regard to their finite resources;

- to enable authorities to respond more readily to the wishes of those who might not want to face the upheaval that making their homes fit might entail or who might not want to leave their home – in cases where those wishes, when weighed with all the other relevant factors, point to deferred action as being the most satisfactory course of action.

32.   These are important and necessary flexibilities that go hand in hand with a discretionary renovation grant system. The Secretary of State expects local authorities to use the deferred action notice option sensibly and in relation to the degree of formal enforcement activity an individual local authority is already undertaking. Examples of where the service of a deferred action notice might be appropriate include where unfit premises are in an area designated by an authority for renewal in the future; where an authority wishes to respond affirmatively to an application for renovation grant to make the premises fit but does not have sufficient funds in the current financial year; where the elderly home owner might welcome minor works of improvement but not the upheaval that making the premises fit might entail; where the nature of unfitness is not considered by the authority to be seriously detrimental to the well being of the occupants.

Provision of advice and assistance

33.   When serving or renewing a deferred action notice local authorities should additionally consider whether it would be appropriate – using their powers under section 169 of the Local Government and Housing Act 1989 – to provide the person on whom the notice has been served with practical advice and assistance. Such help might include advice:

- on how to remedy the unfitness problems;

- on ways that the works might be financed;

- on how to employ a suitable builder;

- on agency services which might be able to assist.

Decision to serve a deferred action notice

34.   In deciding whether to serve a deferred action notice under section 81 of the 1996 Act, or renew a notice under section 84 of that Act, a local authority should in particular :

- consider the circumstances and wishes of the owner and occupants of the premises; the extent to which they are able to carry out repairs and the advice and assistance that might be available, or made available, locally to help with that;

- consider the health and needs of the owner and occupants and the extent to which these might be adversely affected by a deferment of action;

- consider the physical condition of the premises - eg whether it constitutes an immediate health and safety risk to the occupants;

- consider the cost and nature of the works required to make the premises fit and whether, in the case of those likely to qualify for renovation grant, the authority is willing, and has sufficient funds, to provide grant.

Decision to serve a closing order

35.   In deciding whether to make a closing order under section 264 of the 1985 Act, a local authority should:

- consider whether the premises are a listed building or a building protected by notice pending listing - where repair is not the most satisfactory course of action, serving a deferred action notice on or closure of a listed or protected building should always be considered in preference to demolition;

- take account of the position of the premises in relation to neighbouring buildings - where repair is not the most satisfactory course of action and demolition would have an adverse effect on the stability of neighbouring buildings, closure or the service of a deferred action notice may be the only realistic options;

- irrespective of any proposals the owner may have, consider the potential alterative uses of the premises;

- take into account the existence of a conservation or renewal area and proposals generally for the area in which the premises are situated - short term closure may be an option if he long term objective is revitalization of the area;

- consider the effect of closure on the cohesion and well being of the local community and the appearance of the locality;

- consider the availability of local accommodation for rehousing any displaced occupants.

36.   A closing order may be made in respect of a dwelling house (section 264(1) of the 1985 Act) or of a building containing flats, some or all of which are unfit (section 264(2)). The factors listed in paragraph 35 - and the need to have regard to the general factors in paragraph 25 above - will be as relevant to a building containing flats as to a dwelling house. In the case of the former, however, a local authority should also consider the condition of the common parts of the building and the proportion of unfit flats compared with fit flats.

Decision to serve a demolition order

37.   In deciding whether to make a demolition order under section 265 of the 1985 Act, a local authority should:

- take into account the availability of local accommodation for rehousing the occupants;

- consider the prospective use of the cleared site;

- consider the local environment, the suitability of the area for continued residential occupation and the impact of a cleared site on the appearance and character of the neighbourhood.

38.   A demolition order may be made in respect of a dwelling house (section 265(1) of the 1985 Act) or a building containing flats, some or all of which are unfit (section 265(2)). The factors listed in paragraph 37 - and the need to have regard to the general factors in paragraph 25 above - will be as relevant to a building containing flats as to a dwelling house. In the case of the former, however, a local authority should also consider the condition of the common parts of the building, the proportion of unfit flats compared with fit flats and the reasons why certain flats are unfit.

Decision to declare a clearance area

39.   A local authority should consider the desirability of clearance in the context of proposals for the wider neighbourhood of which the premises form part. In deciding whether to declare the area in which unfit premises are situated to be a clearance area under section 289 of the 1985 Act, a local authority should have regard to:

- the degree of concentration of unfit premises within the area;

- the density of the buildings and the street pattern around which they are arranged;

- the overall availability of housing accommodation in the wider neighbourhood in relation to housing needs;

- the proportion of fit premises and other, non-residential, premises in sound condition which would also need to be cleared to arrive at a suitable site;

- whether it would be necessary to acquire land surrounding or adjoining the proposed clearance area; and whether added lands can be acquired by agreement with the owners;

- the existence of any listed buildings or buildings protected by notice pending listing - listed and protected buildings should only be included in a clearance area in exceptional circumstances and only when building consent has been given;

- the results of the statutory consultations;

- the arrangements necessary for rehousing the displaced occupants and the extent to which occupants are satisfied with those arrangements;

- the impact of clearance on, and the scope for relocating, commercial premises - for example corner shops;

- the suitability of the proposed after-use(s) of the site having regard to its shape and size, the needs of the wider neighbourhood and the socio-environmental benefits which the after-use(s) would bring, the degree of support by the local residents and the extent to which such uses would attract private investment into the area.

ANNEX C1

RENEWAL AREAS : DIRECTIONS, SPECIFICATIONS, DETERMINATIONS, REQUIREMENTS AND CONDITIONS IMPOSED UNDER PART VII OF THE LOCAL GOVERNMENT AND HOUSING ACT 1989

1. This Annex reproduces the directions given, determinations made, and matters specified and required, and conditions imposed by the Secretary of State relating to renewal areas under various provisions in Part VII of the Local Government and Housing Act 1989 ("the Act"). The contents of this Annex have statutory force.

Section 89(5):

Consultation and publicity

2. In exercise of his powers under subsection (5) of section 89 of the Act, the Secretary of State hereby directs that, before exercising their power to declare an area to be a renewal area a local housing authority shall:

 (1) (a) publish in two or more newspapers circulating in the locality (of which one at least shall, if practicable, be a local newspaper) and (b) for not less than 7 days display on conspicuous sites throughout the area notices indicating their intentions; identifying the area; naming a place where a map defining the proposed renewal area may be inspected; and indicating where representations concerning the proposed renewal area should be addressed, allowing a period of not less than 28 days for these to be made;

 (2) not more than 7 days after publication of the newspaper notice referred to in (1) above, deliver to each address in the area a statement containing the same information together with a summary of the report referred to in section 89(1) of the Act explaining why they propose to declare a renewal area;

 (3) consider any representations which have been made to them providing a written explanation to the person who made the representation where it is not proposed to accept a point made.

Section 90(1):

Conditions for declaration of a renewal area

3. In exercise of his powers under subsection (1) of section 90 of the Act, the Secretary of State hereby directs that:

 (1) for the purposes of paragraph (a) of that subsection, the specified minimum number is 300;

 (2) for the purposes of paragraph (b) of that subsection, the specified proportion is 75%;

 (3) for the purposes of paragraph (c) of that subsection:

 (i) the condition with respect to the physical condition of the dwellings in the area is that at least 75% of the dwellings are unfit or could qualify for relevant works under sections 12, 17, 27 or 60 of the Housing Grants, Construction and Regeneration Act 1996; and

 (ii) the condition with respect to the financial circumstances of those living in the area is that at least 30% of the households in the area appear to the authority to be eligible for one or more of the following state benefits: Council Tax Benefit; Disability

Working Allowance; Earnings Top Up; Family Credit; Housing Benefit; Income Support; Job Seeker's Allowance.

Section 91(2):

Statement of numbers of dwellings, HMOs and hostels

4.   In exercise of his powers under subsection (2)(b) of section 91 of the Act, the Secretary of State requires that as soon as may be after declaring a renewal area a local housing authority shall send to him a statement of the numbers of dwellings and houses in multiple occupation (as defined in section 100 of the Act) and hostels in the area on the day it was declared.

Section 92(2):

Publication of information

5.   In exercise of his powers under subsection (2) of section 92 of the Act, the Secretary of State directs that as soon as may be after declaring a renewal area and thereafter at intervals not exceeding two years a local housing authority shall:

(1)   (a)   publish in two or more newspapers circulating in the locality (of which one at least shall, if practicable be a local newspaper) and (b) for not less than 7 days display on conspicuous sites throughout the area notices indicating:

(i)   the action they propose to take in relation to the area;

(ii)   the action they have taken in relation to the area, and

(iii)   the assistance available for the carrying out of works in the area.

(2)   not more than 7 days after publication of the newspaper notice referred to in 1 above deliver to each address in the area a statement containing the same information.

Section 95(2):

Exclusion of land and termination of a renewal area

6.   In exercise of his powers under subsection (2) of section 95 of the Act, the Secretary of State directs that, before exercising their power under subsection (1) to exclude land from a renewal area, or declare that an area shall cease to be a renewal area, a local housing authority shall:

(1)   (a)   publish in two or more newspapers circulating in the locality (of which one at least shall, if practicable, be a local newspaper) and (b) for not less than 7 days display on conspicuous sites throughout the area notices indicating their intentions; identifying the area which will be excluded from, or cease to be a renewal area; naming a place where a map defining the area may be inspected; and indicating where representations concerning the proposal should be addressed, allowing a period of not less than 28 days for these to be made;

(2)   not more than 7 days after publication of the newspaper notice referred to in (1) above deliver to each address in the area a statement containing the same information;

(3)   consider any representations which have been made to them, providing a written explanation to the person who made the representation where it is not proposed to accept a point made.

Section 95(3):

Exclusion of land from a renewal area

7. In exercise of his powers under subsection (3)(b) of section 95 of the Act, the Secretary of State specifies that, after resolving to exclude land from a renewal area, a local housing authority shall send to him the following additional information:

> (1) A copy of a map indicating the land which has been excluded from the renewal area.

Section 96(2):

Contributions towards expenditure

8. In exercise of his powers under subsection (2) of section 96 of the Act, the Secretary of State hereby determines that expenditure incurred by a local housing authority under Part VII of the Act and which is certified by that authority as incurred in connection with any of the matters falling within the matters eligible for contributions set out below is expenditure in respect of which he will pay contributions:

(1) Matters eligible for contributions:

(a) *Street works*

Carrying out or assisting street works and traffic management schemes designed to enhance the environment of the area, excluding normal highway maintenance and improvement works carried out for the benefit of road users in general.

(b) *Landscaping*
Improving small areas of land whether by conversion to open space children's play areas, residents' parking or other purposes intended to benefit the environment of the area, or by landscaping, clearing waste land and planting, including the acquisition of land for such purposes.

(c) *Exteriors and Curtilages of Buildings*
Improving the external appearance of buildings in the area and the appearance of their immediate surroundings, excluding work carried out as part of a Group Repair scheme under Part 1 of the Housing Grants, Construction and Regeneration Act 1996 and works such as routine maintenance and structural repairs which owners would normally carry out for their own benefit; but including any other works such as cleaning and colour-washing exterior walls, repair and replacement of decorative architectural features, or improvements to the appearance of garden boundaries and out-buildings which are intended to benefit the appearance of the area as a whole.

(d) *Community Facilities*
The conversion of existing buildings to provide community facilities such a meeting halls and other accommodation for social and recreational activities where such facilities are lacking in the area and are intended to benefit the local community as a whole.

(e) *Miscellaneous Works*
Miscellaneous works not covered by the preceding categories provided:

(i) their primary purpose is the improvement of the environment of the area as a whole;

(ii) they are not eligible for other forms of specific Exchequer assistance; and

(iii) the expenditure on which contribution is claimed does not exceed half the aggregate of the expenditure towards which contribution may be paid in the area.

(2) Matters not eligible for contribution:

    (a) Works to the interiors of housing accommodation;

    (b) Works to improve or provide facilities which are intended primarily to produce revenue for the authority.

    (c) Works to commercial and industrial premises which are likely to increase significantly the profits of the enterprise occupying them.

    (d) Works of routine maintenance.

(3) Meaning of "area":

    In paragraph 1 above "area" means the renewal area.

(4) The contribution shall be 50% of the expenditure incurred and shall be payable annually.

(5) The aggregate of the expenditure towards which such contributions may be made with respect to a renewal area shall not exceed the sum arrived at by multiplying:

    (a) £1,000 by

    (b) the number of dwellings in the area at the date of the declaration or such higher number of dwellings as the authority may subsequently notify to the Secretary of State to include dwellings constructed or otherwise provided after that date.

(5A)(1) After 31st March 1997, the aggregate of contributions paid in respect of matters eligible for contributions (including any payment made to the local housing authority as a result of a prior year adjustment to subsidy already received by the authority) in any financial year (when aggregated with relevant payments) shall not exceed the total provision allocated to the local housing authority towards relevant expenditure for that financial year.

(2) In this paragraph -

    "the 1985 Act" means the Housing Act 1985;

    "the 1989 Act" means the Local Government and Housing Act 1989;

    "the 1996 Act" means the Housing Grants, Construction and Regeneration Act 1996;

    "allocated" means allocated in exercise of the powers in section 132 of the 1989 Act or section 92 of the 1996 Act or any of the powers under which relevant payments are made;

    "relevant expenditure" means expenditure incurred by the local housing authority under -

        (a) section 429 of the 1985 Act (improvement for sale schemes),

        (b) Part IX of the 1985 Act (slum clearance),

        (c) Part VII of the 1989 Act (renewal areas),

        (d) Part VIII of the 1989 Act (grants towards costs of improvements and repairs etc.), other than in relation to disabled facilities grants,

        (e) Part I of the 1996 Act (grants etc. for renewal of private sector housing), other than in relation to disabled facilities grants, or

        (f) section 139 of the 1996 Act (relocation grants); and

    "relevant payments" means contributions and subsidies (other than in relation to disabled facilities grants) paid in that financial year under section 429 of the 1985 Act (contributions for improvement for sale schemes), sections 132 (contributions for improvements and repairs) and 165 (slum clearance subsidy) of the 1989 Act and sections 92 (contributions for renewal of private sector housing) and 139 (relocation grants) of the 1996 Act.

(6) Meaning of "dwelling":

    In paragraph (5), "dwelling" includes a house in multiple occupation or a hostel.

(7) Contribution will be payable in 10 instalments on account on the basis of an authority's estimated expenditure in each financial year. The balance will be payable on receipt of the authority's claim after the end of the financial year to which it relates, subject to any adjustment, if necessary, once the claim has been examined by an auditor appointed by the Audit Commission.

Section 96(3):

Conditions imposed on payment of contributions

9.   In exercise of his powers under subsection (3) of section 96 of the Act, the Secretary of State, with the approval of the Treasury, hereby imposes the following conditions on the payment of contributions under section 96 of the Act:

(a)   Each authority shall maintain adequate records of expenditure to facilitate the completion of claims for payments of contribution. Claims shall be submitted in such form and at such times, as may from time to time be required by the Secretary of State.

(b)   An authority shall permit the auditor appointed by the Audit Commission, or any other officer authorised by the Secretary of State, to have access to and inspect the registers, records and where necessary, accounts, plans and contracts and other relevant documents and vouchers.

Section 96(4):

Payment of contributions at an increased rate

10.   In exercise of his powers under subsection (5) of section 96 of the Act, the Secretary of State hereby determines that any application made to him under section 96(4) before declaration of a renewal area for contributions to be paid at a higher rate than set out in paragraph 4 of the determination under section 96(2) should be accompanied by:

(a)   a full justification of why the higher rate of contribution is necessary;

(b)   detailed costings and specifications of the proposed works;

(c)   a map on which the proposed renewal area is defined and the report referred to in section 89 of the Act.

Annex C2

RENEWAL AREAS : DECLARATION AND POST DECLARATION ISSUES

Conditions for declaration of a renewal area

1.   A renewal area may not be declared without specific approval from the Secretary of State unless it meets the conditions specified in *Annex C1*. It should be clear from the results of the NRA whether the proposed area meets all the conditions. The following sets out the reasoning behind the conditions.

●   **Size of the Renewal Area - minimum 300 dwellings**

It is considered that 500 dwellings represents the minimum size normally necessary for an area to fully reap the benefits of a comprehensive approach of a renewal area and to attract the interest of financial institutions and developers. However, it is acknowledged that outside major urban concentrations there are a number of smaller self-contained settlements which would benefit from the renewal area approach. Therefore the Secretary of State has decided to specify a minimum of 300 dwellings for the purposes of section 90(1)(a) of the Local Government and Housing Act 1989 (the 1989 Act).

All renewal areas should be based on identifiable cohesive neighbourhoods and it is anticipated that areas of substantially fewer than 500 dwellings are unlikely to be viable as renewal areas where they form part of a continuous urban fabric.

The maximum size of a renewal area is not specified but it is considered that an area of more than 3000 dwellings may not achieve a sufficient concentration of effort and may be too large to manage effectively.

When considering the size of a potential renewal area authorities will need to bear in mind what can be achieved in the 10 year lifespan of the renewal area given the resources available to them.

●   **75% of dwellings either privately owned or rented**

Renewal areas are not primarily designed to deal with problems arising from public sector housing and therefore should mainly consist of privately owned or rented property (75% of the dwellings in a renewal area). Privately owned dwellings for the purposes of Part VII of the 1989 Act are defined in section 90(2) of the Act.

●   **At least 75% of the dwellings must qualify for works for the one or more of the purposes mentioned in sections 12, 17, 27 or 60 of the 1996 Act**

This criterion is intended to cover poor housing which is in need of the sort of works for which renovation grants, common parts grants, HMO grants or group repair assistance would be available (irrespective of whether the occupants would qualify for grant): the properties need not be statutorily unfit. Areas in which the housing is not bad enough to meet this condition are unlikely to warrant the commitment of resources implied by a comprehensive approach. Initiatives such as strategically located group repair schemes or targeting of renovation grants are likely to be more appropriate.

and

- at least 30% of the households in the renewal area must appear to the authority to be eligible for Council Tax Benefit, Disability Working Allowance, Earnings Top Up, Family Credit, Housing Benefit, Income Support, or Job Seeker's Allowance;

Again this is to target renewal activity and resources on areas where a significant proportion of the residents (public sector or private sector) are poor. Authorities are not required to means-test all residents: they may, however, wish to carry out a sample survey in order to form a broad view as to whether the criterion is met.

Application for a special direction specifying different conditions for a renewal area

2.   While the Secretary of State has the power under section 99 of the 1989 Act to issue a direction specifying different conditions for the declaration of a renewal area, he will only be prepared to do so in exceptional circumstances. The vast majority of areas will fall within the specified criteria – see *Annex C1*. It is, however, accepted that there may be exceptions (for example, it might be appropriate to declare a smaller area such as a village in an old mining area or other similar identifiable community), but each of these will have to justified on their own merits.

3.   Authorities will need to examine carefully why they consider the declaration of a renewal area to be the most appropriate way of dealing with conditions in areas which fall outside the specified criteria. If it is considered that such an area warrants declaration then an application to the Secretary of State for a special direction should be sent to the appropriate Government Office for the Region. The application should consist of:

- a full justification for the declaration;

- the report referred to section 89(1) and (3) of the 1989 Act;

- a map defining the proposed renewal area;

- a statement that the authority have complied with all the publicity and consultation requirements as specified in *Annex C1*.

4.   The Secretary of State will have regard to any matters which he considers to be appropriate, these will include:

- any particularly severe physical or social problems in the area;

- private sector interest in the areas and whether the renewal area strategy proposes some novel, largely private sector led solution to the area's problem;

- the contribution declaration of a renewal area would make to other initiatives such as employment and training; and

- whether there are any associated schemes eg. regeneration initiatives.

5.   Authorities should be aware that the Secretary of State will not be prepared to make a direction specifying different conditions for the declaration of a renewal area if the only objective is to obtain public funding for the carrying out of environmental works or to facilitate group repair schemes.

Application for a higher rate of Exchequer Contribution

6.   The Secretary of State's specific approval is not required for expenditure which falls within the general determination at *paragraph 8 of Annex C1*. However, if an authority considers that the rate of contribution would be inadequate having regard to the action they propose to take in a particular area they may apply to the Secretary of State for contributions to be paid at a higher rate.

7.   Applications must be made before declaration and should contain the particulars set out in *paragraph 10 of Annex C1*. Any application should be sent to the appropriate Government Office for the Region and will need to be justified by explaining why the normal rate of contribution will not be adequate bearing in mind the action the authority proposes to take and intend to encourage others to take in order to secure the regeneration of the area. Applications will only be considered for works eligible for contribution under the terms of the general determination at *paragraph 8 of Annex C1* and will only be granted in exceptional circumstances. If such an application is made, the authority must not declare the area concerned to be a renewal area until the application has been approved, refused or withdrawn.

Annex C3

NEIGHBOURHOOD RENEWAL ASSESSMENT PROCESS

1. Before declaring a renewal area an authority should carry out a comprehensive appraisal of the area. The Secretary of State recommends a method known as Neighbourhood Renewal Assessment which the following guidance describes. Whether, and the extent to which NRA is used is for authorities to decide; but in reaching that decision they **must have regard to this guidance**. The guidance is supplemented by more detailed non-statutory guidance in the *Neighbourhood Renewal Assessments - Guidance Manual DOE, HMSO, 1992.* This following guidance is given to local housing authorities in accordance with the provisions of section 89(4) of the Local Government and Housing Act 1989.

Neighbourhood Renewal Assessment (NRA)

Principles of NRA

2. The NRA is a series of logical steps which, when taken together, provide a thorough and systematic appraisal technique for considering alternative courses of action for an area or individual dwellings. Whatever the scale on which the NRA is undertaken, the basic steps in the process are essentially the same. The scale of the NRA will affect the approach and, to some extent, the methods and advice adopted in this guidance concentrate on the application of the process to an area large enough to embrace a subsequent renewal area.

3. The NRA was developed to help authorities develop area-based strategies which are both forward looking and wide ranging. It has been designed to:

- help authorities draw boundaries around cohesive neighbourhoods;

- help authorities think about the long term future of the area by encouraging the consideration of cost consequences, over 30 years, of alternative options for the area;

- encourage the consideration of:

  - all the uses of land within the area under consideration, and

  - look at ways of dealing with housing in poor condition within a wider context than hitherto;

- encourage authorities to think broadly about possible alternative courses of action for the area, taking account of both public and private cost implications along with social and environmental factors which cannot be quantified in financial terms;

- encourage authorities to take account of a wide range of views including both those of people who already have an interest in the area (eg. residents, landowners and local businessmen) and those who might want to take an interest (eg. private developers and housing associations);

- help to build up a commitment by all concerned to securing the implementation of the chosen strategy.

4. **It must be emphasised that the NRA process is only an aid to decision making. The authority will still need to make choices. Nor is its purpose simply to find the lowest cost solution for an area. It does, though, make explicit the costs which will be incurred by each of the options considered; and provides a means for comparing these with the unquantifiable social and environmental considerations which also need to be taken into account.**

Setting up the NRA process

5.   An illustration of the NRA process is given in *Appendix 1 to this Annex*. It has been set out as a sequential process but in order for it to work effectively there will need to be some overlap between stages.

6.   The first step is to decide that there are areas of private sector housing within the local authority's boundaries which could be expected to benefit from being declared a renewal area (RA). This decision should be taken in the context of the overall private sector housing strategy adopted by the authority.

7.   Authorities will need to examine the implications for the rest of the private sector stock in their areas. As renewal areas require concentrated investment a decision to focus resources in one or more such areas will inevitably mean that there are other parts of the authority's area which will have fewer resources available to it. It may be necessary, where an authority has more than one potential RA within its boundaries, to decide on an order of priorities.

8.   Once the need to carry out an NRA and the approximate area on which it is to be focussed is identified the next essential step is to set up a core team and identify a team leader. Experience has suggested that the core team need work on the NRA full-time, but people with other skills (eg. valuers) can be co-opted as necessary. As NRAs are not just about housing, any team which is undertaking an NRA should include other disciplines. This arrangement will cut across functional hierarchies. The skills and personality of the team leader will be crucial to the success of the exercise; and it is advisable to bear in mind the need for the leader to be sufficiently senior within the authority to be able to wield some influence and command the use of resources.

Aims, objective and decision rules

9.   Once the decision to undertake an NRA has been taken authorities need to think about the **aims** for the area before they finalise the boundary of the NRA. It is important that they should have a clear idea at this early stage of what they hope to achieve for the area as it will provide the context for the rest of the NRA process. In stating their aim, the authority will also need to identify why they need to intervene in the area. This will help clarify the problems the area faces. An example of an aim might be:

> "To provide a focus and framework to facilitate an increase in confidence levels in and about the area and secure its long term future and positive identity, recognising the social, physical and economic aspirations of those who live, work and visit the area".

10.   The aim needs to be supported by **objectives** which meet specific ends which will contribute to the success of the aim. Examples of objectives could include:

●   to achieve an overall improvement in living conditions within a finite timescale;

●   to preserve a low cost housing market;

●   to enhance the image of the area in order to promote long-term confidence;

●   to assist, promote and support commercial development for an area.

11.   Although the initial list of objectives will be compiled by local authority officers the list should not be fixed at this stage. It is important to the success of the renewal area that the objectives of those people who currently have an interest in the area, or may have in the future are taken into account. The objective setting will inevitably go through a number of stages and may give rise to conflicting objectives.

12. The objectives which are set will subsequently be used as the criteria against which the options are tested. When the renewal area strategy is being implemented the objectives will serve as bench marks to monitor progress.

13. At this stage authorities should also identify decision rules which will apply to the initial sieving of options. Options which do not conform to decision rules can then be rejected. Examples of decision rules might include:

- political acceptability;

- conformity with policy commitments;

- technical feasibility.

Boundary definition

14. In practice this will overlap with the objective setting. As the objectives are set the boundaries will change. It is important to recognise that the boundary may be adjusted during the NRA process and that the boundary of any resultant renewal area will not necessarily be the same as the NRA (although the renewal area will fall within the NRA boundary). The setting of the boundary is not just drawing a line on a map. It is actually the first stage by which the aims and objectives are being translated into a strategy.

15. Authorities should note that at the preparation stage they are not trying to fix the boundaries of the potential renewal area. The boundaries of the NRA do not have to be the same as those of the eventual renewal; in fact they can be much wider. It would be possible for an authority to declare more than one renewal area following an NRA. Where a renewal area is being considered within a small town it may make sense to consider the whole town as being part of the NRA area with the renewal area being selected from within the NRA boundary.

16. At this stage the NRA boundary is flexible and should:

- be outward looking and not just delineate the housing within the area;

- encompass physical facilities which are related to the social, commercial and industrial functions of the area;

- be drawn with a view to identifying opportunities. Areas of vacant or derelict land would be considered for inclusion because of their redevelopment potential;

- be a mix of social and physical barriers to accommodate the social and community network.

Option generation

17. The aim of option generation is to identify different ways of dealing with the problems which face the area in up to a 10 year period. It is recommended that this process should take place before much information has been collected. If it is not undertaken until the detailed survey material is available there is the risk that those undertaking the process will become overwhelmed by too much information.

18. In undertaking option generation it is important that the thinking does not have too narrow a focus and it should not be constrained by existing practice, either consciously or sub-consciously. It may help to think of ways in which the area might be sub-divided and to consider potential options on such a sub area basis. However, it is important that if such an approach is adopted potential options are not eliminated simply because they would not fit in with the boundaries of such sub-areas as initially drawn.

19.   It is essential to include non-housing issues in the options and a "do-nothing" option should also be included. If as a consequence of not taking action the area declines, then there will be future costs. Market values will fall and at some point in the future the authority may have to take statutory action.

20.   Examples of the options which might be included for part or all of the area are:

- clear all pre-1919 houses;
- retain and improve all pre-1919 houses;
- clear the worst pre-1919 houses and improve the rest;
- retain/expand all commercial uses;
- remove all commercial uses from the area;
- redevelop under-used land;
- dispose of all public sector housing;
- improve traffic management;
- improve security;
- decentralise council services.

The ultimate aim will be to put together packages of those options which will form the basis of alternative strategies for the area.

21.   In order to undertake option generation effectively an authority will probably find it helpful to set up one or more workshop sessions at which all the appropriate disciplines can be represented along with elected members. They may find it useful to employ some techniques which help what is essentially a creative thinking process. Authorities may also find it helpful to employ a 'facilitator' to run this part of the process.

22.   Option generation should incorporate the views of those people who have an interest in the area. The ideal model would be to include representatives of the following groups as appropriate in the option generation sessions:

- members;
- residents;
- community groups;
- landlords;
- housing associations;
- local businesses;
- developers;
- Government Offices for the Regions;
- other statutory bodies.

23.   As a final stage in the option generation process, an authority will need to sieve through the options derived as a result of going through the process. As a first step the authority will need to assess each option against the decision rules set when the aims and objectives were developed and if an option fails, it should be considered no further. Where options do accord with the decision rules it will

be necessary to measure them against the objectives which have been set for the area and, again, options which would not contribute towards meeting these objectives should be discarded.

Information gathering

24.   This is the most resource intensive part of the NRA. The key to its success is for authorities to be clear about the use of the information. It would be easy to mount a general purpose survey and to discover that the right questions have not been asked. Experience suggests that data from surveys undertaken for other purposes cannot be successfully used for the purposes of the NRA and that it is less resource intensive to collect the information that is really needed than to try and manipulate that which is already available.

25.   The information needed for the NRA will probably mean that some or all of the following surveys will be required:

- house condition survey;

- residents survey;

- landlords survey;

- commercial users survey;

- employees survey;

- environmental survey.

These surveys are not substitutes for consultation. They are information gathering exercises and ways of establishing what people see as the problems of the area and of identifying their aspirations. The NRA guidance manual provides information on how these exercises can best be undertaken but it will be up to authorities to choose the methods they think will be the most appropriate.

26.   The NRA guidance manual recommends that it is not necessary to carry out a full house condition survey of each dwelling in the RA. Full surveys of 10% of the dwellings should be sufficient with only external surveys on between 50% and 100% of the remaining dwellings. However where, as a result of that survey, it becomes apparent that there are pockets of potentially unfit housing within the NRA boundary, the authority need to undertake full surveys of all the relevant properties. In any survey of unfit properties an authority will need to satisfy itself that the costs produced as part of the survey are robust and can therefore be used as a reliable basis for the assessment of the action which should be taken to deal with the unfit property as part of the overall RA strategy. This will then normally eliminate the need to undertake a further assessment related to the unfit dwelling itself.

Option development

27.   The sieving process which takes place at the end of the option generation stage will have left the authority with a reduced number of options which they will wish to put into "packages" in order to build up alternative strategies for the area. No more than five of these option packages should be produced. These packages can then be worked up in detail using the information obtained from the data gathering exercise. In setting out the detailed packages of options the authority may find that certain options are common to each package. For example, the refurbishment of commercial premises may feature in all five option packages for the area. If this arises, such common elements do not necessarily need to be included in the subsequent option appraisal as they do not affect the overall comparison. However they will need to be included in a final reporting exercise which will include a budget for the implementation of the RA.

28.   The two key parts of the development process are the economic assessment and the socio-environmental assessment.

Economic assessment

29.   The aim of the economic assessment is to enable authorities to consider both the current and future cost consequences of the different options they are considering for the RA. Its principles are to:

- include total, and not just public sector costs. Decisions should consider the overall economics of the action and not just the public sector costs;

- include only those costs for each option which differ from alternative options. For example, if the administrative costs associated with demolition are the same as those associated with retaining dwellings, then administrative costs should not be included in the assessment;

- consider cost consequences over a 30 year period;

- base costs for year 30 on a further major decision for the future of the area for the next 30 years;

- identify the benefits by the change in market values resulting from each action.

30.   All the costs and benefits are expressed in real terms which make no allowance for expected inflation. The costs and benefits beyond the first year (year 0) therefore need to be discounted to present values using a real discount rate. The Treasury rate for trading purposes is currently 8%. This process recognises that costs and benefits accrued today are worth more to individuals or the community than those arising in the future.

31.   The formula to be used in the economic assessment is set out in *Appendix 4 to this Annex*. Although the same formula is used as for individual unfit dwellings, there will inevitably be differences in the scope of the costs to be included and in the scale of the exercise when the formula is applied to the preparation of an RA strategy.

Sensitivity analysis

32.   Monetary values given to the costs and benefits included in the assessment will affect the outcome. The impact of different values can be determined through sensitivity analysis as explained in *Appendix 2 to this Annex*.

Socio-environmental assessment

33.   The socio-environmental assessment is a way of trying to decide which of the options provides the greatest social and environmental benefits for the area. To undertake this exercise a list of socio-environmental criteria need to be set out and each option assessed against them. *Appendix 2 to this Annex* illustrates the use of this technique and demonstrates that it gives a good visual impression of whether one of the options confers more benefits than others.

Option appraisal

34.   The option appraisal brings together the economic assessment and the socio-environmental assessment, along with an assessment of each of the options against the objectives set at the beginning of the exercise, as a basis for rational decision making.

35.   One way of undertaking the assessment of options against objectives is suggested at *Appendix 3 to this Annex*. This uses a similar scoring system to that suggested for the socio-environmental assessment in order to give a quick visual impression of relative levels of performance.

36.   Having undertaken these three assessments, an authority will have obtained three sets of information from which to identify:

- the comparative net present values of each option package;

- the package which appears to confer the most socio-environmental benefits;
- the option package which maximises the achievement of objectives;

and these will then form the basis for preparing recommendations for the adoption of a preferred strategy. The ultimate reconciliation of the three sets of information must remain, however, a matter of judgement and there are no rules set down in the NRA process to govern how an authority should select the "right" option package. All the NRA can do is to provide the tools for informed decision making so that officers, Members and residents can all be made fully aware of the implications of their aspirations and of the ultimate decision.

37.   As part of this appraisal process, the authority will need to consider both whether or not the declaration of an RA is likely to be the most appropriate course of action in the light of the issues and priorities identified in the course of undertaking the NRA and, if so, what its boundary should include.

Reporting

38.   Having identified the RA boundary and their preferred option package the authority will need to produce a costed implementation plan. This should be put together in a report which sets out briefly the findings of the NRA process, identifies the options which were appraised and justifies the final selection. It will then form the basis for the report required in accordance with the provisions of section 89(1) of the 1989 Act.

Annex C 3(Appendix 1)

NRA PROCESS

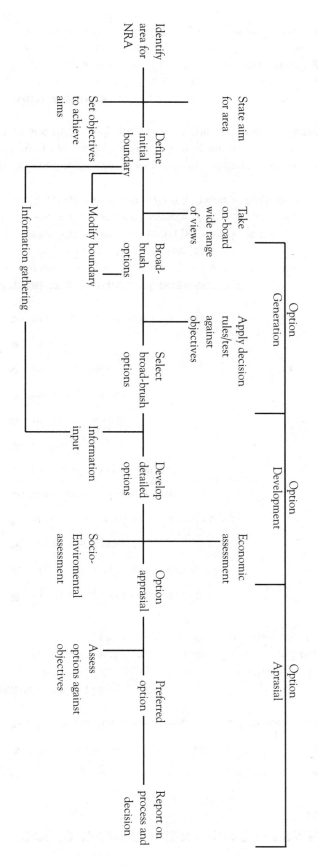

Identify area for NRA

Define initial boundary

Set objectives to achieve aims

Modify boundary

Information gathering

State aim for area

Take on-board wide range of views

Broad-brush options

Option Generation

Apply decision rules/test against objectives

Select broad-brush options

Information input

Option Development

Develop detailed options

Economic assessment

Socio-Environmental assessment

Option Appraisal

Option appraisal

Preferred option

Assess options against objectives

Report on process and decision

Annex C3 (Appendix 2)

NRA - SOCIO-ENVIRONMENTAL ASSESSMENT

1.   The aim of this assessment is to determine which of the options provides the greatest social and environmental benefits. It is undertaken in three stages:

- determine the socio-environmental criteria against which the options can be assessed;
- determine the method of assessment;
- decide whether some criteria carry more weight than others.

Determine criteria

2.   These criteria will largely reflect those issues which cannot be quantified in monetary terms. They will cover the non-economic aspects of the objectives and the social and environmental issues of importance to those people who have, or may have, an interest in the area. Examples of such criteria are:

- maintaining the existing community;
- private sector attractiveness;
- security and safety;
- anti-social behaviour elimination;
- environmental conditions;
- litter and refuse reduction;
- pollution;
- transport facilities;
- traffic arrangements;
- social facilities;
- shopping;
- non-conforming users.

Determine the method of assessment

3.   The preferred means of assessment is to assess all options against each of the criteria. For the former each of the option packages is awarded a value between 0-5 which reflects the extent to which the option meets the criterion. If each option package met one criterion to the same extent then each would have the same score. An example of this option ranking is given below. The extent to which each option meets one of the criteria is a matter of judgement.

4.   The aim of this assessment is to determine whether one option above the others confers the greatest socio-environmental benefits. This assessment will then have to be set alongside the economic assessment and the overall assessment of options against objectives for a decision to be made.

Determine weights

5.   It is unlikely that an authority would choose to give the socio-environmental criteria the same weight. Those criteria which are more important than others should be given a multiplying factor which increases the score of each option against that criterion. As with the ranking the assignments of weights is subjective. It is likely that some criteria will merit different weights depending on whose

perspective they are considered from. An authority will find it helpful to examine different weights to determine whether a change in weights affects the overall score of the options. Where there are significant changes an authority will need to determine which weight takes precedence.

SOCIO-ENVIRONMENTAL RANKING

Example Criteria	Option Packages				Weights	Option Packages			
	A	B	C	D		A	B	C	D
Environmental conditions	***	****	*	*	2	******	********	**	**
Social facilities	**	*****	***	*	1	**	*****	***	*
Traffic arrangements	*	*	*****	*	1	*	*	*****	*
Shopping	***	*****	*	*	1	***	*****	*	*
Private sector attractiveness	****	*	***	*	3	************	***	******	*
Existing communities	**	*	****	*****	2	****	**	********	*****

6.   Under the non-weighted options B and C score the same whereas under the weighted options A has the higher score.

ANNEX C3 (Appendix 3)

NRA – OBJECTIVE SCORING MATRIX FOR OPTION PACKAGES

	IMAGE OF AREA	IMPROVE LIVING CONDITION	PROMOTE COMMERCIAL DEVELOPMENT	PRESERVE LOW COST HOUSING	INVOLVE PEOPLE	NEEDS AND ASPIRATIONS OF RESIDENTS	PRIVATE AND PUBLIC INVEST.	LOCAL AUTHORITY COMMITMENT	OVERALL
OPTION A	5	5	5	2	4	3	4	5	33
OPTION B	3	2	3	4	2	2	3	3	22
OPTION C	2	2	4	3	1	1	2	1	16
OPTION D	0	0	0	0	0	0	0	0	0

Option A has the highest score

SCORES: 0 WORST

5 BEST

Annex C3 (Appendix 4)

Neighbourhood renewal assessment in relation to individual unfit premises

Definition

1. The code of guidance for dealing with unfit premises at *Annex B* recommends that, where authorities do not have sufficient information on which to reach a decision on action on unfit premises they should conduct a survey and assessment based on Neighbourhood Renewal Assessment (NRA). This is a series of logical steps which when taken together provide a systematic appraisal for considering alternative sources of action for unfit premises. The aim is simple – to establish which of the various options produce, or is likely to produce, the greatest net benefit for the community.

2. The steps to be followed are:

- statement of purpose

- definition of aims and objectives

- boundary definition

- option generation to determine the broad range of options for the dwellings in the area

- information gathering

- option development - refining broad options into a workable number for appraisal purposes and ensuring that sufficient information is available

- option appraisal - costing and comparing options using economic formulae and socio- economic assessment

- reporting - selection of preferred option together with explanation. Where a local authority is of the view (following information obtained through a NRA and having regard to other factors mentioned in *Annex B*) that enforcement action is required on a property they should consider making it clear in the "minded to take action notice" required under the Housing (Fitness Enforcement Procedures) Order 1996 – *see also Annex B* – that in reaching their view they have taken account of such evidence supplied by the owner or landlord in response to the NRA consultation.

Principles of NRA for individual unfit premises

3. The application of NRA to an unfit property has been developed to move away from what are often short term, and perhaps rather narrow, views of possible courses of action on unfit property. To achieve this the NRA requires that a number of basic principles are adhered to:

- the local context of the unfit property will need to be considered to identify the neighbourhood relevant to those premises. Unless the property is isolated it cannot be considered on its own;

- authorities should consider all the land uses within the neighbourhood they have defined. For example, the boundary of the NRA around the unfit premises could include some unused land the future of which needs to be considered at the same time as that of the unfit property;

- the long term future of the property will need to be assessed. The cost and benefits of the action on the unfit property will need to be considered over the next 30 years;

- both public and private sector costs should be considered;

- social and environmental factors, the impact of which are not quantifiable in monetary term, must also be considered;

- the NRA should take on board the views of people in the defined neighbourhood who will be affected by subsequent action on the unfit property. Views of those who might subsequently have an interest in the neighbourhood should also be considered;

- NRA is not about trying to find the lowest cost solution for an unfit property, it is about making explicit the costs and benefits which will result from the option chosen.

NRA process

4. The steps in the NRA process are listed above in *paragraph 2* and are illustrated in *Annex C3 (Appendix 1)*. Although presented as sequential steps there is overlap between them. The process is described in detail below.

NRA preparation

5. If the unfit premises are being assessed as part of the NRA for a renewal area then the preparatory stage will be as described in *Annex C3*. Where NRA is undertaken for unfit premises outside a renewal area the authority will need to decide who should be involved in the process and how best this can be organised. Decisions on action for unfit premises may require inputs on a wide range of issues including: relating action on the unfit dwellings to the private sector renewal strategy; the context of the premises; assessment of premises condition and costing of remedial action; valuation; obtaining views and preferences of those affected by the action; environmental assessment; relationship to statutory development plans.

6. To cover these issues authorities need access to a broad spectrum of skills. Once having identified who needs to be involved in a NRA for unfit premises it may be helpful to always use the same people to deal with unfit dwellings. This should streamline the process and help ensure that the authority takes an even-handed approach to its decisions on action on unfit properties.

Aims, objectives and decision rules

7. Having identified unfit premises the first step is to determine the aim of taking action on those premises and the objectives which will contribute to the success of the aim. In the case of unfit premises these are simple. The aim must be to remedy unfitness and the objective is to find the most satisfactory way of doing so.

8. Also at this stage the authority should identify any decision rules which are used to reject options which do not conform. It will be up to the authority to determine appropriate decision rules but these should not be so restricted as to rule out all but one option for development.

Examples of decision rules which may be appropriate are:

- technical feasibility – an unfit flat located in a block for example could not itself be demolished without demolition of all or part of the rest of the block;

- action does not conform to other controls – for example an unfit listed building in a conservation area would not normally be considered for clearance;

- action is inconsistent with other agreed plans – for example the unfit premises may be in the path of an imminent road scheme and repair may not therefore be a sensible course of action.

Boundary definition

9. The aim of defining a NRA boundary is to provide the context for deciding on the most satisfactory course of action for the unfit premises. Where the unfit premises are in a Renewal Area (RA) the context will be the strategy for the area as a whole. But where the unfit premises are outside such an area a boundary of the appropriate scale needs to be drawn.

10. Where the boundary is drawn will depend on the properties in the immediate vicinity. For isolated unfit premises in a rural community the boundary is likely to conform to the curtilage of the premises. Where the unfit premises are in a terrace of otherwise sound housing, with neighbouring streets of equally sound housing, then the boundary would sensibly be drawn around the terrace, or part of the terrace, in which the premises are located. If the premises are in an area of housing in apparently poor condition and where others may appear to be unfit then the boundary should be more widely drawn to include all those properties so defined.

11. In drawing the boundary an authority should consider the inclusion of adjacent non-housing land as this could substantially affect the costs and benefits which are taken into account in the option appraisal. For example, a vacant adjacent plot of land may offer opportunities which would enhance the option of clearance in that a much more useful site could be produced.

Option generation

12. In considering the options for action on an unfit property an authority will need to identify the long term consequences of immediate action taken. Each of the options should include the consequences of the immediate action over the next 30 years. In addition, at the end of 30 years the authority will need to consider the further long-term future of the area within the defined boundary. The actions which are considered, and their consequences, should cover all activity regardless of whether that action would be undertaken by the public or private sector.

Making the property fit

13. The authority will need to consider the long-term future of the premises. If the premises are to be retained long-term further work incurring additional expenditure is likely to be needed at some point between the initial actions and the end of 30 years if the premises are to retain their value.

14. An alternative is to retain the premises for the short-term and only undertake work to make the premises fit.

Making a closing order

15. Making the order will result in further action on the premises as it is unlikely that the property will be left closed for a 30 year period. Such consequential actions could involve inclusion in a clearance area, serving a demolition order, or that the premises are brought back into use.

Making a demolition order

16. Once the property has been demolished consequential action will relate to what is done to the site. This may be left until other land is made available when it could then be used for new building. Alternatively, the site may be used for non-housing purposes.

Declaring a clearance area

17. Clearance action will leave an empty site and there are a range of options for the authority to consider. The site could be temporarily not used, awaiting further clearance, or it could be given over to amenity use, some non-residential building or for new-build.

Issuing a deferred action notice

18.   By issuing such a notice the authority will have in mind what it sees as the long term future of the unfit premises. This should be indicated in setting out the consequential actions.

19. In producing options for unfit premises an authority will find it helpful to consider the views of those who will be affected by the decision. This would include those people who are resident in, or have an interest in, the premises included in the defined boundary. It would also involve people who may have an interest in the outcome of the action - for example in considering clearance the views of those who may be expected to provide any new-build should be obtained.

20. The last stage of option generation is to test options against the decision rules which were set out in the preparation phase. Any options which do not conform to the decision rules can be discarded. This should be undertaken before information is collected. There is little point in obtaining information which is relevant only to those options which cannot practically be implemented. Information which the authority will need to consider obtaining is described in *paragraphs 21 to 24* below.

Information gathering

21.   The key to the success of this part of the NRA is a clear brief for use of the information. This is easier to establish once an authority has determined which options are worth developing. The information required can be obtained from the following:

- an assessment of the condition of the properties within the NRA to provide information which will give costs of making the premises fit, plus costs of other remedial works - here a local house condition survey may be appropriate (see *Chapter 2*).

- socio-economic characteristics of residents to determine household composition and income;

- views and preferences of residents to establish what they feel about the area, whether they would want to stay or move elsewhere;

- views and preferences of people with a commercial interest in the area, either at present or those people who might have an interest following action;

- an environmental assessment of the area which considers the layout and design, appearance, vandalism, noise/pollution and crime/safety.

22.   The NRA manual for RAs provides a description of how this type of information can be obtained. It is important from an authority's point of view that it is seen to reach all decisions about action on unfit properties in an evenhanded way. There is, therefore, considerable merit in employing systematic means of obtaining information. It is recognised however that the scale of the NRA for unfit premises will be such that simplified versions of the information collected for the NRA for RAs may be more appropriate.

23.   The authority will need to obtain detailed information on the unfit premises but may consider it appropriate to obtain less detailed information for the rest of the premises included within the defined boundary. How much detail is collected will be influenced by the options which are being considered.

24.   Authorities should bear in mind that information collected as part of the NRA is not a substitute for consultation statutorily required.

Option development

25.   Here the authority is using detailed data from the information gathering exercise to quantify options and develop them in detail. Where quantification can be undertaken in monetary terms these

aspects are included in the economic assessment and where they cannot they are included in the socio-environmental assessment. The NRA methodology requires only that, for comparative purposes, those quantifiable which differ between options need to be included. For example, if administrative costs are the same for each option in terms of their value and timing then they can be excluded from the assessment.

(a) Economic assessment

28.   The aim of the economic assessment is to consider both the current and future economic cost and benefit consequences of the different options for unfit premises. This is achieved by reducing all the different costs and benefits into a single net cost figure. All the costs and benefits are given in real terms which makes no allowance for expected inflation. The costs and benefits beyond year one need to be discounted to present values using a real discount rate, the current Treasury rate is 8%. This process recognises that costs and benefits accrued today are worth more to individuals or the community than those arising in the future. Thus, all the costs and benefits are given in present value terms and the economic assessment produces a single net present value (NPV) for each option.

29.   The principles of the economic assessment are to:

- include total, and not just public sector costs - decisions should consider the overall economics of the action and not just the public sector costs;

- include only those costs for each option which differ in present value terms from alternative options - for example, if the administrative costs associated with demolition are the same as those associated with retaining the premises, then administrative costs should not be included in the assessment;

- consider cost consequences over a 30 year period;

- base costs for year 30 on a further major decision for the future of the area for the next 30 years;

- identify the benefits by the change in market values resulting from each action.

30.   In notation form the formula (treating the year in which action is first taken as Year 0) is as follows:

(a - b) [Year 0] + c(d - e) [Year 1] + c(d - e) [Year 2] (and so on for Years 3 to 29) + c(f - g)[Year 30] = cost of option (net present value - NPV).

Where:

a = total cost of initial action at Year 0 prices (eg renovation, demolition and rebuild or deferred action) for the individual property or group of properties under consideration. (Where fit properties are included in an assessment, little initial action may be required on them).

b = market value of dwelling or group of dwellings, at Year 0 values, after initial action completed (which, where a cleared site is to be used for non-residential purposes, will be the value of the site in its eventual after-use) MINUS the market value of the dwelling or group of dwellings before the action.

c = the appropriate factor for discounting future values to present values assuming a discount factor of 8 per cent per annum (see *Appendix 1 of Annex D3* for a list of factors). This means that for the interim action described below (c(d-e)), a figure will be derived for each year in which action takes place, and then these will need to be added up to achieve an overall NPV for the interim action.

d = costs arising from action taken between the completion of the initial action and Year 29. These should all be expressed in Year 0 prices but allocated to the year in which each action is expected to commence for discounting purposes. Such costs might include, for example, repair costs required to return the dwelling(s) to the same state as immediately following work in Year 0, or a decision to demolish in, say, 15 years time after an interim renovation programme (ie Year 14). There is no need to include maintenance costs as these are assumed to be the same following renovation or new-build.

e = for each of the years which interim action has been identified in "d" above, an estimate has to be made, in terms of Year 0 values, of the market value of the dwelling or group of dwellings after the interim action has been taken MINUS the market value (in Year 0 values) immediately before that interim action.

f = costs of action at Year 30, using Year 0 prices. It should include the major costs likely to arise as a result of a further major decision in that year about the future of the dwelling for the next 30 years, even though all the costs attributable to that decision will not arise in Year 30. If the assumed action is to retain a dwelling which was retained in Year 0 for a further 30 years, then the costs of the action should be assumed to be the same as in Year 0.

g = the market value of the dwelling after major action taken in Year 30 (expressed in Year 0 values) MINUS the market value of the dwelling (also expressed in Year 0 values) immediately before the Year 30 action. If the dwelling is one which was retained in Year 0, then the market value before the Year 30 action should be assumed to be the same as it was before the Year 0 action.

31. Costs and benefits should only be included in the formula if they are incurred in taking action on the unfit premises or are a direct consequence of that action. It will be up to an authority to choose the costs and benefits which are appropriate. As a guide, *paragraphs 40-42* below identify those costs and benefits which an authority may need to consider.

32. When undertaking a NRA for unfit premises, which is being considered in the context of the group of properties to which it relates, an authority will need to undertake two economic assessments for each of the options being considered. The first will be a detailed calculation of the net present values (NPVs) of each of the alternative courses of action in relation solely to the unfit property. The second will calculate the net present values of alternative courses of action in relation to the group of properties as a whole.

33. This assessment can be less detailed than that for the unfit property alone, provided that the same general assumptions are made in relation to the assessment of each alternative. However, it is important that both sets of calculations should be undertaken as the option with the lowest NPV for the unfit premises may result in a high NPV for the surrounding premises, thus making it an unviable option.

(b) Sensitivity analysis

34. Clearly the monetary values given to the costs and benefits included in the assessment will affect the outcome. The impact of a variation in these monetary values can be determined through sensitivity analysis, examples of which are provided in *paragraphs 43-48* below. This analysis can be undertaken for all monetary values included in the economic formula but it is only necessary where the values are likely to show substantial variation.

35. The aim of the sensitivity analysis is to determine whether changes in values will affect the ranking of the NPVs for each option. If the rankings remain the same when different values are used an authority can be reasonably confident that, for example, the option with the lowest NPV really would produce the lowest costs. Where there is little differential in NPVs for each option the sensitivity analysis is likely to change the rankings of the options. In such cases it may be appropriate for the authority to conclude that each option is likely to generate the same costs and that there is no economic difference between them.

(c)   Socio-environmental assessment

36.   The socio-environmental assessment is the means of trying to decide which of the options provides the greatest social and environmental benefits within the area. To undertake this exercise an appropriate list of socio-environmental criteria need to be produced and each option assessed against them. This assessment can be undertaken by using a simple scale from 0 to 5 and valuing each option on this scale in terms of how well it meets each of the criteria. An example is given in *Annex C3* (*Appendix 2*). This process gives a good visual impression of whether one of the options confers more benefits than others.

37.   Using a simple scale enables an authority to consider whether it wishes to accord different weights to the criteria used. If one of the criteria is felt to be three times more important than the others then all the scores against this criterion would be multiplied by three.

Option Appraisal

38.   At the end of the development process the authority will have a single economic cost for each of the options and a view as to which of the options confers the maximum social and environmental benefits. There are no rules by which the authority can be directed to choose an option from this information. **The NRA is not designed to give a "right answer"**. Ultimate reconciliation of the two sets of information must remain a matter of judgment. The information the NRA generates enables officers and members to be made fully aware of the implications of their decision.

Reporting

39.   Having decided the most satisfactory course of action the authority will wish to produce a report which sets out briefly the findings of the NRA process, identifies the options which were appraised and justifies the final selection.

Costs and benefits which may be considered for inclusion in the economic assessment

40.   The economic assessment includes those costs and benefits which can be described in monetary terms. Costs and benefits which accrue to either the public or private sector are included. It is not necessary to include those items which, being a transfer between two organisations, involve no drain on national resources. For example, the sale of land by a local authority to a developer produces a receipt for the local authority which represents a cost to the developer. But resources are not used up in the process, the ownership of an asset being exchanged.

41.   Costs can also be excluded if they are the same in present value terms as within all the options. For example if the administrative costs of serving a repair notice and any subsequent involvement in making the dwelling fit costs the same as serving a demolition order, and these activities were due to take place in the same year, then there is no need to include these costs in the assessment.

42.   The items listed below under both costs and benefits are provided as examples of what an authority may wish to include in the assessment. The list is not exhaustive neither is it expected that all the costs and benefits would be included in one economic assessment.

Costs are those for:

- works required to make the dwelling fit;

- works required over and above those to make the dwelling fit to secure its long term future;

- works required to maintain the value of the dwelling if it is given a long term future. These costs can be included as an annual cost or as a single lump sum figure for a year mid-way between that in which the action was taken and year 30. However the costs are included they must cover any likely repair and replacement work over and above regular maintenance;

- compensation which is paid to occupants where a closing order or demolition order is served, or where the property is included in a clearance area;

- rehousing, where this is the duty of the local authority. The costs used will depend on the supply of local authority accommodation and the length of time the displaced households makes use of the local authority accommodation. If the authority has surplus dwellings and the accommodation occupied would not otherwise have been used then the costs involved would be those of making that accommodation suitable for use. Where re-housing is temporary then the costs are those associated with the displaced household using that accommodation in preference to another household being housed. Such costs are described as "welfare costs" and are quantified as the annual cost of management and maintenance of a local authority property. If however the authority has to provide permanent replacement housing then the costs must be those of effectively adding another dwelling to the social rented stock regardless of whether a new dwelling is built or an existing property used. The costs should be expressed as the annual interest charges on the debt outstanding /incurred;

- securing a dwelling which is closed or is to be demolished;

- demolition;

- work associated with retaining a vacant site. If the site is in local authority ownership these may include initial site works and future maintenance. Where the site is in private ownership it is difficult to assume what costs may be incurred, costs of site insurance could be included;

- new-build costs of dwellings included on any cleared site.

Benefits for inclusions are:

- increase in market value of dwelling(s) as a result of action;

- increase in land values as a result of action;

- rental income where an authority rehouses someone in a dwelling which was previously vacant and would not otherwise have been used.

Sensitivity analysis: Example calculation

43.   Sensitivity analysis is used to identify whether changes to the costs and benefits used in the economic assessment of different options would result in different NPVs being produced, such that it would affect the decision about which option to choose. This analysis can be used to test the sensitivity of individual costs or components of individual options.

44.   This illustration of sensitivity analysis uses example 1 in *paragraph 52* below. The costs and benefits included in this example are:

Option 1

(i)	serving a demolition order	costs =	£15,650
(ii)	demolition	costs =	£300
		benefits =	£0
		discount factor =	0.93
		Total NPV =	£15,929

Option 2

(i)	refurbishment long-term	costs =	£14,855
		benefits =	£7,500
(ii)	maintaining value of dwelling	costs =	£7,000
		benefits =	£0
		discount factor =	0.34
(iii)	further refurbishment	costs =	£14,855
		benefits =	£7,500
		discount factor =	0.1
		Total NPV =	£10,471

With the above costs option 1 is more expensive than option 2.

45. Sensitivity analysis is undertaken on those costs about which there is greatest uncertainty and are likely to show considerable variation. It is suggested that in this example these are:

(i)   costs associated with maintaining the value of the dwelling;

(ii) the assumption that the dwelling will be further refurbished.

Costs associated with maintaining the value of the dwelling

46.   The cost of £7,000 may be felt to be rather arbitrary. Here the sensitivity analysis should be used to determine how high this cost could go before the NPV of option 2 equalled or exceeded that of option 1. This cost would have to be £23,054 to give an NPV equivalent to that of option 1. As the cost associated with maintaining the value of the dwelling is unlikely to be this high an authority could be fairly confident that the NPV of option 1 would remain less than that of option 2.

Assumption of further refurbishment

47.   It would be reasonable to consider the effect on the NPV of a change to the assumption of what would happen to the dwelling in year 30. The alternative to retaining the dwelling could be assumed to be the same as the action under option 1, i.e. demolition without rebuilding. This would give a cost in year 30 of £1,595. This would increase the cost of option 2 by £859. Therefore a change to the year 30 assumption has little effect on the costs of option 2.

48.   Having carried out both these tests the authority could be fairly confident that option 2 had the lowest NPV. These two tests are purely illustrative. It would be the responsibility of an authority to satisfy itself that sufficient sensitivity analyses had been undertaken such that it could be confident of the relative NPVs produced by different options.

Worked examples of economic formula recommended in code of guidance for dealing with unfit premises

49.   As a guide to using the economic formula, two worked examples have been provided. The first takes an isolated unfit dwelling and the second an unfit dwelling which is part of a terrace. Each example goes step by step through the formula for the options under consideration. The costs and benefits of each action are explained and the NPVs calculated. The costs used are purely illustrative.

50.   The examples are lengthy, but this is simply because they are described from first principles and on a year-by-year basis. The calculations themselves are relatively short and straightforward.

51.   In undertaking an economic assessment an authority will find that it is not necessarily in a position to produce robust costs for components, nor will it be able to put an accurate monetary value on all benefits. Assumptions will have to be made and an authority will have to use those available fig-

ures. In general, the use of net present values makes the costing simpler as all costs can generally be reduced to present day values. An authority may, however, wish to take into account real cost increases over time where these can be reasonably expected.

Example 1

(i)   Situation
52.   An isolated unfit dwelling, built before 1919.

(ii)   Options for Action
53.   These are:

- make the property fit by serving a repair notice;

- to defer action by serving a deferred action notice;

- make a closing order;

- make a demolition order;

- declare a clearance area.

For the purposes of this example it is assumed that the decision rules employed rule out the third and fifth options and that to defer action is not an appropriate course of action. Only the first and fourth options are therefore put through economic assessment.

54.   In detail these two options are:

1.   to demolish the property and not replace it;

2.   to refurbish the property for long term retention.

55.   Fulfilment of either option requires a different sequence of actions, with a different set of costs and benefits. The use of the economic formula enables the different sets of costs and benefits which can be expressed in monetary terms to be compared by reducing each option to a single net cost. Thus, before trying to use the economic formula, the authority should first identify the relevant costs and benefits.

(iii)   Identification of Relevant Costs and Benefits

Costs
56.   A cost is anything which can be identified as a drain on resources, regardless of whether it is met from public or private funds. For the economic formula it is necessary to consider the costs of the action to the unfit dwelling and then any consequent costs arising from this action.

Benefits
57.   A benefit is a release of resources. For the purposes of the economic formula it is identified by an increase in market value resulting from the action taken.

58.   *Paragraph 42* gives examples of the costs and benefits which an authority may include in the economic assessment of an unfit dwelling.

(iv) Cost and Benefits for Option 1

Year 0

Costs

59. For the first option shown above the authority would take action in the first instance by placing a demolition order on the dwelling. This action results in a cost to "society" of a dwelling lost for occupation. This cost can be represented by the statutory payments which the authority has to make to the occupants. These are in the form of a range of compensations:

- "home loss payment"

- "disturbance payment"

- compensation equal to the market value of the property less residual value of the dwelling which reflects the site value. In this example the site has minimal value.

The authority, in this case, has no obligation to rehouse the occupants as it is assumed that the sum of these compensations covers their cost of finding alternative housing.

Benefits

60. There is no monetary benefit from the action of serving a demolition order as there is no enhancement of the market value of the property.

Year 1

Costs

61. The next action is demolition. The cost is that incurred in pulling the property down. It is assumed that the site is then left.

Benefits

62. Here the monetary benefit would accrue from the enhancement of the market value of the site on which the unfit dwelling was located. If the site had the potential for development then its cleared value would be greater than its value with the property still standing. The benefit would be the increase in this value arising from the action of demolition.

63. In this example however it is assumed that development of the site is not a realistic option. Demolition therefore does not result in an increase in value.

Years 2-29

Costs and benefits

64. There are no further costs or benefits as the site is left in the same state as that following demolition.

Year 30

Costs and benefits

65. There are no costs as the site will continue to be left unused.

(v) Calculation for option 1

66. The costs and benefits from each year are brought together in the calculation of the net present value of the option. The economic formula for the NPV of option 1 above is:

(a-b) [year 0] + c(d-e) [year 1] + c(d-e) [year 2] etc for years 3 to 29 + c(f-g) [Year 30]

121

Year 0
(a-b) = (15,650–0)

a = the cost of serving a demolition order. This comprises:
  – £1,350 home loss payment
  – £300 disturbance payment
  – £14,000 compensation from a market value of £15,000 which leaves a residual site value of £1,000.

b = enhancement (if any) of market value of property on which demolition order served. This action results in no enhancement.

Year 1
+ c(d-e) = 0.93 (300-0)

c = discount factor for action taking place in year 1
d = cost of demolition
e = market value of cleared site less the market value of site on which the unfit property was located. There is no change in value.

Year 2 to Year 29
+ c(d-e) = 0.86 (0-0)

c = discount factor for year 2.
d = there are no costs in this period.
e = there are no monetary benefits in this period.

Year 30
+ c(f-g) = 0.1 (0-0)

c = discount factor for costs incurred in year 30.
f and g = there are no further costs.

This would give the following final calculation:

15,650 - 0 + 0.93(300-0) = 15,929 net present value

(vi) Costs and benefits for option 2

67.   To calculate a comparable net cost for option 2, the sequence of actions is represented as costs and benefits in the same way.

Year 0

Costs

68.   The cost of the initial action, renovation of the property, is simply the cost of the works carried out.

Benefits

69.   The value of the dwelling will increase as a result of renovation. The benefit accruing from the renovation is equal to the increase in market value of the property which results.

Years 1-29

Costs

70.   Although the property has been renovated further expenditure will be needed on the property in this period to retain the value of the dwelling. This is represented by the inclusion of a single sum for accumulated repairs at the mid-point of this period (treated as Year 14 since the first year is Year 0). An alternative is to determine an annual cost for carrying out work to the dwelling to maintain it in its refurbished state.

Benefits

71.   The expenditure does not result in an enhancement of the value of the property and thus there is no quantifiable benefit.

Year 30

Costs

72.   The property is to be retained again for the long term. It is assumed that it will need further major renovation to return the dwelling to its condition following renovation in year 0. The costs are assumed to be the same as those for renovation in year 0.

Benefits

73.   This renovation will result in an increase in the value of the property. It is assumed that the increase will be the same as that in year 0.

(vii) Calculation for option 2

74.   The costs and benefits from each year are brought together in the calculation of the net present value of the option. The economic formula for the NPV of option 2 above is:

(a-b) [year 0] + c(d-e) [year 14] + c(f-g) [Year 30] = total NPV.

Year 0	a = the cost of refurbishment.
(a - b) = 14,855 - 7,500	b = enhancement of market value of property refurbished (22,500–15,000).
Year 14	c = discount factor for year 14.
+ c(d-e) = 0.34(7,000 - 0)	d = assumed cost of accumulated repairs.
	e = no enhancement in market value as repairs only maintain value – they do not increase it.
Year 30	c = discount factor for year 30.
+ c(f-g) = 0.1 (14,855 - 7,500)	f = cost of refurbishing the dwelling for further long-term retention.
	g = enhancement in market value of refurbished property (22,500–15,000).

This would give the following final calculation:

$$7,355 + 0.34(7,000 - 0) + 0.1(14,855 - 7,500) = 10,471 \text{ total net present value}$$

75.   On this example option 2 has a considerably lower NPV than option 1. An authority would wish to test the robustness of this conclusion by undertaking sensitivity analysis - see *paragraph 43*. The results of this assessment would then need to be set alongside that of the socio-environmental assessment.

Example 2

(i) Situation

76.   One unfit owner-occupied dwelling in the middle of a pre-1919 terrace of five dwellings. The other four dwellings in the block, three of which are owner-occupied and one of which is privately rented, are in generally poor condition but not unfit.

77.   The block is adjacent to a cleared site of identical size which previously housed a similar terrace. The site has been grassed over and left undeveloped.

78. The housing in the surrounding area is of generally sound condition.

(ii) Options for action

79. These are:

- make the property fit by serving a repair notice;

- to defer action by serving a deferred action notice;

- make a closing order;

- make a demolition order;

- declare a clearance area.

For the purpose of this example the decision rules sieve out options two, four and five. Demolition of a mid-terrace property is not considered technically feasible as it will affect the structural integrity of the terrace. As only one dwelling is unfit the terrace itself cannot be declared a clearance area and there are no unfit properties in the surrounding housing. To defer action is not considered an appropriate course of action for the purposes of this example.

80. In detail the two options are:

(1) renovate the unfit dwelling and retain for the long-term with the aim that the rest of the terrace will be refurbished.

For this option assume:

Year 0: the property is made fit;

Year 1: two of the other four dwellings are privately renovated before deteriorating further;

Year 2: the two remaining dwellings become unfit and because the most satisfactory course of action is to retain the dwellings a repair notice is served;

Years 3-29: undertake repair work to maintain the value of all five dwellings;

Year 30: assume that at the end of 30 years most of the dwellings have become unfit: declare a clearance area - the whole block is demolished; rebuild six family units on the site consisting of the cleared site and the adjacent site; rehouse the tenant from the demolished block in one of the new houses.

(2) serve a closing order on the unfit dwelling.

For this option assume that:

Years 0: closing order placed on property: occupants move out;

Year 1: no action;

Year 2: two more dwellings in the terrace become unfit, declare the whole terrace a clearance area; acquire the unfit dwellings and compensate the four owner-occupiers and one landlord accordingly; rehouse the tenant;

Year 3: demolish the properties;

Year 4: rebuild six family units on a site made up of the cleared site and the adjacent site; rehouse the tenant of the original terrace in one of the new houses;

Years 5-29: undertake repairs to the new dwellings to ensure that they retain their value;

Year 30: retain the dwellings for the long-term. This requires some refurbishment.

In this example each of the primary actions has been assessed with only one set of consequent actions. An authority would normally want to test a range of consequent actions. For example, in the first option the decision may be to retain the dwelling but only for the short term, thereafter assuming the terrace would deteriorate in condition such that it would be included in a clearance area.

(iii) Identification of relevant costs and benefits

81.   Costs and benefits are defined and identified as described in example 1.

(iv)   Costs and benefits for option 1.

Year 0

Costs

82.   The initial action is the renovation of the property; the cost is simply the cost of the works carried out.

Benefits

83.   The value of the dwelling will increase as a result of renovation. The benefit accruing from the renovation is equal to the increase in market value of the property which results.

Year 1

Costs

84.   Two of the other properties which are in generally poor condition but not unfit are renovated. The cost is that of the works carried out. This is a lower cost per dwelling than that associated with the renovation in year 0 as the dwellings are not in as poor condition.

Benefits

85.   The benefit from this action is the increase in market value due to renovation of the two dwellings.

Year 2

Costs

86.   The two remaining properties become unfit and the most satisfactory course of action is to serve a repair notice with the aim of retaining the dwellings in the long-term. The costs are those of the renovation work and it is assumed they are the same as for renovation of the unfit dwelling in year 0.

Benefits

87.   The benefit from this action is the increase in market value of the properties which have been renovated. Because the whole terrace has now been refurbished the effect of this may be to further enhance the value of all the properties in the terrace. This assumption of additional benefit can be included in the assessment by a further increase in market value for all five dwellings. This is the type of assumption which would need to be tested in the sensitivity analysis.

Years 3-29

Costs

88.   Although all of the properties have now been renovated, further expenditure will be needed on the five properties in this period in order to retain their market value. It is the assumption that this sum will be spent as a single payment for each dwelling and that this will occur at the mid-point

between the initial action and year 30. On this basis there is further expenditure on one dwelling in year 14, on two dwellings in year 15 and on two in year 16.

Benefits

89.   As the expenditure is assumed to be aimed only at maintaining the value of the properties there is no quantifiable benefit.

Year 30

Costs

90.   At the end of 30 years this option assumes that the majority of the terrace will have become unfit and that the most satisfactory course of action will be to declare a clearance area. All five properties are now acquired, closed, secured and demolished, with the attendant costs and compensations.

91. Four of the households are owner-occupied and the cost of their losing their homes is accounted for in terms of the market value compensation and other allowances they are paid. The landlord of the other property is also paid market value compensation. The household in rented accommodation is given home loss payment and disturbance payment and is to be re-housed in one of the new properties which will be built on the site. But whilst demolition and rebuild is taking place they have to be found alternative accommodation. This 'welfare cost' can be quantified as six months of council management and maintenance costs and loan charges (that is, the cost of housing one household for six months). In place of the demolished properties, six family dwellings are built: the costs incurred being six times the unit cost of a new dwelling.

Benefits

92.   The benefit accruing from all the actions in this year can be represented by the increase in value of the housing. This is derived from the value of the new dwellings less the value of adjacent site. The value of the unfit dwellings have already been taken into account as part of the costs.

(v)   Calculation for option I

93.   The costs and benefits from each year are brought together in the calculation of the net present value of the option. The economic formula for the NPV of option 1 above is:

(a-b) [year 0] + c(d-e) [year 1] + c(d-e) [year 2] +c(d-e) [year 14] + c(d-e) [year 15] + c(d-e) [year 16] + c(f-g) [Year 30] = total NPV.

Year 0	a = the cost of renovation works.
(a-b) = 14,855 - 7,500	b = enhancement of market value.
	of property improved (22,500–15,000).
Year 1	c = discount factor for action taking place in year 1.
+ c(d-e) = 0.93 (20,000–11,000).	d = cost of renovation works (2 x 10,000).
	e = enhancement of market value of properties improved (2 x [22,500 - 17,000]).
Year 2	c = discount factor for action taking place in year 2.
+ c(d-e) = 0.86(29,710 - 22,500)	d = cost of renovation works (2 x 14,855).
	e = enhancement of market value of properties improved (2 x [22,500 - 15,000]) + enhancement of market value of whole terrace (5 x [24,000–22,500]).
Year 3 to Year 29	c = discount factor for action taking place in year 14
+ c (d-e) = 0.34 (10,000-0)	c1 = discount factor for action taking place in year 15.

+ c1(d-e) = 0.32 (20,000-0)
+ c2(d-e) = 0.29 (20,000-0)

c2 = discount factor for action taking place in year 16.
d = assumed cost of accumulated repairs for 1 dwelling in year 14 and 2 in each of 15 and 16 (10,000 per property).
e = enhancement in market value as a result of the repairs: no enhancement.

Year 30
  + c(f-g) = 0.1 (326,625 - 314,000)

c = discount factor for costs incurred in year 30.
f = cost: compensation ((4 x 16,650) + 15,000 + 1,650); securing (5 x 250); demolition (5x 300); "welfare loss" (0.5 x 1,250) and rebuild (6 x 40,000).
g= enhancement in market value: value of new dwellings (6 x 55,000) less the value of adjacent site (16,000).

This would give the following final calculation:

7,355 + 0.93 (9,000) + 0.86 (7,210) + 0.34 (10,000) + 0.32(20,000) + 0.29 (20,000) + 0.1 (-12,625) = 36,263

(vi) Costs and benefits for option 2

94.   To calculate a comparable net cost for option 2, the sequence of actions is represented as costs and benefits in the same way.

Years 0 and 1

Costs

95.   The first action is to place a closing order on the unfit dwelling, the property would then need to be made secure. The latter would result in a small cost.

96. At this stage, the occupants would be paid compensation and would move. The compensation is assumed to cover all rehousing costs in this case. The cost incurred is equivalent to the sum of the home loss payment, the disturbance payment, and a compensation paid. The last of these is based on market value compensation less the value of the closed property.

Benefits

97.   There is no quantifiable benefit from the action of serving a closing order and securing the property, as there is no enhancement of the market value of the property.

Year 2

Costs

98.   Two of the remaining properties become unfit. The whole block is now declared a clearance area. All five properties in the block are now acquired. The owner of the closed property is given compensation to match the residual value of the dwelling, the landlord is given market value compensation and the three remaining owner-occupiers are given market value compensation, home loss payment and disturbance allowance.

99.   The three owner-occupiers move, their rehousing costs being covered by the compensations they received. The one tenant household in the terrace is to be rehoused in one of the new dwellings to be built on site. Until these are available temporary rehousing is provided by the local authority. This is calculated as a "welfare loss" cost and is quantified as one year of council management and maintenance costs.

100.   The cost of securing the four dwellings ready for demolition is also incurred in this year.

Benefits

101. There are no benefits as there is assumed to be no increase in market value attributable to this activity.

Year 3

Costs

102. The block is now ready to be demolished—the next action is demolition itself. The cost is that incurred in pulling the five properties down.

103. "Welfare loss" costs in respect of the tenant household are again incurred in this year as one more year's management and maintenance charges.

Benefits

104. Any benefit derived from the provision of the cleared site can either be included in the assessment as an increase in value of the land or, when dwellings are built on the site as an increase in the value of the new dwellings compared with the old. This benefit must not be included on both occasions. In this example the benefit is included when the dwellings are built. Therefore at this stage there is no monetary benefit.

Year 4

Costs

105. The costs are those incurred in building 6 new dwellings on the site. The tenant household is rehoused immediately in one of the new houses, so no more "welfare loss" costs are incurred.

Benefits

106. The monetary benefit accrues from any increase in value as a result of building these dwellings. It is calculated from the market value of the new dwellings less the original value of adjacent site. The value of the dwellings which were on the site are not included in this part of the equation as they have already been taken account of in the costs under earlier years. They must not be counted twice.

Years 5-29

Costs

107. It is assumed that further expenditure is needed on the new properties in this period. The costs included are in the form of a single sum in year 17. This accumulated repairs cost will be less than that for renovated pre- 1919 dwellings in option 1.

Benefits

108. The expenditure therefore does not result in an enhanced value and there is no quantifiable benefit.

Year 30

Costs

109. The properties are to be retained for the long term. It is assumed that they will need significant renovation to be returned to their original condition. The cost of this is likely to be less than that incurred for pre- 1919 dwellings in option 1.

Benefits

110.   Significant renovation will increase the value of the properties. This increase is assumed to be the same as that derived for option 1 in year 30.

(vii)   Calculation for option 2

111. The economic formula for the NPV for option 2 above is:

(a-b) [year 0] + c(d-e) [year 2] + c(d-e) [year 3] + c(d-e) [year 4] + c(d-e) [year 17] + c(f-g) [Year 30] = total NPV.

Year 0 (a-b) = 13,900–0	a = cost of securing (250) and compensation comprising: – home loss 1,350 – disturbance allowance 300 – market value (less residual value) 12,000 b = enhancement of market value of property: no enhancement.
Year 2 + c(d-e) = 0.86 (71,850 - 0)	c =discount factor for year2. d = cost of securing (4 x 250), full compensation for owner occupiers (3 x 16,650), for landlord (15,000) and tenant household (1,650), compensation for residual value (3,000), and "welfare loss" (1,250). g= enhancement in market value: none.
Year 3 + c(d-e) = 0.79(2,750 - 0)	c=discount factor for year 3. d = cost of demolition (5 x 300) and"welfare loss" (1,250). e = no enhancement in market value.
Year 4 +c(d-e) = 0.74(240,000 - 314,000)	c = discount factor for year 4. d = cost of rebuilding (6 x 40,000). e = enhancement in market value = market value of new-property (6 x 55,000) less original value of additional site (16,000).
Year 5 to Year 29 +c(d-e) = 0.27 (24,000 - 0).	c = discount factor for action taking place in year 17. d = assumed cost of accumulated repairs (6 x 4,000). e = enhancement in market value as a result of the repairs: no enhancement.
Year 30 + c(f-g) = 0.1 (72,000 - 45,000)	c = discount factor for costs incurred in year 30. f = cost of major renovation (6 x 12,000). g = enhancement of market value due to improvement (6 x 7,500).

This would give the following final calculation:

13,900 + 0.86(71,850) + 0.79(2,750) + 0.74(-74,000) + 0.27(24,000) + 0.1(27,000) = 32,284 total NPV.

112.   On the basis of the costs used and assumptions made in comparing option 1 with option 2 the most economic solution would be to retain and refurbish the properties. The cost difference between the two options is small. Before reaching a decision on which option gave the best economic result an authority would undertake sensitivity analysis to test the effect of changing some of the more crucial assumptions.

Annex C4

POWERS AVAILABLE TO LOCAL AUTHORITIES IN RENEWAL AREAS

Acquisition of Land and Property

1.   Section 93(2) of the Local Government and Housing Act 1989(the 1989 Act) empowers authorities to acquire premises consisting of, or including, housing accommodation to achieve or secure their improvement or repair; their effective management and use; or the well-being of residents in the area. They may provide housing accommodation on land so acquired.

2.   Section 93(2) of the 1989 Act also provides that authorities may acquire properties for improvement, repair or management by other persons. Authorities acquiring properties compulsorily should consider subsequently disposing of them to owner-occupiers, housing associations or other private sector interests in line with their strategy for the Renewal Area (RA).

3.   Where property in need of renovation is acquired, work should be completed as quickly as possible in order not to blight the area and undermine public confidence in the overall RA strategy. In exercising their powers of acquisition authorities will need to bear in mind the financial and other (eg manpower) resources available to them and to other bodies concerned.

4.   Section 93(4) of the 1989 Act empowers authorities to acquire land and buildings for the purpose of improving the amenities in a RA. This power also extends to acquisition where other persons will carry out the scheme. Examples might include the provision of public open space or community centres either by the authority or by a housing association or other development partner. Where projects involve the demolition of properties, regard should be had to any adverse effects on industrial or commercial concerns.

5. The powers in sections 93(2) and 93(4) of the 1989 Act are additional powers and are without prejudice to other powers available to local housing authorities to acquire land which might also be used in RAs.

6.   The extent to which acquisitions will form part of an authority's programme will depend on the particular area. In some cases strategic acquisitions of land for amenity purposes will form an important element of the programme. However, as a general principle, the Secretary of State would not expect to see authorities acquiring land compulsorily in order to secure improvement except where this cannot be achieved in any other way. Where acquisition is considered to be essential by an authority, they should first attempt to do so by agreement.

7.   General advice on the submission of compulsory purchase orders for decision by the Secretary of State is given in DOE Circular 14/94. Compulsory purchase orders are considered on their merits but should not be made unless there is a compelling case in the public interest. Where an authority submits a compulsory purchase order under section 93(2) or 93(4) of the 1989 Act, their statement of reasons for making the order should seek to demonstrate that the reasons for which compulsory purchase is considered necessary are in order to secure the objectives of the RA. It should also set out the relationship of the proposals for which the CPO is required to their overall strategy for the RA; their intentions regarding disposal of the property; and their financial ability, or that of the purchaser, to carry out the proposals for which the order has been made.

Power to Carry Out Works

8.   Section 93(5)(a) of the 1989 Act gives a local housing authority power to carry out works (including works of demolition) on land which they own. Section 93(5)(b) gives an authority power to assist others in carrying out works on land which is not owned by the authority. Work for which assistance is being or has been provided under Part VIII of the 1989 Act is specifically excluded. Section 93(6) allows an authority to contract out either of these functions on an agency basis.

Power to extinguish Rights of Way

9.   Normally a local housing authority will be able to exercise its powers as a local planning authority under section 212 of the Town and Country Planning Act 1971 to apply to the Secretary of State for an order. However, by virtue of section 94 of the 1989 Act, a local housing authority which is not also the local planning authority for the area is able to apply to the Secretary of State for an order with the consent of the planning authority.

Powers of Entry

10.   Section 97 of the 1989 Act provides powers of entry which an authority may need to use, for example, while undertaking the survey work necessary to assess whether the declaration of an RA is the most effective way of dealing with an area. These powers may also need to be used to examine individual properties in order to determine whether to acquire them or to value them in instances of compulsory acquisition. Authorities will wish wherever possible to obtain entry by agreement and these powers should only be used where absolutely necessary.

Annex D1

GUIDANCE ON GROUP REPAIR SCHEMES

Introduction

1.   This Annex contains details of:

- the provisions of Chapter II of Part I to the 1996 Act relating to group repair schemes;

- the rationale behind the criteria specified in the Secretary of State's general approvals set out at *Annex D2*;

- the procedure to be followed for obtaining specific approval for schemes which fall outside the specified criteria.

Purpose of group repair

2.   Group repair will often form an important part of an authority's strategy for improving the external condition of groups of properties either within or outside renewal areas. The object of a group repair scheme is to secure the external fabric of a group of properties so that they are in reasonable repair on completion of the works. Under the 1996 Act, group repair can now also cover works to make a property structurally stable even where there is no associated external disrepair. Where such works are included the authority must ensure that, on their completion, the properties are structurally stable.

3.   Not only will a coordinated proactive approach often give economies of scale but the enhancement of the visual amenity of the area may encourage private investment and a wider revitalisation of the local community. Group repair may therefore be a particularly useful tool in renewal areas where a more holistic approach to problems of an area has been adopted and where the overall effect can be complemented by environmental works. But it can also be useful as an effective way of preventing the deterioration and eventual loss of poor condition housing in other areas.

Qualifying buildings

4.   Under the **Group Repair (Qualifying Buildings) Regulations 1996**, a building can be included in a group repair scheme if :

(a)   the whole or some part of the exterior of the building is not in reasonable repair, or

(b)   the whole or some part of the structure of the building is unstable.

Each scheme must contain at least one **primary** building which, as well as meeting one or other of the above two conditions must comprise at least **two** dwellings. In theory, the minimum permitted scheme would therefore comprise a single pair of semi-detached houses, or a single house which had been converted into 2 flats, or a purpose-built block of 2 flats. Since a building can be part of a terrace as well as the whole block, two houses or flats in a terrace could also count.

5.   **Additional** buildings can also be included in a scheme if:

(a)   each building comprises at least **one** dwelling (ie a house or flat - whether or not part of a terrace - so a detached house or a detached building comprising a single flat over a shop could also be included); and

(b)   carrying out the works to the building and to the primary building at the same time is the most effective way of securing the repair or structural stability of each of them.

General and special approval

6.   Authorities should note, however, that schemes which meet the prescribed conditions can only go ahead if they are approved by the Secretary of State. The Secretary of State has given his **general approval** to all schemes which meet the criteria set out in *Annex D2*. Schemes which do not meet these criteria must be submitted, **before commencement of works**, to the appropriate Government Office for the Region in order to obtain the Secretary of State's **special approval**. Any such submission should include the following documents:

- a plan showing the properties included in the scheme and indicating tenure, vacant properties, properties in non-residential use and any previous public sector input - eg individual renovation grants;

- a report specifying the works proposed and providing justification for those aspects where the schemes fall outside the terms of the Secretary of State's general consent, as outlined below;

- detailed costing of the works for each property including fees and keying-in costs;

- a statement showing the total scheme costs, together with the amount of public subsidy and the amount of private sector contributions;

- an appraisal of the alternative courses of action considered having regard to the guidance in *Annex D3*.

Approval criteria

7.   An explanation of the general approval criteria and advice on any additional information which should be provided in support of any applications for special approval are given below. Where all of the qualifying buildings to which the scheme relates are situated within a renewal area, the criteria are that:

- **the scheme must relate to four or more houses**: this is similar to the previous requirement in the Local Government and Housing Act 1989 except that the question of whether a property is a house must now be determined as at the time the scheme is prepared (rather than as it was at the time of its construction).

   Note that, for the purposes of the general approval, the term 'house' does not include houses in multiple occupation. All schemes involving HMOs will require special approval (for treatment of flats, see further criterion below). This is because the circumstances in which group repair would be a better option than HMO grant are not clear. Once the Secretary of State has experience of schemes which include HMOs it may be possible to relax this requirement. Meanwhile, schemes which include HMOs and which are submitted for special approval will normally be expected to comply with the criteria in paragraph 5(b), (d), (e) and (f), and (if outside a renewal area) paragraph 6(b) of the Group Repair Schemes (England) General Approvals 1996 as though references in those paragraphs to houses included references to HMOs. If any of these criteria cannot be met, reasons should be given.

   The Secretary of State also takes the view that the higher level of public subsidy involved under group repair will normally only be justified if the scheme makes a significant impact on the visual amenity of an area or where there are likely to be useful economies of scale. For this reason, authorities are discouraged from undertaking 'pepper-potting' of small isolated groups of properties. The Secretary of State will, nevertheless, be willing to consider the case for special approval of schemes with fewer than four houses if the authority can demonstrate that:

- the visual amenity impact of the scheme is significant despite the small number of properties involved (eg because the work complements work previously carried out to neighbouring properties, or because the properties are strategically located and present a real eyesore); or

- group repair has any other advantages over alternative options.

- **at least 60 per cent of the houses to which the scheme relates must be affected by lack of reasonable external repair or structural instability**. In this context, a house is to be treated as being affected by lack of reasonable external repair or structural instability if -

(i) it comprises or is contained in a building which is wholly so affected; or

(ii) where only part of a building is so affected, it comprises or is contained in that part.

The effect of this is that if a whole terrace block suffers from roof problems, for example, all the houses in the terrace can be counted towards meeting the 60% requirement. But if only a few houses in the block are affected, only houses in the affected part can count. Note also that the requirement relates to the scheme as a whole so that, even if the primary building does not contain 60% of affected houses, the scheme could still go ahead under the general approval if other qualifying buildings can be added to meet the criterion.

Since this rule is a relaxation of the previous 75% criterion, it is not envisaged that there will be much need for further relaxation. However, the Secretary of State will look at applications for special approval on their merits.

- **the scheme must not include any flats**. The Secretary of State is concerned to ensure that group repair is not carried out to flats if the use of common parts grants would be more practicable. Authorities may experience particular problems in putting together schemes which involve flats because the repairing obligation will sometimes rest with the landlord and in other cases with the individual flat owners. In the latter case, authorities will need to ensure that sufficient of the owners consent to the works to make the scheme worthwhile and that the proposals for works or for financial contributions from participants do not cut cross any contractual arrangements between them or with their landlord.

For these reasons, group repair may have few, if any, advantages over common parts grant where all the flats in the scheme are in a single high-rise block. However, it may have some attractions where the layout of the flats is analogous to terraced housing (eg those known as 'Tyneside flats'). As with HMOs, once the Secretary of State has experience of schemes which include flats, it may be possible to relax this criterion. Meanwhile, schemes which include flats will normally be expected to comply with the criteria in paragraph 5(b), (d), (e) and (f), and (if outside a renewal area) paragraph 6(b) of the Group Repair Schemes (England) General Approvals 1996 as though references in those paragraphs to houses were references to flats. If any of these criteria cannot be met, reasons should be given.

If a scheme comprises **fewer than 8 flats**, the case for special approval should also include the matters mentioned above for schemes with fewer than four houses.

- **if a qualifying building to which the scheme relates includes houses or other (eg commercial) premises that are not affected by lack of reasonable external repair or structural instability, their inclusion must be necessary in order to give satisfactory visual or structural effect to scheme works on houses that are so affected**: this is to ensure that schemes are coherent and likely to have a good visual impact. For example, a terrace of 5 houses may have structural problems which are currently affecting only the middle 3 houses but where it may make sense to deal with the whole block at the same time. The whole building can be included in the scheme since 60% of the houses are affected and the coherence criterion is met with respect to the rest.

Although the aim of group repair is primarily to improve the condition of the private sector housing stock, commercial premises such as shops, offices or garages may also be included if they are part of a qualifying building and their inclusion is necessary to give satisfactory visual or structural effect to other scheme works. If this condition cannot be met, any application for a special approval should give the reasons.

- **the authority are satisfied that the scheme of group repair is the most satisfactory course of action for remedying the lack of reasonable external repair or structural instability**. In order to satisfy themselves on this matter, authorities must take into account the following:

  (i) the cost of the scheme works;

  (ii) the estimated cost of any other works (excluding maintenance) which may be required to the buildings which comprise or contain the houses to which the scheme relates;

  (iii) the estimated cost of any reasonable alternative course of action (including the demolition or renovation of some or all of those buildings) for remedying the lack of reasonable external repair or structural instability; and

  (iv) the benefits reasonably foreseeable (including enhancement of the market value of those buildings after the completion of works), of group repair and such alternative courses of action as may be identified for the purposes of paragraph (iii).

  Authorities must also have regard to guidance from the Secretary of State in relation to the matters mentioned in paragraphs (i) to (iv) above. That guidance is given in *Annex D3*.

  This is one of the most important criteria for the approval of schemes and it is not envisaged that the criteria would be relaxed other than in the most exceptional of cases.

- **the authority's estimate of the fees to be incurred in connection with the scheme must not exceed 15 per cent of the cost of the scheme**. This follows the criterion under the previous legislation and is self-explanatory. Again it is envisaged that the requirement would only be relaxed in very exceptional cases.

8.   Schemes where one or more of the qualifying buildings in the scheme are outside a renewal area must meet the additional criterion that:

- **at least 25 per cent of the households residing in the buildings included in the scheme are in receipt of one or more prescribed benefits**. These are:

  council tax benefit;

  disability working allowance;

  earnings top-up;

  family credit;

  housing benefit;

  income support;

  job seeker's allowance.

This is intended to be a relatively straightforward test of whether the potential participants in a scheme are in need of assistance and obviates any requirement to carry out a full means test of each before a scheme can be prepared. The requirement does not apply where any buildings in the scheme are in a renewal area because it is already a condition of renewal area declaration that 30% of the households in the area must appear to the authority to be eligible for these benefits (see *paragraph 3.7.1 of Chapter 3*).

Although the Secretary of State is concerned to ensure that group repair is targeted on areas of greatest need, it is recognised that there may be cases for relaxing this rule eg in areas where incomes are just above the level which would qualify owners for benefits but would still qualify them for 100% renovation grants. In such cases, the application for special approval should be supported by details of the incomes of those who it is proposed to include in the scheme and show why the benefits criterion cannot be met.

9.   There is now **no longer any requirement as to the maximum unit costs of scheme works** above which schemes need special approval. Authorities will nevertheless appreciate it is incumbent on them to scrutinise scheme costs carefully in order to get the best possible value from the limited resources available. The economic analysis required under paragraph 5(d) of the general approval will help authorities to choose between different options but cannot of itself ensure that costs are reasonable. Competitive tendering is obviously important as a means of controlling costs and authorities should cast their net as wide as possible in order to ensure a good price.

10.   Authorities should also be rigorous in excluding from the cost of schemes any works which fall outside the purposes mentioned in sections 62(2) and (3) of the 1996 Act: no Exchequer contribution is payable on ineligible items. If an authority wishes to carry out internal renovation works in conjunction with group repair, those works should be clearly identified separately.

General approval to variations of group repair schemes

11.   Once a scheme has been approved (either because it meets the criteria in the general approval or has received special approval) it may subsequently be varied, subject to the provisions of section 68 of the 1996 Act. Before varying a scheme the authority must consult the existing participants and consider any representations made by them. If anyone's interests are adversely affected by the variation (eg because of an increase in scheme costs), their fresh scheme consent is required: otherwise, their existing consent will be treated as applying to the varied scheme.

12.   In any event, however, any variation requires the fresh approval of the Secretary of State. This approval is given generally under paragraph 7 of the Group Repair Schemes (England) General Approvals 1996 (see *Annex D2*) where the scheme as varied:

   (a)   fulfils the criteria for general approval; or

   (b)   where the original scheme required special approval, does not depart from the criteria for general approval any more than is allowed for in that special approval.

For example, a scheme may receive special approval because, say, only 20% of the participants are in receipt of benefits. The special approval may indicate that variation of the scheme will only be possible without further special approval if **at least** 20% of the participants are in receipt of benefits and that the other criteria of the general approval are met.

Selection of schemes – general

13.   In addition to the formal requirements for scheme approval, authorities will need to be satisfied that the scheme fits in with its wider private sector renewal strategies - see *Chapter 3*.

Eligible works

14. As mentioned above, works may be carried out to put the exterior of the scheme buildings in reasonable repair or to render the buildings structurally stable or both. Works may also include additional works to other parts of the buildings if they are necessary to give satisfactory effect to the repair or stabilising works.

15. To determine whether the whole or part of the exterior of a building is not in reasonable repair, authorities should take into account the factors mentioned in section 96 of the 1996 Act, bearing in mind the provision set out in section 62(6) of that Act that a building should not be regarded as being in reasonable repair unless the exterior is substantially free from rising or penetrating damp. The exterior of the dwelling is defined in section 62(4) of the Act and includes work to the curtilage of the building and retaining walls, as well as any part of a building exposed to the elements. Additional works can also be carried out on land outside the curtilage. For cavity walls, works to both the inner and the outer skin can be regarded as eligible works if the outer skin faces the open air.

Preparation of schemes

16. It is the responsibility of the local authority to:

- initiate the scheme in consultation with owners;
- make the necessary arrangements for the execution of, and payment for, the works required; and
- collect contributions due from participants.

17. Consultation will ensure that:

- the wishes of residents are taken into account;
- they appreciate the extent of the proposed works and any arrangements for decanting, etc; and
- they fully understand the arrangements for the payment of contributions where appropriate.

Whilst pursuing the matter of contributions with potential participants, the authority may also be able to ascertain how many of them are in receipt of the benefits specified in the Secretary of State's general approval

Eligible participants

18. No scheme can go ahead unless and until all those eligible to participate have signified their agreement ('**scheme consent**') to take part. A person is eligible to participate as an assisted participant if they:

- have an owner's interest in a scheme property;
- can give the authority access to any part of the building to which it is proposed to carry out scheme works, or have the consent of the occupier to enable those works to be carried out; and
- give an owner-occupation certificate (that they, or a member of their family, intend to live in the property for five years after completion of the works), a certificate of intended letting (if they intend to let it for that period) or a certificate of future occupation (if they intend to use it as an HMO for that period).

19.   Owners who are unable to give the necessary certificate may participate as unassisted participants. Certain public sector and other bodies listed in section 64(7) of the 1996 Act are also unable to participate as assisted participants but may do so as unassisted participants.

20.   By giving their scheme consent, participants agree to the works being carried out and become liable to pay an apportioned contribution towards the cost. They also become liable to the clawback provisions described in *paragraph 29 below*. For these reasons, local authorities are advised to obtain such agreements **in writing**.

21.   Works may only be carried out to a property without the consent of the owner if :

- the local authority are unable to trace anyone with the appropriate owner's interest; or

- an eligible person does not wish to participate but consents to works being carried out to his premises so that the works to the rest of the building may be satisfactorily completed.

Implementation and completion of works

22.   Once the decision has been taken to proceed with a scheme, the authority is responsible for letting and managing the contract. Authorities will need to monitor the works as they progress and to carry out the necessary building control inspections. They should also maintain close contact with the participants in order to resolve any difficulties which might arise, and they may wish to consider ways of encouraging participants to prepare for their on-going maintenance responsibilities.

23.   Once the works have been completed to their satisfaction, authorities are required to issue assisted participants with a certificate specifying the **completion date**. This date marks the start of a five year period during which the participants must either fulfil the intention expressed in the relevant certificate mentioned in *paragraph 18* above or else may be required to pay the balance of the cost of the works (see below).

Payment of contributions

24.   In determining the contribution required from each participant in a scheme, the cost of the works must be apportioned amongst all the buildings and premises in the scheme in a way agreed by the owners. Costs may include fees, which should not normally exceed 15% of total costs; and keying-in works to other properties, which should not normally exceed 5%. Costs should be apportioned to each house on the basis of the value of work to be undertaken within its curtilage. Where a house has been converted to include flats, bed-sits or commercial activities, the costs will need to be apportioned appropriately. Section 67(2) of the 1996 Act provides that, if agreement cannot be reached, the cost should be apportioned equally. In practice, however, it is expected that authorities will need to agree the apportionment of the costs before the work commences: if any of the parties disagree, they are unlikely to be willing to participate.

25.   Unassisted participants are required to meet the full cost attributable to works on their property. For assisted participants, the **maximum** contribution is:

- 25 per cent, where the building is in a renewal area; and

- 50 per cent, in any other case.

26.   For owners of dwellings or HMOs, the authority may determine a percentage contribution of any amount up to the maximum. In making their determination, the authority must have regard to the way in which the means-testing rules for renovation grants or HMO grants would apply if the person concerned were an applicant for such a grant. The authority must also have regard to the following guidance which is given by the Secretary of State in exercise of his powers under section 67(7) of the 1996 Act, namely that **authorities should not charge a contribution which is less than the maxi-**

mum except insofar as the application of the means-test rules for renovation or HMO grants would justify a lower contribution.

27.   Any test of resources carried out in connection with a group repair scheme should be undertaken separately from any assessment carried out in relation to an application for a renovation grant for the same property. However, in the case of an owner-occupier, any contribution made by such an assisted participant towards a group repair scheme must be taken into account in determining the contribution towards subsequent grant-aided works, and vice versa (*see Regulation 11 of the House Renovation etc Grants (Reduction of Grant) Regulations 1990 (S.I.1990 No. 1189)*.

28.   Authorities should bear in mind that, once costs have been agreed with the participants, they will not be able to increase the costs without seeking fresh scheme consent from the participants affected. The authority may therefore themselves become liable to meet any additional expenditure incurred. However, if the final cost of works proves to be lower than the costs agreed with the participants, then proportional refunds should be passed on to the participants.

Clawback provisions

29.   It is a condition of participation in a group repair scheme that:

- if an assisted participant **disposes of their property** at any time after signifying scheme consent and up to five years after completion of the works (where the disposal is a 'relevant disposal' within the meaning of section 53 of the 1996 Act and is not an 'exempt disposal' under section 54); or

- the dwelling is **not occupied, let, or kept available for letting or residential occupation** in accordance with the intention stated in the relevant certificate given under *paragraph 18* above; or

- the owner of the dwelling or house does **not comply with a notice** requiring a statement showing how the previous condition is being fulfilled within 21 days of its service;

the owner must pay on demand the difference between the cost of the works attributable to his premises and the amount of his contribution towards that cost. These conditions are local land charges which are also binding on anyone who takes over ownership of the dwelling or house if the obligation has not already been discharged.

30.   **The authority may, however, determine not to demand payment or to demand a lesser amount**. In deciding whether or not to reclaim the full amount, the authority will need to take into account all the circumstances of the disposal or breach of conditions, as well as their fiduciary duty to their council tax payers. Circumstances in which abatement or waiver might be justified include cases where the person has to move for good reason but repayment of the full amount of the balance would leave them unable to afford another home reasonably suitable for their needs in the new location.

31.   The Government recognises that the requirement to pay the balance on disposal may deter some people from participating in a scheme if they cannot be certain that they will be able to fulfil the intention expressed in the certificate provided with their application. Although authorities cannot fetter their discretion by giving any cast-iron assurances in advance of any disposal, they may, however, wish to give participants some general indication of their policy on waiver or abatement in hardship cases so that they know broadly what to expect.

32.   The three conditions of participation mentioned above will come to an end once the amount has been paid or any demand for payment has been satisfied. The conditions will also cease to apply if there is an exempt disposal of the premises, unless the disposal is to an associate of the person. The requirement to pay the balance on disposal (but not the other conditions) will also continue to apply

where the property is bequeathed to someone else under a will or on intestacy. This is because, whilst it may be reasonable to require payment if someone who inherits a renovated property quickly sells it, they should not be required to live in the property or to continue to let it meanwhile.

Exchequer contributions and requirement as to records

33.   Under *paragraph 2 of the Housing Renewals Grants, Etc.(Exchequer Contributions) (England) Determination 1996* the Government will pay a contribution of 60% towards the net costs (ie the cost of works and fees less any costs met by assisted or unassisted participants) incurred by authorities in carrying out schemes – see *Annex J3*. Claims may be made as soon as expenditure becomes payable by the authority – it is not necessary to wait until the scheme has been completed. *Paragraphs 8 and 13* of the determination require authorities to keep registers giving prescribed particulars of each group repair scheme completed.

Annex D2

THE GROUP REPAIR SCHEMES (ENGLAND) GENERAL APPROVALS 1996

This Annex reproduces the **general approval to group repair schemes** given by the Secretary of State under section 63(2) and (3) of the Housing Grants, Construction and Regeneration Act 1996. It also sets out the **general approval to variations of group repair schemes** given under section 68(2) of the Act. **The contents of this Annex have statutory force.** *Annex D1* explains the criteria and gives general guidance on the preparation and submission of schemes for special approval where necessary. *Annex D3* gives the guidance to which, under paragraph 5(d) of this Annex, local authorities must have regard when carrying out their assessment of the costs and benefits of group repair compared with other options.

Citation

1.—(1) The approval in paragraph 4 below may be cited as the Group Repair Schemes (England) General Approvals 1996.

(2) The approval in paragraph 7 below may be cited as the Group Repair Scheme Variations (England) General Approval 1996.

(3) The approvals referred to in sub-paragraphs (1) and (2) may together be cited as the Group Repair Schemes (England) General Approvals 1996.

Application and extent

2. The Group Repair Schemes (England) General Approvals 1996 -

    (a) extend only to local housing authorities in England; and

    (b) do not apply to any group repair scheme approved before 17 December 1996.

Interpretation

3.—(1) In this and the following paragraphs -

        "the Act" means the Housing Grants, Construction and Regeneration Act 1996;

        "house" has the same meaning as in Part V of the Housing Act 1985 but does not include a house in multiple occupation;

        "flat" means a dwelling which is not a house.

(2) For the purposes of the following paragraphs -

    (a) a house is affected by lack of reasonable external repair or structural instability if -

        (i) it comprises or is contained in a building which is wholly so affected; or

        (ii) where only part of a building is so affected, it comprises or is contained in that part.

General approval to group repair schemes

4. The Secretary of State for the Environment, as respects England, in exercise of the powers conferred on him by section 63(2) and (3) of the Act, hereby approves group repair schemes which fulfil the criteria specified -

(a) where one or more of the qualifying buildings to which the scheme relates are situated within an area which is for the time being a renewal area within the meaning of Part VII of the Local Government and Housing Act 1989, in paragraph 5;

(b) in any other case, in paragraph 6.

Criteria for paragraph 4(a) purposes

5.   The criteria for the purposes of paragraph 4(a) are -

(a)   that the scheme relates to four or more houses;

(b)   that at least 60 per cent of the houses to which the scheme relates are affected by lack of reasonable external repair or structural instability;

(c)   that the scheme does not relate to any flats;

(d)   that, if a qualifying building to which the scheme relates includes houses or other premises that are not affected by lack of reasonable external repair or structural instability, their inclusion is necessary in order to give satisfactory visual or structural effect to scheme works on houses that are so affected;

(e)   that, having taken into account the following matters, the authority are satisfied that the scheme of group repair is the most satisfactory course of action for remedying the lack of reasonable external repair or structural instability:-

(i)   the cost of the scheme works;

(ii)   the estimated cost of any other works (excluding maintenance) which may be required to the buildings which comprise or contain the houses to which the scheme relates;

(iii)   the estimated cost of any reasonable alternative course of action (including the demolition or renovation of some or all of those buildings) for remedying the lack of reasonable external repair or structural instability;

(iv)   the benefits reasonably foreseeable (including enhancement of the market value of those buildings after the completion of works), of group repair and such alternative courses of action as may be identified for the purposes of paragraph (iii); and

(v)   such guidance from the Secretary of State in relation to the matters mentioned in paragraphs (i) to (iv) above as may then be in force;

(f)   that the authority's estimate of the fees to be incurred in connection with the scheme does not exceed 15 per cent of the cost of the scheme.

Criteria for paragraph 4(b) purposes

6.   The criteria for the purposes of paragraph 4(b) are -

(a)   those specified in paragraph 5; and

(b)   that at least 25 per cent of the households residing in the buildings included in the scheme are in receipt of one or more of the following -

council tax benefit;

disability working allowance;

earnings top-up;

family credit;

housing benefit;

income support;

job seeker's allowance.

General approval to variations of group repair schemes

7.   The Secretary of State for the Environment, as respects England, in exercise of the powers conferred on him by section 68(2) of the Act (and, as applied by that section, section 63(2) and (3) of the Act), hereby approves the variation of a group repair scheme where the scheme as varied -

(a)   fulfils the criteria in paragraph 5 or, as the circumstances require, paragraph 6 above ("the relevant criteria"); or

(b)   in any case where approval to the scheme was given otherwise than pursuant to paragraph 4 above, fails to fulfil the relevant criteria only to the extent provided for in that approval.

Annex D3

ECONOMIC APPRAISAL FOR GROUP REPAIR

1.   This guidance is given for the purposes of paragraph 5(e) of the **Group Repair Schemes (England) General Approvals 1996** (*see Annex D2*) which makes it a condition for the general approval of schemes that authorities must be satisfied that group repair is the most satisfactory course of action for remedying the lack of reasonable external repair or structural instability. In deciding this, authorities must take into account the costs and benefits of group repair and of any reasonable alternative courses of action, having regard to guidance from the Secretary of State in relation to these matters. **The guidance in this Annex therefore has statutory force.**

2.   The purpose of the economic assessment is to ensure that group repair is the most satisfactory option over the long term, taking account of non-financial as well as financial costs and benefits. The Secretary of State recognises, however, that a full-blown cost-benefit analysis of all options will not always be appropriate where the works to be undertaken are fairly minor and it is obvious to the authority that other options would be impracticable or far more expensive. Further, where the costs and benefits of a group repair scheme have already been considered as part of a Neighbourhood Renewal Assessment (NRA) in preparation for the declaration of a renewal area, and group repair has already been identified as a satisfactory course of action, there will be no need to undertake a further economic appraisal unless there has been a marked change in circumstances since the NRA was completed. Authorities should nevertheless be able to demonstrate in all cases that they have considered other options and to justify any decision not to carry out the more rigorous analysis set out below.

Determination of options

3.   The first step in the analysis is to identify the reasonable courses of action which might be taken as an alternative to, or together with, group repair. The main options will be:

- group repair on its own;

- renovation of the properties on an individual basis;

- group repair and interior renovation at the same time;

- demolition and the provision of alternative accommodation (whether by rebuild for sale or otherwise);

- some combination of these, depending on the nature of the problems under consideration.

4.   In most cases, group repair might be expected to be cheaper than renovating the individual properties using grants, if only because of the economies of scale. However, if the properties require extensive internal works as well as works to the exterior, or if the need for a coherent approach is not a decisive factor, authorities might find it preferable to encourage individuals to apply for discretionary grants, either in conjunction with, or instead of, group repair. Authorities should also bear in mind that any additional expenditure on renovation works may have a more significant effect on the market value of the property than might be achieved by group repair alone: if this is properly taken into account in the analysis, it may show that carrying out group repair on its own is not the most satisfactory option.

5.   In determining the costs of demolition works and the provision of alternative accommodation, authorities should take into account the cost of any compensation payable for loss of the property, including home loss and disturbance payments, any relocation grants payable from 1997/98 under Part

IV of the 1996 Act, together with the cost of any temporary accommodation pending permanent re-housing.

Analysis of options

6.   In order to compare financial costs and benefits meaningfully over a long period, the Secretary of State requires that all costs be discounted to their present value. Having chosen suitable options, authorities should normally calculate the net present value (ie discounted costs less benefits) in accordance with the following formula (taking the year of initial action as Year 0):

$$NPV = (a - b) [Year 0] + c (d - e) [Year 1] + c (d - e) [Year 2] \text{ (and so on for years 3 to 29)} + c (f - g) [Year 30] \text{ where } -$$

NPV =   the net present value of the option

a =   the total cost, at Year 0 prices, of the initial action (eg group repair, renovation, demolition and rehousing) for the properties under consideration;

b =   the market value, at Year 0 values, of the dwellings or other premises under consideration after the initial action is completed less the market value, at Year 0 values, of those properties before the initial action began;

c =   the appropriate factor for discounting future values to present values assuming a discount factor of 8 per cent per annum (see *Appendix 1*);

d =   costs arising from action taken between the completion of the initial action and the end of Year 29;

e =   the market value, at Year 0 values, of the dwellings or other premises under consideration after any action taken between the completion of the works and the end of Year 29 *less* the market value, at Year 0 values, of those properties immediately before that action began;

f =   the estimated cost, at Year 0 prices, of works likely to be required during Years 30 to 59 inclusive (on the assumption that all such works are, in fact, carried out in Year 30);

g =   the market value, at Year 0 values, of the dwellings or other premises under consideration after completion of the works likely to be required in Years 30 to 59 inclusive (on the assumption that those works are, in fact, carried out in Year 30) *less* the market value, at Year 0 values, of those properties immediately before those works are assumed to be carried out.

7.   In carrying out the above calculations, note that:

- the calculation of c(d-e) must be carried out for every year for which costs are expected to arise between the completion of the initial action and the end of Year 29, applying the appropriate discount factor for each such year in question *(see Appendix 1)*;

- where a cleared site is to be used for non-residential purposes, the market value after clearance will be the value of the site in its proposed eventual after-use;

- maintenance costs should be excluded, as these are assumed to be the same under all options.

8.   In carrying out these calculations, authorities may find it helpful to refer to the principles and examples set out in *Appendix 4 of Annex C3*. Authorities should also ensure that sufficient sensitivity analysis has been undertaken on the basis of the guidance in that Appendix.

9.   It is important to ensure that the same assumptions are adopted in assessing the costs and benefits of each option; and where there is uncertainty about the magnitude of costs it will be necessary to test whether options are sensitive to alternative assumptions. It is not necessary, however, to include items which represent simply a transfer of resources between bodies, (for example, where the sale of land by the authority to a developer would feature in the equation as both a cost and a receipt); and costs can also be excluded if they would be the same for each option.

10. An example of the application of this methodology is given at *Appendix 2* to this Annex.

Non-financial assessment

11. In deciding, in the light of the economic assessment, whether group repair is the most satisfactory course of action, authorities should also take into account the non-financial costs and benefits of the different options. The methodology used for the appraisal of options under the Neighbourhood Renewal Assessment process is recommended for consideration here, although a full formal analysis will not normally be necessary unless the choice between two options on financial grounds is a narrow one. In any event, authorities should be clear as to the reasons for their choice, particularly where it is not the cheapest solution.

Annex D3 (Appendix 1)

GROUP REPAIR ECONOMIC ASSESSMENT: DISCOUNT FACTORS

Year	Discount factor
(0)	(1.00)
1	0.93
2	0.86
3	0.79
4	0.74
5	0.68
6	0.63
7	0.58
8	0.54
9	0.50
10	0.46
11	0.43
12	0.40
13	0.37
14	0.34
15	0.32
16	0.29
17	0.27
18	0.25
19	0.23
20	0.21
21	0.20
22	0.18
23	0.17
24	0.16
25	0.15
26	0.14
27	0.13
28	0.12
29	0.11
30	0.1

" __ " indicate most commonly used years and discount rates

Annex D3 (Appendix 2)

EXAMPLE OF ECONOMIC ASSESSMENT FOR GROUP REPAIR SCHEMES

1.   The example given here is provided simply to illustrate the methodology required under the main Annex. It therefore deals only with the costs and benefits of group repair itself despite the fact that it would, of course, be necessary in practice to carry out a similar exercise for the other two options in order to be able to compare their net present values (NPVs).

2.   Group repair scheme of 5 houses. Internal works to be carried out to bring properties up to the fitness standard.

Year 0

Costs

   (i)   The initial action is the renovation of these properties. The cost is that of work carried out. The works did not require residents to be decanted.

   (ii)   Internal work is started; cost of works so far completed; cost of making good external works.

Benefits

   (i)   Increase in market value due to renovation.

Year 1

Costs

   (i)   Internal works are completed; houses brought up to fitness standard.

Benefits

   (ii)   Increase in market value of houses fully renovated and fit.

Year 2-29

Costs

Although the properties have been renovated, further expenditure will be needed in this period to retain the value of the dwellings. This is represented by the inclusion of a single sum for accumulated repairs at the mid-point of this period (Year 14). An alternative is to determine an annual cost for carrying out work to the dwellings to maintain them in their refurbished state.

Benefits

The expenditure does not result in an enhancement of the value of the property and thus there is no quantifiable benefit.

Year 30

Costs

The properties will need to be retained again for the long term. It is assumed that they will need further major renovation to return the dwellings to their condition following renovation in year 0. The costs are assumed to be the same as those for renovation in year 0. (It may be that the satisfactory course of action in year 30 will be to demolish and rebuild, all attendant costs should in that case be included).

Benefits

This renovation will result in an increase in the value of the properties. It is assumed that the increase will be the same as that in year 0.

Calculation for group repair option

3. The costs and benefits from each year are brought together in the calculation of the net present value of the option. The economic formula for the NPV of the option above is:

(a - b)[year 0] + c(d-e) [year 1] + c(d-e) [year 14] + c(f-g) [year 30]

Year 0
(a-b) = 25,000   a = cost of refurbishment:£50,000 external works
                                            £5,000 internal works
                                            b = increase in market value:
                                            £30,000

Year 1
+ c(d-e) = 0.93(15,000-10,000)   c = discount factor for action taking place in year 1
                                            d = costs of refurbishment:
                                            £15,000
                                            e = increase in market value:
                                            £10,000

Year 14
+ c(d-e) = 0.34(35,000-0)   c = discount factor for year 14
                                            d = assumed cost of accumulated repairs:
                                            £35,000
                                            e = there are no monetary benefits in this period

Year 30
+ c(f-g) =0.1(70,000 - 40,000)   c = discount factor for year 30
                                            f = costs of refurbishing the dwellings for further long-
                                            term retention £70,000
                                            g = enhancement in market value of £40,000

This would give the following final calculations:
25,000 + 0.93 (15,000 - 10,000) + 0.34 (35,000 - 0) + 0.1 (70,000 - 40,000) = £44,550

Annex E1

CLEARANCE AREAS : COMPULSORY PURCHASE AND OTHER ISSUES

Compulsory purchase orders (CPOs)

1.   Clearance area CPOs are made under section 290 of the Housing Act 1985. They are regulated by the provisions of:

- the Acquisition of Land Act 1981

- the Compulsory Purchase of Land Regulations 1994 - SI 1994 No 2145

- the Compulsory Purchase by Non-Ministerial Acquiring Authorities (Inquiries Procedure) Rules 1990 - SI 1990 No 512

2.   Authorities submitting clearance area CPOs for confirmation should follow the general guidance in Circulars:

- 14/94 - Compulsory Purchase Orders: Procedures

- 1/90 - The Compulsory Purchase by Non-Ministerial Acquiring Authorities (Inquiries Procedure) Rules 1990

- 5/93 - Compulsory Purchase Orders made under Housing Powers

Certificates should be submitted in the form shown in Circular 14/94.

3.   Compulsory purchase orders are considered on their merits, subject to specific criteria which may apply to different powers, but should not be made unless there is a compelling case in the public interest. An authority submitting a clearance area CPO will be expected to deal with the following matters in their statement of case:

- the declaration of the clearance area and its justification, having regard to the Code of Guidance for dealing with unfit premises in *Annex B*;

- the unfitness of buildings in the clearance area: incorporating a statement of the authority's principal grounds for being satisfied that the buildings are unfit as required by Rule 22(2) in the 1990 Inquiries Procedure Rules;

- the justification for acquiring any added lands included in the CPO;

- proposals for re-housing and for re-locating commercial and industrial premises affected by clearance;

- the proposed after-use of the cleared site. Where it is not practicable to table evidence of planning permission, the authority should demonstrate that their proposals are acceptable in planning terms and that there appear to be no grounds for thinking that planning consent will not materialise.

4.   Authorities promoting clearance area CPOs will need to demonstrate that they have fully considered the economic aspect of clearance and that they have responded to any submissions made by objectors regarding that.

Right of Way Extinguishment Orders

5.   The procedural changes introduced by Schedule 9 to the Local Government and Housing Act 1989 for Right of Way Extinguishment Orders remain extant. The effects are that:

- the date on which the right of way is extinguished is specified by the Secretary of State in approving the order;

- the statutory period for objection to an order is 4 weeks;

- forms of order and notice of the Making of an Order are prescribed in "The Housing (Prescribed Forms) Regulations S.I. 1990 No. 447".

NB: "The Housing Act (Extinguishment of Public Right of Way) Regulations 1937 (S.R. & O. 1937/79)" continue to apply to orders made on or before 31 March 1990.

Authorities applying for approval of Right of Way Extinguishment Orders should submit them to the Government Office for the Region at the time they publish notice of the making of the order. They should provide with their application:

- the sealed order and map, with two additional copies of each;

- a copy of the published notice of the making of the order;

- a certificate that the order has been published in the manner prescribed by the Housing (Prescribed Forms) Regulations 1990;

- details of the clearance area in which the right of way is situated and the position regarding the purchase of land over which the right of way exists;

- the date on which they wish the right of way to be extinguished if the Secretary of State approves the order.

Compensation

6.   Compensation for the compulsory acquisition of unfit houses is paid on the same basis as for acquisition of a fit property and assessed in accordance with the provisions of the Land Compensation Acts 1961 and 1973 and the Planning Compensation Act 1991. In practice this means market value compensation.

7.   Where a property is tenanted, compensation will be payable on the basis of the interest in that property subject to tenancy. If a property was tenanted at the date on which the notice to treat was served, but the tenants have left before date of entry, then the interest will normally be valued with the benefit of vacant possession except where the tenants were rehoused by the local housing authority, in which case it will be valued as though subject to tenancy. Tenants and owner occupiers qualify for all payments, such as home loss and disturbance payments, to which they would be entitled in the case of the compulsory purchase of a fit house. Acquiring authorities are normally liable to pay a claimant's surveyor's fees (based on Ryde's Scale) and their legal expenses.

8.   Compensation for properties on added lands will normally be open market value subject to any tenancies which may exist. Business owner occupiers and tenants will normally be entitled to compensation for disturbance where they relocate. This may include the cost of acquiring alternative premises - eg surveyors and legal fees, and, in some cases, for the proprietor's time. Where the business is extinguished they may be entitled to compensation based on its open market value. As for residential owner occupiers, they will normally be entitled to recover their surveyor's fees and legal costs in dealing with their claim.

Slum clearance subsidy

9.   The method of calculating slum clearance subsidy is set out in the determination at *Annex E2*.

Valuations of land

10.   For the purposes of calculating slum clearance subsidy, all valuations of land and buildings acquired (whether for acquisitions, exchanges of land or appropriations to or from the slum clearance function) must be made at the market value assessed in accordance with the provisions of the Land Compensation Acts 1961 and 1973 and the Planning and Compensation Act 1991. The valuation of land disposed of or given in exchange for other land shall be the amount certified by the valuer to be the open market value, or best price reasonably obtainable, for that land. This includes valuations for the appropriation to the slum clearance function following declaration of the relevant clearance area of:

- land acquired under other powers in advance of the declaration of a clearance area;

- adjoining land acquired pursuant to a blight notice served on the grounds specified in paragraph 11, or 22, (including the Notes) of Schedule 13 to the Town and Country Planning Act 1990;

- dwellings already owned by the local authority;

as well as appropriations of land from the slum clearance function to any other function (including open space, school playing fields, allotment gardens and highways).

Special determination for the nil value appropriation of slum clearance land

11.   Although the slum clearance subsidy determination does not provide for authorities to appropriate land for open space, school playing fields or allotment gardens at nil value for subsidy purposes, the Secretary of State recognises that there may be circumstances where such a provision might exceptionally be justified on social or environmental grounds. Therefore, he is prepared to consider on individual merits and with the consent of the Treasury, applications from authorities for special determinations including provisions for such nil value appropriations.

12.   Such applications must:

- relate to specific named clearances;

- be submitted in the first instance to the appropriate Government Office for the Region;

- set out a full description of, and justification for, the proposed after-use of the site. This includes an indication of the need for the type of open space proposed in the area in which the cleared site is situated and the arrangements to be made for the management and maintenance of the site once the open space has been created.

13.   Authorities should be aware that any special determination issued under these arrangements can be expected to include a provision enabling the Secretary of State to recoup any subsidy paid towards land appropriated at nil value for open space, school playing fields or allotment gardens if, within 5 years of the date of the relevant appropriation, the authority resolve to sell the land or to use it for any other purpose.

After declaration of a clearance area

14.   Section 289(5) of the Housing Act 1985 provides that, following the declaration of a clearance area, authorities must send a number of documents to the Secretary of State. The documents, which should be sent to the appropriate Government Office for the Region, are:

- a copy of the resolution passed by the authority;

- a statement of the number of persons who on a day specified in the statement were occupying the buildings comprised in the clearance area;

- a map defining the area (although this is not a requirement of legislation it is important that it is provided);

- a copy of the formal report confirming that the publicity provision of S.289(2B) of the 1985 Act have been carried out (again this is not a legal requirement but will aid the Government Office for the Region in satisfying itself that the clearance area declaration is valid).

Annex E2

DETERMINATION OF SLUM CLEARANCE SUBSIDY

This Annex reproduces the Slum Clearance Subsidy Determination 1990 (as amended) in its application to housing authorities in England which remains in force.

Introduction

The Secretary of State for the Environment in exercise of the powers conferred on him by section 165(4) and (5) of the Local Government and Housing Act 1989, and of all other powers enabling him in that behalf, and with the consent of the Treasury, hereby makes the following Determination:–

1. Citation and Commencement

This Determination may be cited as the Slum Clearance Subsidy Determination 1990 and shall have effect for the financial year beginning on 1st April 1990 and for subsequent financial years.

2. Interpretation

2.1   Any reference in this Determination to a numbered paragraph is a reference to the paragraph bearing that number in this Determination.

2.2   In this Determination, unless the context otherwise requires–

"authority" means a local housing authority within the meaning of section 1 of the 1985 Act;

"compulsory purchase value", in relation to land, means the compensation which would be payable in respect of the compulsory acquisition of land if it fell to be assessed in accordance with the Land Compensation Act 1961 and the Land Compensation Act 1973;

"expenditure" means any expenditure incurred, or deemed by paragraph 7.2 or 7.5 to be incurred by an authority in, or in connection with, the exercise of their slum clearance functions;

"receipt" means any receipt due, or deemed by paragraph 7.4 or 7.6 to be due, to an authority in, or in connection with, the exercise of their slum clearance functions;

"slum clearance functions" has the same meaning as in section 165(3) of the Local Government and Housing Act 1989;

"slum clearance land" means land for the time being held by an authority for the purposes of their slum clearance functions;

"the 1985 Act" means the Housing Act 1985;

"the 1989 Act" means the Local Government and Housing Act 1989;

"valuer" means the District Valuer or a qualified valuer employed by an authority whether under a contract of service or otherwise.

3. Payment of Subsidy

3.1   Slum clearance subsidy shall be payable where an authority incur a loss, as hereinafter calculated, in any financial year in connection with the exercise of their slum clearance functions.

3.2   An authority incur a loss in any financial year if, in accordance with paragraphs 5 to 8, their aggregate expenditure for the year exceeds their aggregate receipts for the year, the loss being equal to the excess expenditure.

3.3   The rate of subsidy shall be 60 per cent. of the loss.

3.4   The Secretary of State will pay slum clearance subsidy in 10 instalments on account on the basis of the authority's estimated expenditure in each financial year; and the balance will be payable on receipt of the authority's claim after the end of the financial year to which it relates, subject to any adjustment, if necessary, once the claim has been examined by an auditor appointed by the Audit Commission.

3.5 (1)   After 31st March 1997, the aggregate of subsidy paid under paragraph 3.1 (including any payment made to the local housing authority as a result of a prior year adjustment to subsidy already received by the authority) in any financial year (when aggregated with relevant payments) shall not exceed the total provision allocated to the local housing authority towards relevant expenditure for that financial year.

(2)   In this paragraph -

"the 1996 Act" means the Housing Grants, Construction and Regeneration Act 1996;

"allocated" means allocated in exercise of the powers in section 132 of the 1989 Act or section 92 of the 1996 Act or any of the powers under which relevant payments are made;

"relevant expenditure" means expenditure incurred by the local housing authority under -

(a)   section 429 of the 1985 Act (improvement for sale schemes),

(b)   Part IX of the 1985 Act (slum clearance),

(c)   Part VII of the 1989 Act (renewals areas),

(d)   Part VIII of the 1989 Act (grants towards costs of improvements and repairs etc.), other than in relation to disabled facilities grants,

(e)   Part I of the 1996 Act (grants etc. for renewal of private sector housing), other than in relation to disabled facilities grants, or

(f)   section 139 of the 1996 Act (relocation grants); and

"relevant payments" means contributions and subsidies (other than in relation to disabled facilities grants) paid in that financial year under section 429 of the 1985 Act (contributions for improvement for sale schemes), sections 96 (contributions relating to renewal areas) and 132 (contributions for improvements and repairs) of the 1989 Act and sections 92 (contributions for renewal of private sector housing) and 139 (relocation grants) of the 1996 Act.

4.   Repayment of Subsidy

4.1   Where an authority incur a surplus, as hereinafter calculated, in any financial year in connection with the exercise of their slum clearance functions, they shall pay to the Secretary of State in respect of that surplus an amount equal to 60 per cent. of the surplus.

4.2   An authority incur a surplus in any financial year if, in accordance with paragraphs 5 to 8, their aggregate receipts for the year exceed their aggregate expenditure for the year, the surplus being equal to the excess receipts.

4.3 Where an authority incur a surplus, the amount due to the Secretary of State will be recovered on receipt of the authority's claim after the end of the financial year to which it relates, subject to any adjustment, if necessary, once the claim has been examined by an auditor appointed by the Audit Commission.

5. Items to be taken into account

Expenditure

5.1 Subject to paragraphs 6 to 8, the aggregate expenditure for any financial year shall be the aggregate of an authority's expenditure in that year in respect of the following matters:

5.1.1 the payment of compensation or purchase money for the acquisition of land for the purposes of slum clearance functions

5.1.2 the payment of any interest on such compensation or on such purchase money

5.1.3 payments made under sections 29, 37 or 43 of the Land Compensation Act 1973

5.1.4 the payment of compensation under sections 295(3) or 296 of the 1985 Act or Parts II or III of Schedule 2 to the Acquisition of Land Act 1981

5.1.5 the declaration of a clearance area under section 289 of the 1985 Act including the cost of publishing, displaying or serving statutory notices

5.1.6 the making and confirmation of compulsory purchase orders under Part IX of the 1985 Act including the cost of hiring premises for local inquiries where suitable premises owned by an authority are not available, the cost of publishing, displaying or serving statutory notices and the Secretary of State's costs in connection with a local inquiry (where payable by an authority)

5.1.7 legal and professional fees, other than remuneration, including stamp duty, arbitration costs and land registry fees

5.1.8 remuneration directly attributable to work carried out in connection with an authority's slum clearance functions after the appropriate date. The appropriate date for work carried out in connection with a function relating to a matter specified in column (1) of the following Table shall be the date specified in relation to that matter in column (2) of that Table.

TABLE

(1)	(2)
(a) The demolition or closing of unfit premises.	(a) The date of the making of the demolition or closing order.
(b) The purchase of unfit premises.	(b) The date of the making of the compulsory purchase order or the date of the decision to purchase by agreement.
(c) The demolition of obstructive buildings.	(c) The date of the making of the obstructive buildings order.
(d) Clearance areas.	(d) The date of service of a notice of intention under section 289(2B) of the 1985 Act.

5.1.9   the demolition and removal of buildings on slum clearance land including-

weather proofing and shoring up of buildings adjacent to those demolished

filling in of basements to ground level and levelling off surfaces

disconnection and removal of sewers and service mains

the removal of material and rubbish arising from the demolition

5.1.10   the watching, lighting and fencing of slum clearance land

5.1.11   the appropriation of land to slum clearance functions

5.1.12   the acquisition of land for the purposes of slum clearance functions in exchange for other land.

Receipts

5.2   Subject to paragraphs 6 to 8, the aggregate receipts for any year shall be the aggregate of an authority's receipts in that year in respect of the following matters -

5.2.1   the disposal of slum clearance land other than by way of exchange

5.2.2   the disposal of materials resulting from the clearance and demolition of buildings on slum clearance land

5.2.3   the appropriation of slum clearance land to some other function of the authority

5.2.4   the exchange of slum clearance land for other land.

Relevant Date

5.3   Subject to paragraph 5.4 and 5.5, expenditure shall be taken into account under this paragraph on the date on which it is incurred and a receipt shall be taken into account on the date on which it is received.

5.4   Expenditure shall be taken into account under paragraph 5.1.11 on the date of the resolution to appropriate the land to slum clearance functions and a receipt shall be taken into account under paragraph 5.2.3 on the date of the resolution to appropriate slum clearance land to another function or the date the land is first used for the purpose of that function, whichever is the earlier.

5.5   Expenditure shall be taken into account under paragraph 5.1.12 and a receipt shall be taken into account under paragraph 5.2.4 on the date of the contract for the exchange of the land in question.

6.   Items not to be taken into account

6.1   In calculating a loss or a surplus for the purpose of paragraphs 3 or 4, no account shall be taken of–

6.1.1   any expenditure or receipts in respect of–

(a)   remuneration not directly attributable to work carried out in connection with an authority's slum clearance functions or remuneration directly attributable to such work carried out before the appropriate date specified in paragraph 5.1.8

(b)   administrative overheads or overheads attributable to any remuneration

(c)   the temporary use of slum clearance land

(d)   emergency repair work, water charges, and payments for the supply of gas or electricity to premises used for temporary housing accommodation under section 300 or 301 of the 1985 Act

(e)   any interest or other debt management charges incurred by an authority in borrowing money to enable them to carry out any slum clearance function

6.1.2   expenditure incurred and receipts due or deemed to have been incurred or due before 1 April 1990

6.1.3   receipts due after 1 April 1990 in respect of the disposal of slum clearance land, or deemed to be due after that date in respect of the appropriation of such land, where the land was acquired and all the buildings on the land were demolished before that date

6.1.4   expenditure incurred in respect of the costs of any person (other than the Secretary of State or the authority) in connection with a local inquiry in relation to a compulsory purchase order where those costs are payable by the authority

6.1.5   any money paid or received by an authority for equality of exchange in relation to the exchange of land

6.1.6   expenditure incurred or receipts due in respect of land acquired other than for the purposes of slum clearance functions where the land has not been appropriated to those functions

6.1.7   any part of a receipt set aside by an authority under section 59 of the 1989 Act as provision to meet credit liabilities

6.1.8   any amount required to be set aside under section 61(4) of the 1989 Act in respect of the land received by way of exchange for slum clearance.

7. Valuation

7.1   Expenditure taken into account under paragraph 5.1.1 shall not exceed the amount certified by a valuer as the compulsory purchase value of the land acquired as at the date when the value of the land is agreed or is assessed by the Lands Tribunal or the date when possession is taken by the authority whichever is the earlier.

7.2   Where land is appropriated by an authority to slum clearance functions from another function of the authority, they shall be deemed to have incurred expenditure of an amount equal to the amount certified by a valuer as the compulsory purchase value of the land at the date of the resolution to appropriate the land; and expenditure taken into account under paragraph 5.1.11 shall not exceed that amount

7.3   A receipt taken into account under paragraph 5.2.1 shall, subject to paragraph 6.1.7, not be less than the amount certified by a valuer as the best price reasonably obtainable for the land disposed of at the date of the disposal.

7.4   Where slum clearance land is appropriated by an authority to some other function of the authority, they shall be deemed to have received an amount equal to the amount certified by a valuer as the compulsory purchase value of the land at the date of the resolution to appropriate the land or the date the land is first used for the purpose of that function, whichever is the earlier; and the receipt taken into account under paragraph 5.2.3 shall not be less than that amount.

7.5   Where land is acquired by an authority for the purposes of their slum clearance functions in exchange for other land, the authority shall be deemed to have incurred expenditure of an amount equal to the amount certified by a valuer as the compulsory purchase value of the land acquired at the date of the contract for the exchange; and expenditure taken into account under paragraph 5.1.12 shall not exceed that amount.

7.6   Where slum clearance land is exchanged by an authority for other land, the authority shall be deemed to have received an amount equal to the amount certified by a valuer as the best price reasonably obtainable for the land at the date of the contract for the exchange; and the receipt taken into account under paragraph 5.2.4 shall, subject to paragraph 6.1.8, not be less than that amount.

8.   Apportionment

Where an authority incur or are deemed to have incurred expenditure or any receipt is due or deemed to be due partly in the exercise of their slum clearance functions and partly in the exercise of some other function, only such part of the expenditure or receipt as may fairly be regarded as attributable to the exercise of their slum clearance functions shall be taken into account in accordance with the provisions of this Determination.

9.   Conditions of subsidy

9.1   Each authority shall maintain adequate records of expenditure and receipts to facilitate the completion of claims for slum clearance subsidy. Claims shall be submitted in such form and at such times as may from time to time be required by the Secretary of State.

9.2   The authority shall maintain records in respect of each clearance area declared under section 289 of the 1985 Act showing:

9.2.1   the expenditure incurred or deemed to be incurred in connection with the acquisition, appropriation and clearance of all land included in, surrounded by or adjoining the clearance area;

9.2.2   the receipts due or deemed to be due in connection with the disposal or appropriation of the slum clearance land.

9.3   The authority shall maintain records to show for each financial year:–

9.3.1   the number of properties acquired or appropriated for the purposes of slum clearance functions for which subsidy has been claimed;

9.3.2   the number of properties demolished in respect of which subsidy has been claimed.

9.4   The authority shall permit the auditor appointed by the Audit Commission or any other officer authorised by the Secretary of State to have access to and inspect any records maintained in accordance with this paragraph.

9.5   The authority shall provide such information in connection with those records or a claim for subsidy as the Secretary of State may require.

Annex F

MAIN GRANTS - GENERAL

Operation of New System - General

1.   This part provides advice on the general framework of the new grant system and the information which follows applies equally to renovation grants, common parts grants and HMO grants. Where the detailed operation of the grant system differs for one particular type of grant, that information is set out in *Annex G*. Advice on implementation of the new provisions of the grant system in respect of disabled facilities grant is set out in *Annex I*.

Preliminary enquiry system

2.   Local authorities are encouraged to use a preliminary enquiry system for dealing with applications for grant assistance. An effective enquiry system will help to minimise the number of abortive applications, thus conserving resources and avoiding disappointment to applicants. Authorities should try to establish sufficient preliminary information to enable them to provide applicants with a reasonable indication of grant eligibility and their likely contribution. The main factors governing grant eligibility are the age and tenure of the property, the applicant's interest in it, and the nature of works required. Subject to these, grant entitlement will be governed by the cost of the proposed works and the financial resources of the applicant.

3.   Authorities are encouraged to help prospective applicants to understand how their grant entitlement, if any, will be assessed. This might involve providing appropriate literature, perhaps in the form of an information pack, or running an advisory service on grants and renovation generally to offer support in answering queries. If forms are used to process preliminary inquiries it must be made clear that these do not constitute a formal application. Such an enquiry system should not be used to prevent potential applicants from submitting formal applications where it is their wish and it should at all times be made clear that no commitments about the availability and the amount of grant can be given until a formal application has been submitted. Potential applicants should be made aware of the authority's published policy for allocating discretionary grants, and the sequence for assessing applications such that they understand that grant could be approved but no money given if the means test establishes that they are able to contribute to the full cost of the works.

4.   Advice at this preliminary stage on which grant, if any, is appropriate to an enquirer's particular situation may help to avoid future confusion or uncertainty. In particular, authorities might draw to the attention of elderly, disabled and infirm people the availability of home repair assistance (see *Annex H*) as an option which might meet their needs less expensively than a full-scale scheme of improvement. Authorities may also receive enquiries from the owners of houses designated as defective under Part XVI of the 1985 Act uncertain as to their eligibility for renovation grant. Authorities should ensure that potential applicants understand that grant cannot be given towards the cost of any works for which an applicant is eligible for assistance under Part XVI of the Housing Act 1985, and where the relevant works are works required to reinstate that defective dwelling (section 6 of the 1996 Act). Grant may, however, be given if the applicant is no longer eligible or has never been eligible for such assistance.

Making an application

5.   The particulars to be included in an application for grant (see paragraph 7) and the forms of application to be used are set out in the Housing Renewal Grant Regulations 1996 and the Housing Renewal Grant (Prescribed Forms and Particulars) Regulations 1996. An application must be made

in the prescribed form, or one substantially similar, to be valid. It is the Department's view that an application should be regarded as made on the date on which it is submitted to the authority completed in the form prescribed and that where information and evidence required in the form is missing or incomplete it should be treated as made when that information and evidence to support the application have been supplied. Authorities must decide what additional information or evidence they reasonably require, if any, to verify the information given in the application. Authorities must approve or refuse the application within six months of the date it is made.

Charges for applications

6.   Local authorities cannot make charges for processing of grant applications or for responding to inform enquiries. These costs are taken into account in calculating the other services block of the Revenue Support Grant (RSG). However where a local authority offers an agency service for grant applicants, section 169 of the 1989 Act enables authorities to levy a charge for providing professional, technical and administrative services on the applicant's behalf to help applicants. Such a charge is at the local authority's discretion and maybe included within the fee element of the grant approval so long as it meets the provisions for preliminary or ancillary services and charges, as set out in *Annex J4*.

Particulars to be included in an application

7.   The main requirements of the application are:-

   ● *particulars of the relevant works*: the relevant works are the works in respect of which grant is sought. The precise details of the works involved in a renovation scheme are likely to differ from contractor to contractor, and depend upon the methods and materials they use. This will be clear in the estimates accompanying the application. Therefore the application need only state the particulars in broad terms, with the estimates submitted providing the clear indication of the proposed works. It is expected that local authorities will make maximum use of their discretion, under section 37(3), to determine a specification with which the eligible works should comply. Where there has been a preliminary enquiry, a detailed schedule of works drawn up on the basis of the authority's inspection could be passed to any contractor approached for the purposes of submitting estimates.

   ● *estimates*: at least two estimates from different contractors are normally required in an application - see paragraph 72.

   ● *preliminary or ancillary services or charges*: see paragraph 13.

   ● *other prescribed particulars*: these particulars, including those necessary to apply the test of resources, are described by reference to the prescribed forms (see paragraph 5). Applicants are therefore required to provide all the information requested in the forms. Although it is not a requirement, applicants are requested to supply copies of plans and of relevant planning permission and building regulation approval documents.

Duty to consider

8.   Once a formal application has been validly made, authorities are under a duty to consider it. An authority could be open to legal challenge if they were to refuse to entertain a valid application or to comply with any reasonable request by a potential applicant to be furnished with the necessary application forms.

Applications by prospective purchasers

9.   Authorities do not have to be satisfied that a grant applicant has the requisite interest in the property until they are actually approving the grant. This means that an application for a grant may be submitted at any time from the point at which the applicant identifies a property as one which he proposes to acquire (although where the three year prior ownership qualification applies this is overridden). Where the application is for a common parts grant the authority must be satisfied that at the

date of the application at least the required proportion of the flats in the building concerned are occupied by occupying tenants. Authorities may give any indication they wish about grant availability when entertaining such an application but it may not be approved until the applicant has the necessary interest. An application which has been validly made must be refused if the applicant has not obtained the necessary interest after six months. The legislation allows for authorities to make a realistic interpretation of the commitment and progress of the applicant to secure ownership of the property.

Applications after commencement or completion of works

10.   Under the provisions of section 29(1) a local authority shall not approve an application for grant if the relevant works have begun before the application is approved . Where the works are commenced but not completed before the application is determined, other than where these are required to comply with a statutory notice, a local authority may approve an application where there were good reasons for commencing the work. However in doing so the Secretary of State would normally expect the authority to seek to vary the application, with the consent of the applicant, in accordance with the provisions of section 29(3) and (4) so as to exclude from the application any works which have already been completed. In such cases the assessment of the condition of the property will be based on its condition at the time of the original application - that is, irrespective of the works which have been carried out.

11.   The above does not apply to works undertaken in advance to comply with a statutory notice – section 29(5) applies. In such cases, the person on whom the notice was served will usually be obliged to comply with start and completion dates specified in the notice. Local authorities should therefore aim to process such applications expeditiously.

12.   Local authorities should ensure that their grants literature carries clear warnings of the consequences for grant if applicants commence works prior to receiving written approval of their application. Special attention may be needed in this regard where the application is for a disabled facilities grant and where the works are required urgently, perhaps to enable a disabled person to be discharged from hospital.

Fees and other ancillary costs

13.   In addition to the actual costs of carrying out works of improvement or repair, other charges necessarily incurred in undertaking grant-aided works are also eligible for grant. These preliminary or ancillary services or charges are specified by order of the Secretary of State and the full specification is set out in *Annex J4*. It includes costs such as architects' and surveyors' fees and charges for planning permission or building regulations approvals. Charges made by agency services for advising on or assisting with a client's application will also be admissible expenses. Grant applicants should be encouraged to use professional advisers to obtain a high standard of completed work.

14.   Particulars of the fees towards which grant is sought are required in an application and authorities must determine which of these are eligible for grant in the same way as they assess the eligible works. In doing so they should consider the reasonableness of the fees and whether they are properly incurred. As with the works themselves, the payment of grant in respect of these fees is dependent on the provision of a satisfactory receipt or invoice (see paragraph 64).

15.   For guidance on the treatment of VAT see paragraph 75.

Age limits

16.   Authorities may not entertain an application for grant unless the property concerned was built or provided by conversion at least ten years before the date of the application. Properties which are less than ten years old are normally covered by builders warranties in respect of any defects arising as

a result of poor design, materials or workmanship. This age limit does not apply to HMOs provided by conversion (section 4 of the 1996 Act).

17.   Applicants must be aged 18 years or over on the date of the application to be eligible for grant (section 3(1)).

NHS Trusts

18.   Authorities should note the exclusion from assistance of those properties in the residential estate whose funding for maintenance comes from Department of Health. This is provided for by section 3(2) of the 1996 Act. This replaces the Direction issued by the Secretary of State for Health in March 1993. This does not affect the power of local authorities under Parts VI and XI of the 1985 Act to serve notices on health authorities and NHS trusts, and special health authorities for works to residential accommodation such as nurses hostels. The Secretary of State hopes that a local authority will work with health authorities to ensure accommodation is brought up to required standards through an agreed programme of works having regard to the availability of resources to fund the works.

Owners interest

19.   Except for common parts grant (*see Annex G2*) authorities must satisfy themselves that an applicant has, or proposes to acquire, an owner's interest in all the land on which the relevant works are to be carried out. An owner's interest means a freehold interest or a leasehold interest where there is at least five years of the lease left to run. Participants in shared equity schemes may be regarded as having an owner's interest provided that the scheme involves at the outset the grant of a long lease. Persons with a shared interest in a property will be eligible to apply for grant with or without the other person being a signatory to the application, although it should be borne in mind that the financial resources of all joint owners with a grant eligible interest and resident in the property will be taken into account when determining the amount of grant payable. The written consent of all other joint owners should be obtained by the grant applicant before works commence.

Grants to tenants

20.   Renovation grants are only available to tenants where they are required by the terms of their tenancy to undertake the proposed works. Grant aid is available towards works that a tenant is required to carry out so long as they are eligible for grant. In the case of buildings containing flats, an obligation to meet the cost of works may apply to parts of the building outside the flat and a common parts grant may be appropriate.

21.   Where a tenant has an obligation to undertake works, he may still need to seek his landlord's permission before carrying out works (section 9). Where a local authority decides to entertain an application for grant from a tenant, not only will the tenant be required to provide a tenant's certificate as to future occupation, but the landlord will also be required to provide a certificate of intended letting for the dwelling. Local authorities have the discretion not to require a certificate from the landlord if they consider it would be unreasonable to do so in the circumstances (section 9(3)). However authorities are advised to waive this requirement only in exceptional circumstances, taking into account the fact that the provisions of sections 43 and 49 would then be unenforceable against the landlord, and the future continued availability for letting of the dwelling would not be safeguarded. Another reason is that where the renovation grant application is supported only by a tenant's certificate there is no grant recovery should the tenant subsequently leave the property after completion of the works.

22.   There may be cases where a local authority serves notice on the person having control of a dwelling-house requiring works to be carried out, but where a tenant of the person having control has a repairing obligation in relation to his dwelling. In such cases the responsibility to carry out the works required by the notice would rest with the person having control of the dwelling-house, and it would

be open to him to apply for grant in the normal way. If appropriate, he might seek recovery of such costs as are not met by grant from his tenant under the terms of the tenancy, if necessary through the Courts. Alternatively, it would be open to the tenant to apply for grant and to carry out the works but in such a case the person having control would be obliged to ensure that the terms of the notice were observed.

23.   A tenant making an application for a disabled facilities grant does not need to have a repairing obligation in order to be eligible for that grant. The application must, however, be accompanied by a tenant's certificate. The landlord's consent will be required before adaptation works can be carried out to his property, and local authorities should ensure that written permission has been obtained by the applicant before approving grant, especially in any cases where they have used their discretion not to require an owner's certificate from the landlords (section 22 (3)). Such discretion may be used where the authority consider the landlord is unreasonably withholding an owner's certificate. Where a landlord withholds his permission for the works to be undertaken a grant cannot be given. Local authority secure tenants are not eligible to apply for renovation grant because they do not have a repairing obligation or an obligation to contribute to the repair of the common parts. However a local authority secure tenant may apply for a disabled facilities grant.

Certificates and conditions of occupation

24.   All applications for main grants other than common parts grants and for applications made in respect of certain types of ecclesiastical property or by a charity, must be accompanied by a certificate relating to the future occupation of the property, and the local authority may not entertain an application unless such a certificate is provided. There are three different types of certificate and they are set in the legislation with the provisions for each grant. The general principles are described below, together with the grant conditions which relate to each:

(a) Owner-occupiers

(i)   An "owner-occupation certificate" certifies that the applicant has, or proposes to acquire, an owner's interest (as defined in section 7(1)(a) for renovation grant) in the dwelling, and that he, or a member of his family, intends to live in the dwelling as his (or that person's) only or main residence from the certified date for the grant condition period (section 8(1) & (2)). The grant condition period is currently set at 5 years. The certified date is the date, certified by a local authority, on which the eligible works were satisfactorily completed. The intentions stated in this certificate differ from those contained in the certificate of owner-occupation under the 1989 Act in that this becomes a condition against which grant is recoverable where there is a breach of agreed occupancy (section 48). Where the property is sold during the grant condition period, section 45 sets out the procedure for recovery of grant which is described in paragraphs 34 to 37 below.

(ii)   An "owner's certificate" certifies that the applicant has, or proposes to acquire, an owner's interest (as defined in section 21(2) for disabled facilities grant) in the dwelling, and that he intends that the disabled occupant will live in the dwelling as his only or main residence from the certified date throughout the grant condition period or for such shorter period as his health and other relevant circumstances permit. The certificate serves to confirm the intention on application, and does not require repayment of grant where there is a breach of condition.

(b) Tenants

(i)   A "tenant's certificate" certifies that the applicant is a tenant of the dwelling who falls within one of the qualifying categories in section 7(1)(b) and that he or a member of his family intends to live in the dwelling as his (or that member's) only or main residence (section 9(1) and (2)).

    (ii)   There are no conditions as to future occupation attached to the tenant's certificate, nor would a tenant be liable for repayment of any grant in the event of a disposal of the dwelling, by the landlord or anyone else, of which he is the tenant. A tenant's application must, however, normally be accompanied by a certificate of intended letting (section 8(3)) provided by his landlord, and the conditions related to that certificate will be registered as a local land charge in relation to that property and binding on the landlord and successive owners for a period of five years from the certified date (section 49). A tenant may also be required to provide his landlord with information to enable him to inform the authority as to how the certificate of intended letting is being complied with. That condition is binding on the tenant under section 49(6).

(c) Landlords

    (i)   A "certificate of intended letting" (section 8(3)) certifies that the applicant has or proposes to acquire an owner's interest in the dwelling, and intends to, or already has, let the dwelling as a residence, for a period of at least five years, beginning on the certified date, to someone who is not a member of his family and, except where the grant is a disabled facilities grant, on a tenancy which is not a long tenancy. These provisions apply equally to situations where a dwelling is already let, and will continue to be let after the grant works are carried out, and to those where letting will only commence or resume after works have been carried out. There may be any number of individual successive lettings during the five-year 'initial period'. Separate certificates may be given in relation to each dwelling provided or improved with grant aid. If a landlord intends himself to occupy one of several dwellings provided by conversion of a building as his only or main residence, he may provide a certificate of owner-occupation for that dwelling.

    (ii)   The intention behind the grant conditions is that the dwelling will be let or licenced, and there are no restrictions as to the type of letting or licence other than that it must be for residential purposes (and not for a holiday) to a person who is "not connected" with the landlord, and that the tenancy must not be a long tenancy.

25.   "Not connected" in this context means that the tenant must not be a member of the owner's family or, where personal representatives or trustees are the owner, a person who is, under the will or intestacy of the terms of the trust, beneficially entitled to an interest in the dwelling or to the proceeds of sale of the dwelling.

26.   Lettings or licences of the whole dwelling which are, for example, on existing regulated tenancies, and existing or new assured tenancies (including assured shorthold tenancies), will all be capable of complying with the grant conditions. Should the property be subsequently let or licensed as an HMO rather than as a dwelling it is possible that a breach of conditions would occur.

27.   For both renovation grant and HMO grant in order to satisfy themselves as to the manner in which a grant-improved dwelling or house is being occupied, the local authority may serve notice on the owner requiring him to provide within 21 days a statement showing how the property is occupied (section 49(6) and 50(6)). It is a condition of grant that the owner comply with any such notice. Similarly, if the owner requires information from the tenant to enable him to comply with such a notice, the tenant must provide such information as it is reasonable for the owner to request and this requirement can be enforced as if it were part of the terms of the tenancy.

28.   The grant conditions remain in force for a period of five years beginning on the certified date, and are binding (unless they cease to have effect for one of the reasons mentioned below) not only on the person who provided the certificate, as well as joint owners of the property, but also on any sub-

sequent owner of the dwelling. The conditions are not binding, however, if the owner is a housing authority or a registered housing association.

29.   In the event of a breach of the availability for letting grant condition, the local authority may demand repayment of the grant with interest, but the authority does have discretion not to demand repayment, or to demand a lesser amount. Once a demand for repayment on breach of letting conditions has been satisfied, the conditions cease to have effect as do the conditions relating to disposal of the property as do all other grant conditions (section 55(1)) except where specifically provided for otherwise (section 45(6)).

Properties held in trust

30.   There are no specific provisions governing grant applications in respect of dwellings owned by trusts and such applications are, therefore, subject to the conditions applying to applications by owner-occupiers, landlords or tenants. Eligibility for grant is likely to depend on the terms of the individual trust and authorities must consider any such application on its merits based, as necessary, on their own legal advice. Section 76(4) enables authorities to consider an application for home repair assistance from a person who does not have an owner's interest in, or who is not a tenant of, the dwelling, but who occupies it under a right of exclusive occupation for life or for a period of more than five years (*see Annex H*).

31.   A trustee or beneficiary applying for a grant must be able to fulfil all the normal grant conditions. So, for example, the applicant must be able to demonstrate a relevant interest in the property, either as an owner or a tenant, and to meet the conditions associated with either interest, including providing the appropriate certificate of future occupation.

Disposals

32.   A disposal, of either the whole or part of the property, is a relevant disposal (section 53) if it is a conveyance of the freehold or an assignment of the lease, or the grant of a long lease for a term of more than twenty one years other than at a rack rent. An applicant shall be treated as having made a relevant disposal if he gives to some other person the right to call for a relevant disposal of the dwelling.

33.   For the purposes of the grant system some "relevant disposals" are then termed "exempt disposals". An exempt disposal is defined as a disposal, whether it is of the whole or part of the premises to which the application relates, of any of the descriptions set out in section 54 of the 1996 Act.

Repayment upon disposal

34.   If an owner-occupier or a landlord makes a relevant disposal before the certified date or on or after the certified date but before the end of the grant condition period, ie the period of five years beginning on the certified date, he will be required to repay grant to the authority on demand. The repayment required will be repayment of any instalment that has been paid, or the whole grant. In the case of a conversion application the grant shall be treated for this purpose as apportioned equally between the dwellings provided (section 45(2)). Liability is binding, in the form of a local land charge, on any person who is the owner of the dwelling during the grant condition period or, in the case of a common parts grant, is a successor in title to the interest in the building which entitled the applicant to make his application, but excluding a local housing authority or social landlord in the case of HMO grants.

35.   Repayment of any grant is subject to the authority making a demand. Authorities are given discretion not to demand repayment of renovation grant or to demand a lesser amount in two specific circumstances (set out in section 45(5) of the 1996 Act). Advice on these is given in *paragraph 4 in Annex G1*. In all other cases authorities may decide not to demand repayment or to demand a lesser

amount with the consent of the Secretary of State (sections 45(4)(b), 46(4) and 47(4)). It is expected that authorities will use this discretion only sparingly. A general consent covering circumstances where the grant applicant has to move for reasons of employment or where sale of the property is required by a lender is set out in *Annex J4*.

36.   The conditions for repayment upon disposal do not apply if the relevant disposal was an exempt disposal except for two specific cases relating to renovation grant (section 45(6)). Guidance on these is set out in *paragraph 5 and 6 of Annex G1*.

37.   A disposal of a property for no consideration or at less than full consideration is also liable to the conditions for repayment where it is not an exempt disposal. The provision under section 121(5)(b) of the 1989 Act whereby such disposals did not trigger repayment has not been retained in the new system because of the possibility of abuse. However, in such cases authorities would be able to apply for consent to waive a demand for repayment where they consider repayment would be unreasonable (see paragraph 35). Any applications for such consents must be fully supported by the local authority with a reasoned justification.

Conditions imposed

38.   By virtue of section 52 of the 1996 Act, where an authority has approved an application they are able to impose grant conditions in addition to those set out in sections 45 to 50, with the consent of the Secretary of State, relating to works or other matters both before and after the certified date. The Secretary of State has issued a general consent to certain conditions being applied and that is set out in *Annex J4*. In exercising their discretion on imposing these conditions authorities need to be mindful of the practicalities of and their ability to monitor compliance with the conditions, as well as their willingness to recover grant where the condition has been breached. While it remains open to local authorities to seek the Secretary of State's consent to impose further conditions, it has been the objective of the general consent to include all those conditions which the Secretary of State considers are appropriate to meeting the purposes of the legislation.

39.   Conditions applied under the powers contained in section 52 require repayment of any grant or instalments of grant that have been paid. Authorities may also require that the amount is repaid with compound interest from the date of payment, at a reasonable rate to be determined by them and with yearly rests. As with the main grant conditions, authorities may exercise discretion not to demand repayment or to demand a lesser amount. A condition under section 52 is also a local land charge, binding on any person who is the owner of the dwelling for the time being (see paragraph 28) and any other person specified by the authority with the Secretary of State's consent.

Certified date

40.   Section 44 defines the certified date as the date certified by the authority as the date on which the execution of the works is completed to their satisfaction. The certified date is the date from which the grant conditions relating to certificates of future occupation, and other certificates, and disposals of grant-improved property will apply.

Works outside the curtilage of a dwelling

41.   Under sections 7(1)(a), renovation grant, 19(1)(a), disabled facilities grant and 25(1), HMO grant, a local housing authority may not entertain an application for grant unless they are satisfied that the applicant has, or proposes to acquire, an owner's interest in all the land on which the relevant works are to be carried out. However, the Secretary of State may direct that the authority may treat this condition as fulfilled by a person who has or proposes to acquire, an owner's interest in only part of the land. This is required to enable an authority to entertain an application in respect of works, part of which will take place outside the curtilage of a dwelling or of an HMO.

42.   The Secretary of State has issued a direction under sections 7(3), 19(3) and 25(2) permitting, subject to certain conditions, local authorities to approve grant for works outside the curtilage of a dwelling or HMO without having to apply to the Department for a special direction. This direction is at *Annex J4*.

43.   The direction limits the type of works outside the curtilage of the dwelling or HMO for which the authorities may decide to give grants for works in respect of utilities provided from public or private sources and for works under section 23(1)(a) to facilitate access to and from a dwelling by a disabled person. Where any of the conditions set out in the Direction are not met, an authority will need to apply to the Department for an individual direction before a decision on a grant can be determined.

Purpose of grant

44.   Grant must still make property fit but all grants (with exception of mandatory DFGs) are available at the discretion of authorities. The purposes for which renovation grant may be given is provided for in section 12 of the 1996 Act, common parts grant in section 17 and HMO grant in section 27. Authorities might find helpful the following guidance on the main purposes for which grant other than a conversion application (see paragraphs 50 to 53 below) is intended:

- *render a property fit*

     (i) Where an authority considers that a dwelling is not reasonably suitable for occupation because it fails to meet one or more of the requirements of the fitness standard (see *Annex A*) it must be declared unfit for human habitation. If the authority consider that the dwelling is capable of being made fit by carrying out a particular scheme of works (other than for the provision of one or more dwellings by conversion), and that to complete such works is the most satisfactory course of action having regard to the guidance issued by the Secretary of State in exercise of his powers under section 604A of the 1985 Act and section 85 of the 1996 Act (see *Annex B*), then a renovation grant **may** be given. Also where authorities were obliged to award mandatory grant in these circumstances under the provisions of the 1989 Act, the award of grant is now at their discretion. A dwelling does not have to have been unfit for any length of time in order to be eligible for grant. Grant must not be given on an unfit dwelling which, following completion of the grant aided works, will remain unfit.

- *put a property into reasonable repair*

     (i) Grant towards works for the improvement and repair of existing dwellings is intended to assist in bringing properties up to a good standard, taking into account among other things the anticipated life of the building. Provided the property is put into reasonable repair an applicant and authorities have flexibility as to the range of works included in a scheme at any particular time, so long as the works undertaken fall within one of the purposes for which grant may be given. It remains the Department's view that a grant should not be given for works to improve or repair a dwelling which include the complete or substantial demolition of the dwelling as this would breach the requirement that carrying out the works is the most satisfactory course of action (sections 13(6), 18(4) and 28(5)).

     (ii) Section 96 defines reasonable repair in relation to matters such as the age, character and locality of the property, but disregarding its internal state of repair. Relevant considerations might include planning restrictions or other restrictions due to listed status or architectural or historical interest of the building. Authorities may require that the eligible works are carried out in accordance with such specifications as they determine (section 37(3)). While the preservation of the architectural heritage or historical character of a dwelling is generally desirable, a sensitive balance may need to be struck in some cases when drawing up the specification.

(iii)   The extent of repairs justified for grant purposes in any individual case is a matter for the authority's judgement, especially where the property's life span is being extended by a number of years. In trying to strike a balance between the minimum repairs needed to put a house in reasonable condition and those which could be justified on the grounds that they would substantially reduce the owner's future liability, it would seem reasonable, where properties are expected to have a long life, for authorities to allow for repairs that would be likely to be needed within a few years of the present scheme if not carried out as part of that scheme.

- *provide adequate thermal insulation*

(i)   The Government is firmly committed to encouraging greater energy efficiency in the home. Authorities are encouraged to use grant aid for insulation to achieve optimum energy efficient solutions compatible with achieving value for money. In particular, authorities should consider approving grant for such works where they will form a useful adjunct to works being carried out to make a dwelling fit, for example works in connection with provision for heating.

(ii)   There is a question as to what constitutes adequate thermal insulation for existing housing. Current building regulations require higher standards of thermal insulation than has been the case previously and, for practical purposes, it might be reasonable to regard these as a target to be aimed for. It may be unreasonable though, and in many cases impracticable, to expect all works of insulation carried out with the assistance of renovation grants to achieve levels comparable with new housing standards.

- *provide adequate facilities for space heating*

(i)   Similar considerations to those outlined above may apply to applications covering the installation of facilities for space heating. These might range from separate gas convector fires or night-rate electric storage heaters up to full central heating installations. The practical purpose of grant aid is to assist in achieving satisfactory conditions of thermal comfort and this will normally be best achieved by an appropriate combination of insulation levels and heating provision. In general, in cases where it is practicable and economical to install insulation, the heating system will be correspondingly more economical both to install and to use. In assessing cases, authorities should give high priority to considerations of energy efficiency and economy of use. Where the optimum energy efficient package of measures cannot be achieved, either because of excessive cost or impracticability, achieving satisfactory conditions of thermal comfort may well be considered to have a higher priority and a less energy-efficient solution may be acceptable.

- *provide satisfactory internal arrangements*

(i)   Whether internal arrangements are satisfactory or not must be judged in the circumstances of the particular case. The main objective in giving grant for this purpose is to help achieve the best use of the existing space in a dwelling, for example additional space may be required to replace space used to provide facilities for a disabled person, where a bedroom is used to create an accessible bathroom or to accommodate a through-floor lift.

(ii)   Works to overcome an inconvenient arrangement in an otherwise adequate dwelling, where this is practicable and can be achieved at reasonable cost, may be eligible for grant, for example, the provision of partitioning to allow separate access to a bathroom or second bedroom in a rear extension which is otherwise only accessible through another room.

Bringing empty properties back into use

45. Local authorities should only be grant aiding the renovation of an empty property where it is clear that the market has been given a sufficient opportunity to deal with the particular property and failed. This includes ensuring the property is realistically priced given its condition. In reaching any decision on grant aiding the renovation of an empty property a local authority will wish to consider:

> the impact on the local area of the property remaining empty for a prolonged period of time;

> the role renovation could play in securing wider strategic objectives;

> the environmental benefit of making use of existing built resources;

> the cost benefit to the authority of providing through grant assistance a home for someone who would otherwise be looking to a local authority for help in securing rented accommodation.

46. A property will have to be fit on completion of the works. It is for the authority to decide, given the particular circumstances, whether it is appropriate to grant aid works beyond fitness. Where the empty property will be for owner occupation a local authority will need to be assured that there are sufficient grounds to waive the three year ownership and/or residency conditions. The means test for owner occupiers applies. Where the property is to be used for private rented accommodation there is no three year prior qualifying period and a local authority has the discretion to decide the most appropriate level of grant.

Radon

47. In some circumstances it may be appropriate for local authorities to provide renovation grants or home repair assistance to help owners with the cost of radon remedial works. A new map identifying those areas in England most affected by the naturally occurring radioactive gas was published by the National Radiological Protection Board (NRPB) on 16 May 1996.

48. Prolonged exposure to radon gas within a house is believed to increase the risk of developing lung cancer. The Department's booklet "Radon: A householders guide" and "Radon: A guide to reducing levels in your home" (Department of the Environment), issued in May 1996, explain more fully what radon is, how it gets into the home, what the effects on health might be and how levels of radon can be reduced. Under the provisions of section 12(1)(g) the Secretary of State has specified the level which radon in a dwelling or a building should not exceed. The specification is set out in *Annex J4* of this Circular. The effect of the specification is that authorities may make grants available to applicants where the annual averaged radon levels present in a dwelling or building exceed the current "action level" of 200 Becquerels per cubic metre (Bq/m3). Authorities should give serious consideration to applications supported by the results of a survey carried out, for at least three months, by the NRPB, or by a survey to a standard specified by the NRPB, showing that the level of radon present exceeds 200 Bq/m3. The authority must be satisfied that the remedial works for which grant aid is sought are necessary to reduce the radon level below the specified level.

49. Authorities are reminded that before paying grant they need to satisfy themselves that the approved works have been completed satisfactorily. Provided this is the case, there is no reason why grant should not be paid at the earliest possible opportunity. Authorities should be aware, however, that, on completion of the approved works, a minimum screening period of three months may be necessary to demonstrate the required reduction in radon levels and in many cases a survey period of six months to one year could be advisable. Where radon levels remain above the action level, authorities will need to consider whether a further grant may be paid either for new work or for modifications which constitute new work.

Provision of dwellings by conversion

50.   Section 58(1) defines "conversion" for the purposes of the Act. It is the Department's view that works for the provision of dwellings by the conversion of a house or other building are distinct from new construction of dwellings. "Conversion" is more a matter of the change of use of a building, for example, from non-residential to residential use or a change in the number of dwellings provided. A conversion may not actually involve a change in the number of dwellings provided in a building, but could involve alterations to the way it is sub-divided or arranged. Works involving complete demolition and rebuilding of a house or other building would not in the Department's view constitute works of conversion.

51.   Where the works involve the conversion of a non-residential building, authorities are asked to consider whether the dwellings provided by the conversion would be a useful addition to the general housing stock, and whether it is appropriate for the applicant to receive help from public funds, having regard to the scale and cost of the proposed works, the return the applicant would be likely to see on his investment on the open market, and the demand for accommodation of the type to be provided, whether for rent or owner-occupation. If the grant is for a property that will be owner occupied rather than let, the applicant or a member of his family must live in the property on completion of the works. Particular attention should also be paid to the special requirements of conversion schemes involving basements (or other underground rooms) and attic floors of houses or other buildings. Such conversions must comply with the building regulations and be carried out to a reasonable specification such that the completed dwelling or dwellings comply with the requirements of the fitness standard.

52.   The main reason for providing for grant towards conversions is to secure an increase in private sector housing accommodation by bringing under utilised space into use. Careful thought should be given where the conversion involves a reduction in the number of dwellings. Authorities should only consider approving a grant if it can be shown that the scheme proposed is the most satisfactory course of action, for example because it will produce more satisfactory accommodation for a large or extended family than any alternative scheme which would not involve a reduction in the number of dwellings.

53.   The enlargement of a house which is already adequate in other respects, for example to provide additional living or bedroom space, cannot be regarded as a high priority. However, it would be reasonable to make an exception in the case of dwellings in isolated locations occupied by families who, because of the nature of their livelihood, cannot be expected to seek alternative accommodation. Exceptions might also be considered in cases where accommodation suitable for extended families is not available within a reasonable distance of the area in which their community is situated.

54.   The Department considers that works of improvement of dwellings would cover smaller extensions to dwellings, with larger extensions, on the whole, falling outside the proper purpose of renovation grants. While a grant for conversion would normally be expected to increase the number of housing units, authorities may also consider awarding grant in cases where a local need could be met by extending into a neighbouring property.

Estimated expense

55.   Authorities should consider four elements in the process of determining the estimated expense and calculating grant (section 34(2)):

- (i) which of the relevant works are eligible for grant - the "eligible works".

- (ii) the amount of the expenses which, in their opinion, are properly to be incurred in the execution of the eligible works.

● (iii) the costs properly attributable to preliminary or ancillary services or charges incurred in relation to the grant application (see paragraph 13). These costs combine with those relating to the execution of the eligible works ((ii) above) to form the "estimated expense".

● (iv) the amount of grant they will pay . This will be subject to the elements set out above and the means test, which is explained in *Annex J2*.

Approvals procedure

56. Authorities must notify the grant applicant as soon as is reasonably practicable, and in any event not later than six months after the date of the application, whether the application is approved or refused. Authorities are also statutorily required to notify the applicant as to how the estimated expense is arrived at or why a grant is refused (section 34(3) and (4)) *(see paragraph 5.1.3 of Chapter 5)*. Clear and efficient procedures for processing applications will therefore need to be established. Several Departments and sections of an authority's administration are likely to need to be instructed on grants procedure, such as those responsible for building regulations approval, planning permission and various financial matters. Authorities may wish to consider the establishment of a multi-practice unit to streamline the procedures.

57. Authorities are under a duty to consider in relation to a grant application whether the property is fit for human habitation. A full inspection should be carried out before grant approval is given to determine the works which need to be carried out. It is most important to ensure that the grant applicant has in place satisfactory financial and other arrangements for carrying out those works. There is no duty on authorities to carry out inspections of a property at any other stage during the works, but authorities should consider whether additional inspections are necessary, particularly where payments are to be made in instalments. Inspection should be made as soon as possible after completion of the works and, subject to other requirements, payment of grant should be made as soon as possible after the works have been certified as satisfactorily completed.

Assessment procedure and supervision of works

58. A local authority should operate adequate systems to ensure that the works specified are appropriate to the circumstances of each case. Close scrutiny of individual applications should therefore be routine as poor procedures can increase the cost of grant aided works and create the risk that inappropriate works will be funded. This is particularly important where a local authority has a strategy that advocates varying extent of works in recognition of policy priorities. A local authority should therefore ensure that where grant is conditional on the works being carried out in accordance with any specification they may determine under section 35 of the 1996 Act, that the terminology is precise with well defined expressions. In addition this will ensure that the requirements of section 34(3) have been fulfilled.

Revisions of grant after approval

59. To provide flexibility authorities may redetermine the estimated expense and the amount of grant if they are satisfied that, owing to circumstances beyond the control of the applicant, the eligible works cannot be, or could not have been, carried out on the basis of the amount of the expenses determined by them (section 34(5)(a)). Where works have yet to commence, local authorities are advised generally to exercise this discretion only if the fact that the original contractor is no longer prepared to carry out the work on the basis of his tender is due entirely to matters beyond the control of the applicant and if further estimates are submitted from both the same and a different contractor. However, there may well be exceptions to this general rule, such as where a non-VAT registered builder becomes registerable for VAT in the period between the submission of the estimate and the commencement of the works, or where this period is sufficiently long to make it unreasonable to expect the builder to adhere to his estimate.

60.   Once a contract has commenced most builders will normally be prepared to honour their estimate, but there could be exceptions, for example where a builder becomes registered for VAT before completing the works or where significant increases in the cost of materials may have to be passed on to their clients. Authorities may consider redetermination of the estimated expense to be justified in cases where meeting in full any such increases would place the grant applicant in undue hardship. It may be appropriate to make any redeterminations at or near completion stage where the works have already begun.

61.   Authorities may similarly redetermine an approval where the eligible works cannot be or could not have been completed without carrying out additional unforeseen works (34(5)(b)). Redetermination may be made retrospectively where it is not possible to delay completion of the works. Local authorities should be aware that in such cases there are no powers enabling them to reconsider whether grants should be given or whether another course of action would now be more appropriate. Comprehensive surveys of properties, the precise identification of fitness and detailed specifications of the proposed remedies should reduce the risk of unforeseen works.

62.   Authorities are also able to withhold or demand repayment of grant in various circumstances after an application has been approved (section 42). These circumstances are:

- where the authority ascertain that they determined an application on the basis of inaccurate or incomplete information and awarded the applicant more grant than that to which he was entitled;

- where the works are not carried out by the contractor, or one of the contractors, whose estimate accompanied the application;

- where the eligible works and associated costs are or are likely to be carried out at less than the estimated expense;

- where the works are not completed to their satisfaction within twelve months or whatever longer period may be specified, or are started before the application was approved.

63.   In all these circumstances, authorities have the discretion to reduce or refuse grant and to require repayment of any grant or instalment of grant that has been paid together with interest. Authorities should bear in mind that these provisions are designed to prevent abuse of the grant system.

Payment of grant

64.   Authorities may pay grants either in whole after the completion of the eligible works, or in instalments as the works progress. In either circumstances the payment of grant is conditional upon the works in question having been executed to the local authority's satisfaction, and upon the applicant or someone appointed to act on their behalf providing the authority with an acceptable invoice, demand or receipt for those works. It is up to each local authority to decide what they regard as a satisfactory invoice, demand or receipt, but **section 37(4) specifies that one given by the applicant himself or by a member of his family is not acceptable**. If the applicant himself does the work, therefore, grant would only be payable in respect of the materials used for which invoices etc. provided by someone else could be submitted. Where grant is paid in instalments, the aggregate amount of grant paid at any point prior to the completion of all the eligible works must not exceed nine tenths of the amount of the grant. Grant may be paid direct to the contractor (see paragraph 80). It is essential that authorities have effective systems in place to secure probity and identify any issues of fraud or abuses of the grant system (see *Annex J1*).

Insurance claims

65.   Section 51 is a new provision to address those cases where there are likely to be insurance payments in respect of works for which grant applications have been submitted. The Department accepts

that there may be cases where there could be an urgent need for works to be undertaken to a property, such as structural instability or to meet the needs of a disabled person, and that grant assistance could be sought. However, in some cases the cost of the works may be covered either by an insurance payment or a claim against a third party. The Department believes that it may be appropriate for the authority to give grant aid to ensure the works are completed at the earliest opportunity. However, where subsequently the grant applicant receives a payment on an insurance or damages claim in respect of the grant aided works, then they should repay to the authority the grant, so far as is appropriate, out of the proceeds of any claim.

66.   The Secretary of State has consented to conditions under section 51 being imposed in the following cases:

- claims for personal injuries in respect of works required under a mandatory disabled facilities grant;

- claims on the applicant's property insurance or on a third party in respect of works for which renovation grant, common parts grant and HMO grant have been given;

and therefore a general consent covering these circumstances is provided at *Annex J4.*

67.   Claims in such cases can be protracted and therefore there is no time limit attached to the provision covering the recovery of grant where compensation has subsequently been paid. A local authority has the discretion in section 51(4) not to demand repayment or to demand a lesser amount where this is appropriate. In operating this discretion a local authority should take full consideration of the terms of any settlement received by the grant applicant.

68.   Where insurance claims have been made and payment received in advance of grant applications a local authority will need to take a view as to whether it would be an appropriate use of resources to give grant aid. Where the grant is mandatory or the local authority decide to proceed in approving the application, details of the insurance payments should be included in the prescribed grant application form.

Successive grants

69.   There are no restrictions on successive applications for grant on the same property, from the same or different applicants. However, authorities should avoid, as far as possible, giving grant assistance on more than one occasion towards works intended to eliminate a particular problem contributing to the unfitness of the dwelling, although exceptions might be made such as where a considerable period of time has elapsed since the earlier grant application or where the same problem occurs in another part of the dwelling in such a way as could not reasonably have been foreseen at the time of the earlier application. Where, despite the carrying out of grant-aided works, a particular problem - such as structural instability - recurs causing a dwelling once again to be become unfit for human habitation, authorities will wish to consider whether renovation is still the most satisfactory course of action, or whether alternative action such as demolition, closing or clearance would now be more appropriate. Authorities should also consider the standard of any previous scheme of works. A dwelling which has been improved to a thirty year life should not normally become unfit again within that period.

70.   Authorities are encouraged to adopt a flexible approach to successive applications for grants involving different works. Where it would appear to be a sensible approach and cost effective, there is no reason why works relating to more than one of the grant purposes should all be carried out at the same time, provided the relevant works in relation to any one purpose are carried out satisfactorily at one time. This sort of flexibility can help householders to carry out works over a period of time which, for financial and other considerations, they may prefer not to have done all at once.

Statistical returns

71.   As part of the Department's continuing policy of collecting data on the renovation of private sector housing in England, statistical return forms, eg P1D and P3D, will continue. However, they are being reviewed to take into account the legislative changes incorporated within the 1996 Act and where possible streamlined to help in the completion of the forms. A guidance note will accompany any revised forms.

Contractors Issues

Estimates for the cost of the relevant works

72.   Grant applications are normally required to include at least two estimates from different contractors of the costs of the relevant works. Local authorities would not be expected to require more than two estimates other than in exceptional circumstances, for example, where the proposed works are very extensive and expensive. Local authorities have also been given the discretion to require one estimate, and it may be reasonable for them to exercise this discretion in cases where the proposed works are either small or very specialised, where an estimate is submitted as part of the application co-ordinated by a recognised agency service (who has satisfied the local authority in respect of the contracting procedures) or where there is a known local difficulty in finding contractors willing to undertake particular kinds of work. The discretion to require only one estimate should be used sparingly.

Assisting applicants with lists of contractors

73.   Section 38(2) and (3) allow the Secretary of State to make regulations setting up lists of approved builders and make it a condition of grant that a contractor from the list carries out the eligible works. We are aware that there are recognised lists of accredited contractors established. However, none either provide sufficient coverage for natural adoption at present or are sufficiently comprehensive to warrant use by local authorities for grant work. However, given the pace at which ideas like this develop, the powers have been taken to enable local authorities to establish their own or use accredited lists in the future without recourse to primary legislation. At present there are no plans to use these powers.

74.   The Department is aware that some authorities already provide lists of contractors to assist applicants in choosing contractors. Nothing in the 1996 Act prevents the continuance of this practice. The principle of assisting applicants by supplying lists of contractors is one the Department would support but without a legislative mandate in the form of regulations under section 38(3) authorities may not make it a condition of grant that applicants are required to use a contractor from a list. Authorities must also be aware of the responsibility for vetting and approving contractors implicit in running an approved list both in terms of fair access for contractors and the expectations of applicants who use a contractor from such a list. Describing a list of contractors as "approved by" an authority implies an endorsement of those contractors and possible legal liability if the work is not of a reasonable quality. It is for authorities that wish to operate lists of contractors to decide, perhaps in consultation with their legal services, what level of service they wish to provide for applicants and then clearly explain to applicants their position when providing them with a list of contractors.

Value Added Tax and assessing estimates

75.   Most improvement or repair works are taxable at the standard rate of VAT, the exception being certain works for the benefit of disabled people (see *Annex I*). In the Department's view VAT should be admissible for grant aid. When assessing estimates submitted with applications authorities must ensure there is genuine and full competition. Authorities should seek to obtain the best package available, with price generally only being one of the relevant considerations in coming to a judgement. Therefore, in considering the estimates it would, in the Department's view, be reasonable to address issues such as VAT registration, the reputation of the contractor and his ability to carry out the works to a good standard and in good time. In providing for equal treatment of competing estimates in

respect of VAT liabilities, factors which authorities should bear in mind are that contractors who charge VAT may be able to recover VAT they pay, whereas contractors who are not registered for VAT are still required to pay VAT on the materials they acquire for carrying out works and have to absorb these costs.

76.   Authorities should be aware of the potential difficulties which may arise where a contractor becomes registered for VAT between providing the estimate and completing the works. Advice on the scope for authorities to redetermine grant in such cases is contained in paragraph 59.

Conditions as to contractors who undertake works

77.   Section 38(1) of the 1996 Act requires that the eligible works are carried out by one of the contractors who provided the estimates included with the application. This condition will assist local housing authorities in maintaining control over the specifications supplied by contractors, to reduce misunderstandings about the works to be undertaken and also to minimise wasted effort in providing estimates on the part of contractors. In recognition of the fact that there may be occasions where exceptions may be required, local authorities may dispense with the requirement if they have good reason. Examples could be where the contractors who provided estimates are unable to undertake the work at the time required; or where both estimates are in excess of what the local authority consider reasonable for the works.

Works undertaken by family members

78.   Section 37(4) prevents applicants from submitting invoices for grant aided work which are from applicants or members of their family. Allowing grant aided work to be carried out by members of the applicant's family would in some cases provide value for money. However, there is also the possibility of collusion and fraud between the applicant and a builder who is a relative. There are opportunities for applicants who are builders or who have relatives who are builders to undertake the works on a DIY basis. Although the legislation prevents applicants or their relatives charging for their labour costs, invoices for materials from a third party should normally be acceptable to a local authority in this type of situation.

The quality of grant aided work

79.   The effectiveness of renovation policies depends on the quality of work carried out on the properties concerned. Authorities are reminded that the payment of all or part of a grant is conditional upon the works being executed to their satisfaction (section 37(4)(a)). Their procedures should ensure that payment including interim payments cannot take place until they are so satisfied. A local authority should not certify as satisfactorily completed any works displaying an unacceptable quality of workmanship, or where the objectives of the grant are not met. These matters are not always fully appreciated by applicants. Authorities might therefore consider this when preparing the information and guidance provided by them to ensure that it sets out clearly the respective responsibilities of authority and applicant. Authorities will also wish to ensure that applicants do not gain the impression that inspections carried out by staff of the authority are done on the applicant's behalf. Where an authority agrees to execute the works on behalf of the applicant, it would have to do so under arrangements made under section 57.

Payment of grant to contractors

80.   In order to reduce the possibility of abuses of the grant system by applicants not passing the grant money they receive on to the contractor or seeking to secure additional works within the same contract price, two new measures have been introduced in section 39. The first of these allows authorities to make payment direct to the contractor. If authorities wish to reserve the right to pay the contractor direct, then they are required to make this clear to the applicant prior to the grant being approved. Therefore the authority must inform the applicant that this **will, or may, be the manner of payment before the application is approved**. Where both the local authority and the applicant are

satisfied with the works there should be no problem with this option. By contrast there will be difficulties where there is a difference of view. If the applicant is satisfied but the local authority is not, the grant must not be paid until the defects are remedied. If the local authority is satisfied under section 37(4)(a) but the applicant is not, the authority should take particular care - in the light of the applicant's expressed concerns - that they have arrived properly at their section 37(4)(a) judgement as to the satisfactory execution of works. If they are content that this is the case the grant should be paid direct to the contractor notwithstanding the applicant's dissatisfaction.

81.   There may be situations where the eligible works are completed to the satisfaction of the authority but the applicant is not fully satisfied with those works. Authorities have the power under section 39(2) to withhold payment to the contractor at the applicant's request, should they consider it appropriate. In these circumstances they may make payment to the applicant instead. Care needs to be exercised when paying contractors direct where a local authority is not meeting all the cost of the works. Further information on the quality of grant aided works is contained in paragraph 79 above.

82.   Authorities also have the option under section 39(1) of making payments to the applicant in the form of an instrument (a cheque) made payable to the contractor. Once again the authority must inform applicants that this will, or may, be the method of payment, prior to the application being approved.

Annex G1

RENOVATION GRANT

1.   Renovation grant is available for the improvement or repair of a dwelling or for the provision of dwellings by the conversion of a house or other building. The information contained in Annex F offers guidance on the basic administration of the grant but there are some details specific to this grant on which authorities might find the following advice helpful.

Prior qualifying period

2.   Section 10 of the 1996 Act introduces a three year ownership and residence qualification for most applicants for renovation grant. Unless authorities have exercised the discretion described in paragraph 3 below, they should not entertain an application unless the applicant is able to show that he has lived in the dwelling as an owner or tenant for the preceding three years. The prior qualifying period does not apply to landlords or to properties in a renewal area. Authorities might find these exemptions particularly helpful if they wish to give discretionary landlords' renovation grants as part of an empty property strategy or if they have plans for renovating run down areas. Other exceptions to the prior qualifying period are conversion applications and works for fire precaution or to provide a means of escape from fire.

3.   Authorities also have the discretion to dispense with the prior qualifying period either generally or for particular cases or types of cases. This will allow authorities to develop clear strategies against which individual applications can be measured and a decision made. The circumstances in which authorities might exercise this discretion would include those where to give grant would accord with their local strategy or where the authority considers that a deserving case would otherwise be excluded from grant. It should be borne in mind, however, that the residence qualification, in conjunction with the five year grant condition period, is intended to prevent applicants from profiting from the sale of properties improved with grant aid. Legally there is a presumption that the three year qualifying period will apply. It is important that where this rule is disapplied in any individual case that the local authority has good reason which forms part of the authority's housing strategy and operational plan.

Relevant disposals where recovery of grant is not required

4.   Section 45(4) and (5) sets out the circumstances relating to a relevant disposal where a local authority has the discretion not to recover grant. These relate to a sale to enable an elderly or infirm person to move to be cared for either in an institution; to be cared for by another person; or to enable a person to move to care for a member of his family or a partner's family. Local authorities can also seek the Secretary of State's consent not to recover grant where they believe it inappropriate.

Transfer of property between family members

5.   Where a renovation grant has been given to an owner occupier for the improvement of his home it is repayable if the property is disposed of or there is a change of use within the five year grant condition period. There are however a number of relevant disposals which are classed as exempt disposals and grant repayment is not required. Disposals under 54(1)(a) to a family member (as set out in section (54(2))) and disposals which are vested under a will or intestacy (54(1)(b)) have in the past been exempt. However it has been evident that these disposal routes have been used to circumvent the grant recovery conditions. Transfers have taken place between family members for the purpose of onward sale to a third party or a change of use from renting to owner occupation. In addition where grant has been given and within the grant condition period it is transferred under the provisions of a will this has had the potential to bring a windfall gain to the beneficiary if the property was subsequently sold.

6. Therefore sections 45(6) and 48(8) provide that where there is an exempt disposal under 54(1)(a) and (b) the grant recovery conditions remain in force for any subsequent disposal within the original grant condition period.

Annex G2

COMMON PARTS GRANT

1.   The common parts grant covers works of improvement and repair to the common parts of a building. The general framework for the operation of the grant is broadly as for renovation grants, but the detailed operation of the grant differs in several important respects. All references to the common parts grant are based on the assumption that an application is made in respect of works to the common parts of a building containing flats, and "relevant works" should be construed on that basis.

Preliminary conditions

2.   As in Part XV of the 1985 Act and Part VIII of the 1989 Act, a common parts grant application can normally only be made in respect of a building containing flats, where at least a specified proportion – namely, three-quarters – of those flats are occupied by "occupying tenants" at the time of the application. An "occupying tenant" is a person who occupies as their only or main residence a flat in the building in respect of which they have, either alone or jointly with others, one of the types of tenancy listed in section 14(2) of the 1996 Act. The Secretary of State does not intend at present to vary the specified proportion. He will, however, consider applications from individual local authorities under the provisions of section 14(3) for the substitution of some other proportion in a specific case or description of case. Such applications should be submitted to the Department and should be accompanied by a full justification of the particular circumstances.

3.   There are two types of common parts grant application:

> a "landlord's common parts application": This procedure is open to someone who has, either alone or jointly with others, a freehold or specified leasehold interest in the whole of the building in question, and who has either a duty or a power to carry out the relevant works;

> a "tenants' common parts application": It is possible for someone who might otherwise make a landlord's common parts application to join in with a tenants' common parts application and such a person is described in the legislation as a "participating landlord".

4.   Whether or not there is a participating landlord, a tenants' common parts application requires the participation of a least three-quarters of the occupying tenants of the building who, under the terms of their tenancies, have a duty to carry out, or to contribute to, the costs of carrying out (whether by service charges or otherwise) some or all of the relevant works. Persons who hold a joint tenancy are treated as a single occupying tenant for these purposes. Thus, if a building contains 10 flats, 8 of which are occupied by occupying tenants who have a duty to carry out works or contribute towards their cost, a tenants' common parts application would require the participation of at least 6 of those occupying tenants. An application may not be made, therefore, by one tenant on behalf of some or all of the other tenants who occupy flats in the building. Tenants with a duty to contribute to the costs of carrying out works should be aware that unless they also have a power to carry out works, either in the terms of their leases or expressly given by the owner of the building, they would not be able to proceed with the works. Tenants will also require their landlord's consent to undertake the works.

5.   All applicants for common parts grants are required to sign a certificate stating the nature of their interest in the building, or in their flat in the building, and certifying that the required proportion of the flats in the building is occupied by occupying tenants (sections 16(1) and (2)).

Eligible works

6.   The works for which common parts grant may be given are set out in section 17(1) of the Act. Problems of various sorts in the common parts of a building can cause one or more of the flats in the building to become unsuitable for occupation, and thus unfit. Section 604(2) of the 1985 Act (see paragraph 83 of Schedule 9 to the 1989 Act) sets out a number of requirements relating to the condition of parts of a building outside any particular flat which, if not met, may contribute to making a flat in the building unfit, and common parts grant may therefore be given towards works which will enable the common parts of a building to meet those requirements. Grant may not be approved if those requirements are not met on completion of the relevant works. If the works are required to comply with a statutory notice under sections 189, 190 or 352 of the 1985 Act, the application would usually be made by an owner of the building, as the person on whom the notice was served.

7.   Local authorities have the same powers as for other main grants to vary applications for common parts grants, with the applicants' consent, where the relevant works are more or less extensive than, in their opinion, is required to achieve the purpose or purposes specified.

Grant conditions

8.   The normal conditions as to the payment of grant and completion of works apply to common parts grants but there are no conditions as to the future occupation of a building on which a common parts grant is given. There are, however, conditions governing the repayment of grant instalments in the event of a disposal of a building before the certified date and repayment of the whole grant if the building is disposed of during the grant condition period (five years from the certified date). These conditions apply only to a landlord's common parts application, and closely resemble the conditions relating to the disposal of a dwelling where a certificate of intended letting has been provided. As with other grants, these conditions are local land charges for the duration of the grant condition period, and are binding on any person who is for the time being an owner of the building – that is, the grant applicant or any successor in title. There is discretion for a local authority not to make a demand or to demand a lesser amount, but only with the consent of the Secretary of State (section 46). A general consent has been issued by the Secretary of State which is explained in *Annex F paragraph 35*.

9.   There are no conditions laid down as to occupancy or availability for letting for common parts grants. However, grant conditions may be imposed under section 52 of the Act with the consent of the Secretary of State. A general consent has been issued by the Secretary of State as explained in *Annex F paragraphs 38 and 39*.

Calculation of grant

10.   The way in which the amount of grant is calculated will depend on whether the application is a landlord's application or a tenants' application, with or without a participating landlord. For a landlord's application the appropriate method of calculating grant is the same as for any other landlords' applications and is governed by the provisions of section 31 (*see Annex J2*). Authorities are reminded that under section 20A of the Landlord and Tenant Act 1985, as amended by paragraph 90 of Schedule 11 to the 1989 Act, landlords will be obliged to pass on to tenants and long leaseholders the benefits of any grant received via a reduction in any service charge which they would otherwise have to pay in respect of the works. Authorities are therefore advised not to take into account the value of service charges in these circumstances.

11.   For tenants, the calculation of grant payable is based on the test of resources described in *Annex J2 and J6*. Each applicant must be individually tested in relation to his share of the cost of the works. Calculation of grant for a tenants' common parts application is therefore potentially more complex because the liabilities and resources of a number of persons need to be established in calculating the overall grant aid and the amount payable to each participant.

12.   Each participant in a tenants' common parts application will normally be liable only for a proportion of the total cost of works. Not all persons with a liability to carry out works or contribute to their cost will necessarily participate in the grant application. Works may nevertheless need to be carried out to parts of the building for which non-participants are liable in order that the requirements of the grant are met. In these circumstances, consent would be required from the non-participants for works to those parts for which they are liable to be included in the renovation scheme. The cost of those works, however, will not be part of the "attributable cost" (see paragraph 13 below) and no grant will be payable in respect of them.

13.   To calculate grant payable authorities must decide how much of the cost of the relevant works can be attributed to those who do participate in a tenants' common parts application: this is called the "attributable cost". They therefore need to ascertain the extent of the participants' liability to carry out, or contribute to the cost of carrying out, those works. In all cases, occupying tenants' leases will specify the extent of their individual liabilities in this respect, some liability may also rest with persons who are not occupying tenants, for example the lessees of commercial premises in a building also containing flats. The aggregate of the grant applicants' liabilities will therefore be a proportion of the overall liability shared by all liable persons. The attributable cost will be the same proportion of the total costs that would be borne by all liable persons, and this will then be apportioned among the applicants according to their respective liabilities.

14.   Where the proportion that the applicants' liabilities bears to all liabilities cannot be ascertained (for example, where leases have been improperly drawn) the proportion used for calculating the attributable cost is the proportion that the number of applicants bears to the total number of persons who are liable to carry out, or contribute to the costs of carrying out, works to the common parts of the building (treating as a single person two or more persons who hold an interest jointly). The attributable cost would then be apportioned equally amongst the applicants.

15.   In some cases, the responsibility for carrying out or paying for the relevant works may be shared between the landlord and some of the tenants. This is likely to be the case where the dwellings in the building are let on different kinds of tenancies, for example some long leasehold and some short term. In these cases in particular the landlord may wish to join in the application as a "participating landlord": but a landlord can also participate in a tenant's application (section 15(4)). The calculation of grant would be similar to that in respect of an application made by tenants alone. The "attributable" cost must therefore be calculated and each participant in the application individually assessed in relation to their share. The calculation of that portion of grant which relates to the landlord's share would be made on the basis of the provisions of section 31 (*see Annex J2*). If the landlord did not participate, grant would not be payable in respect of that part of the works for which he was solely responsible.

Annex G3

HMO GRANT

Definition

1.   HMO grant is the main form of grant available towards works to houses in multiple occupation (HMOs). The definition of an HMO used for grant purposes is contained in section 100 of the Local Government and Housing Act 1989. This is a modified version of the definition used for enforcement purposes contained in Part XI of the Housing Act 1985. In practice the effect of the definition for grant purposes is to exclude from the HMO any part of the house occupied as a separate dwelling by persons forming a single household.

2.   Where the HMO in question is a flat, HMO grant is only payable in respect of works to the flat itself, and not to any common parts of the building in which the flat is situated. The occupants of a flat in multiple occupation are unlikely to be "occupying tenants" (*see paragraph 2 of Annex G2*), and thus would be ineligible to participate in a tenants' common parts application; but where the landlord of a flat in multiple occupation also owns the rest of the building in which the flat is situated, it would be open to him to make a separate landlord's common parts application in respect of works to the common parts.

3.   Further advice on the definition of HMOs is given in DOE Circular 12/93 - *Houses in Multiple Occupation - Guidance to local housing authorities on managing the stock in their area*, which also gives advice on registration schemes, management issues, and on procedures for enforcement of HMO standards. Advice on fitness standards for HMOs can be found in DOE Circular 12/92 - *Guidance to local authorities on standards of fitness under section 352 of the Housing Act 1985* .

Preliminary conditions

4.   HMO grant is only available to HMO landlords, and an applicant for HMO grant must provide a "certificate of future occupation" with the application, stating that they have, or propose to acquire, an owner's interest in the house in question. This requirement stands even where the grant is for works required to comply with statutory notices, and whilst such notices may be served either on the person having control or the person managing the house, a person managing an HMO may not have the necessary interest to apply for HMO grant. In the second part of the certificate of future occupation the applicant must certify their intention to let or license the use of the house, or specified part of it, as a residence in a manner similar to that for a landlord's renovation grant.

Eligible works

5.   HMO grant is given on a discretionary basis towards works to achieve one of the purposes laid out in section 27 of the 1996 Act. Before they may approve an application for HMO grant the local authority must be satisfied that the relevant works are necessary for one or more of those purposes and that after the relevant works are completed the house concerned will be fit for human habitation and fit for the number of occupants.

6.   Fitness for the number of occupants relates to the provision of adequate fire precautions and means of escape from fire, as well as cooking, food storage, washing and toilet facilities. It is for authorities to decide what works may be necessary to provide adequate fire safety standards, cooking and washing facilities for the occupants in the light of the size of the property and the number and characteristics of its occupants. They should, however, consult Circular 12/92 (see paragraph 3 above) when considering what works may be necessary. Grant may not be given in respect of works to provide means of escape from fire or other fire precautions which the applicant is obliged to carry out by

virtue of a statutory requirement. An exception is made in respect of works which are required by a notice served under section 352 of the 1985 Act.

7. Local authorities may not approve an HMO grant unless they are satisfied that, where the relevant works form part of a larger programme, there are satisfactory financial and other arrangements in place for **all** the works. The intention of this is to ensure that the works funded from the public purse and to make the property fit are not jeopardised by the failure, for any reason, of the larger programme.

Grant conditions

8. HMO grants are subject to the usual conditions governing disposal by the owner (section 47 of the 1996 Act). These are that any instalments of grant be repaid if a property is disposed of before the works are complete and that any grant given is repaid if the HMO is disposed of within the grant condition period. There is discretion, however, for a local authority not to make a demand or to demand a lesser amount with the consent of the Secretary of State (section 47(4)). Where there is a disposal that is exempt under section 54 then this condition ceases to be in force.

9. In addition to the condition for repayment on disposal there are conditions as to the future occupation of the HMO in accordance with the certificate of intended letting (section 50). These conditions generally replicate those for other grants. One of these conditions is peculiar to HMOs, and concerns local authorities' powers under section 354 (power to limit the the number of occupants in a house) and 353A (duty to keep premises fit for number of occupants) - inserted by section 73 of the Housing Act 1996 - of the 1985 Act. Where a direction under section 354 has not been revoked or varied under section 357 of the 1985 Act, or where the duty under 353A is breached, or one of the occupation conditions is breached, the local authority may demand repayment of the grant with interest. There is discretion for a local authority not to make a demand or to demand a lesser amount but in this case *without* reference to the Secretary of State.

10. In addition grant conditions may be imposed under section 52 with the consent of the Secretary of State. A general consent has been issued by the Secretary of State as explained in *Annex F, paragraphs 38 and 39*. These grant conditions remain in force, as a local land charge throughout the initial five-year grant condition period and are binding on any person who is for the time being an owner of the house.

Calculation of grant

11. In the same way as for other grants applied for by landlords (see Annex J2), the level of HMO grant to be given is at the discretion of the local authority (section 31). The local authority may however wish to take account of the rental income stream likely to be available to the landlord, based on advice from the Rent Officer Service.

Annex H

HOME REPAIR ASSISTANCE

General Policy Background to Home Repair Assistance

1. Home repair assistance replaces minor works assistance. It is intended, like its predecessor, to complement the mainstream assistance available through the house renovation grant system. It is primarily designed to provide assistance in the form of either grant or materials with small scale works of: repair, improvement and adaptation to a dwelling. That dwelling may be either: a building of traditional construction, a house-boat or mobile home (sections: 76, 77 and 78 of the 1996 Act).

2. Where major work is required, there may still be circumstances where it is appropriate to award home repair assistance as an interim measure, notably where an applicant is unwilling or unable at the time to undertake the full range of work to bring the property up to the desired standard but is prepared to do a few small but essential works. Urgent minor repairs might also be justified on properties earmarked for demolition where such measures would provide basic comfort and safety in the period prior to vacation. As was the case for minor works assistance the property does not have to be fit on completion of the works.

Purposes of Assistance

3. Section 76(1) of the Act enables local authorities to provide home repair assistance by grant or provision of materials for works of: repair, improvement or adaptation to a dwelling, which may be owned or rented by eligible applicants. Although it is for each authority to assess individual applications on their merits, it is important for authorities to establish guidelines similar to those for mainstream grants against which to assess applications; eg a local authority may particularly wish to target such works associated with care in the community, radon, energy efficiency, or lead pipe replacement. Such guidance should be consistent with the strategic aims of an authority's community care plan.

4. Assistance is also intended for works to adapt a dwelling to enable an elderly, disabled or infirm person, who lives or proposes to live in the dwelling as his only or main residence, to be cared for (section 77(2)). When determining a grant for this purpose, a local authority should be satisfied that the works would not be more appropriate for either disabled facilities grant or assistance from the social services authority under their obligations from the Chronically Sick and Disabled Persons Act 1970.

Strategic Objectives

5. Those local authorities making home repair assistance available to eligible residents are responsible for determining how this grant can be used to maximum effect. In doing so, they should consider their own private sector housing renewal strategy and the role home repair assistance can play along side disabled facilities grant and house renovation grant, together with wider strategic objectives which include Care in the Community, energy efficiency, and crime prevention, etc.

Amount of Assistance

6. The maximum grant or cost of materials that may be provided on any one application or in respect of the same dwelling in any period of three years is dependant upon the order making provision in section 76(2). The Disabled Facilities Grants and Home Repair Assistance (Maximum Amounts) Order 1996 places a limit of £2,000 per application and a maximum limit of assistance of up to £4,000 in respect of the same dwelling in any three year period. The Secretary of State believes that authorities may find it appropriate, typically, to apply a minimum period of three months between applications, although a shorter period might be appropriate. The Secretary of State considers that authorities should only entertain simultaneous applications for home repair assistance totalling more

than £2,000 where they are satisfied that this is more cost effective or socially practicable than using major renovation grant: the higher the sum above £2,000 the more likely it is that the works might be tackled through a major grant. It is anticipated that in many cases the cost of works will be well below the £2,000 limit. The Secretary of State will keep the grant maxima under review.

Eligible Applicants

7.   Home repair assistance is available to owner occupiers and private tenants. Newly included within the category of tenants are those employees who occupy a dwelling or flat for the better performance of their duties, eg. a landlord of a public house or resident caretaker (section 77(3)(c)). It is not available to landlords (unless they are wholly or mainly resident in the dwelling in question), or tenants of public sector bodies as defined in section 3(2).

8.   The qualifying criteria for entitlement are set out in section 77(1). Qualifications to the criteria are set out in section 77(2)-(5). Subsection (1)(b) shall be regarded as satisfied where an application is received for works to adapt a dwelling to enable an elderly, disabled or infirm person to be cared for, provided that the elderly, disabled or infirm person (whether or not the applicant) lives or proposes to live in the dwelling as his only or main residence (section 77(2)). Subsection (1)(e) does not apply if the applicant fulfils any or all of the criteria in section 77(5). Section 77(3) provides a definition of tenant. Section 77(4) enables an application to be made by a person who does not satisfy the condition in subsection (1)(c) but who occupies the dwelling under a right of exclusive occupation granted for life or for a period of more than five years. Such applicants are required to satisfy the authority that they have occupied the dwelling for a period of at least three years prior to the date of the application except where the required works are to:

- adapt a dwelling to enable an elderly, disabled or infirm person, who lives or proposes to live in the dwelling as his only or main residence, to be cared for by his relatives or friends;

- provide a means of escape from fire or other fire precautions;

- provide works to a dwelling in a renewal area.

9.   Home repair assistance is also available to applicants in lawful occupation of house-boats and mobile homes. The legislation relating to house-boats can be found in sections 78(1),(2) and (3) while for mobile homes it is contained within sections 78(1), (2) and (4).

10.   The Secretary of State is of the opinion that where home repair assistance is given in respect of house-boats it should not cover works relating to access ways, service ways or jetties which are likely to be the responsibility of the site owner.

Eligible Works

11.   Home repair assistance is available towards works fulfilling the purposes set out in section 76. Where assistance is given the property does not have to be fit on completion of the works. Assistance may be granted towards the cost of materials and/or labour or the provision of materials by the local authority. The Government envisages that assistance will normally take the form of grant, but the power to provide materials is available to ensure flexibility. It may also go towards the cost of any advice (for example fee based advice by agencies and professional advice) which is incurred directly in relation to any application for assistance or the works subsequently performed under that application.

12.   The Secretary of State does not consider it appropriate to suggest a definitive list of works which might be eligible within these purposes, nor the standards to be attained on their completion, as he believes that authorities themselves are best placed to decide these matters. However, some possible areas are set out below.

Grants for Repair and Improvement

13. Intended to secure the basic fabric of the property from the entry of wind or rain or to protect the occupants from immediate exposure to dangerous insecure building elements or foul drainage. Such works might include the replacement of lead pipes, removal of radon gas, the replacement of loose roof tiles or slates, repairs to windows and doors and repairs to the drainage system.

Grants for Adaptations

14. Adaptations can take many different forms and serve equally as many purposes. The Secretary of State expects local authorities to use their judgement and foresight when awarding home repair assistance for this purpose. Where the application is in respect of a piece of equipment and the use of the disabled facilities grant is not appropriate, an authority should have regard to the duties placed on the local social services by the Chronically Sick and Disabled Persons Act 1970. Nevertheless, authorities may award grant for this purpose, if they choose to. Where an applicant's prognosis implies that degeneration in the short term will occur, then eligible works should allow for this.

Grants for Energy Efficiency

15. Home repair assistance may be given for energy efficiency works, including: loft, hot water tank and pipe insulation, draught proofing and secondary glazing, etc. In considering whether to make home repair assistance available for energy efficiency, authorities should always consider the extent to which the person might be eligible for grant assistance under the Home Energy Efficiency Scheme (HEES) and the extent to which a HEES grant would be able to cover the works concerned.

Grants for Crime Prevention

16. Authorities may wish to make home repair assistance available to the elderly, infirm or disabled applicants for the purposes of improving their home security through such works that may include: the provision and installation of improved door locks (both internal and external), window locks and where appropriate an optical enhanced intercom system. Authorities might like to suggest to such applicants that they obtain independent security advice from the Crime Prevention Officer based at their local police station.

Prior Residence Requirements

17. There is no prior residency requirement in the general routine applications. However, a number of non-standard dwellings (house-boats and mobile homes (section 78) and non-standard tenancies (section 77(4)) which are newly eligible for assistance do as a general rule carry a prior residency requirement.

Prior Residence Requirement for a House-Boat

18. Section 78(1) and (2) cross refers to sections 76 and 77, while section 78(3) is concerned with the prior residency requirements. An authority must satisfy itself that the applicant can satisfy these requirements. In determining the applicant's three year occupancy, an authority may wish to liaise with their Treasurer's Department to confirm resident status via the use of council tax records, or refer to the electoral register. In establishing the mooring requirement authorities should adopt a flexible attitude which allows for the mobile nature of house-boats. Provided the applicant is able to demonstrate that they have spent the majority of the required occupancy at the same site, or a mooring within the boundary of the authority, then section 78(3)(b) should be viewed as being met. In confirming the legality of the site of the mooring(s), authorities should use their local knowledge; where necessary referring to relevant Bye-Laws and an appropriate water authority. Exceptions to this are set out at section 78(2).

Prior Residence Requirement for a Mobile Home

19. Section 78(1) and (2) cross refers to sections 76 and 77, while section 78(4) is concerned with the prior residency requirements. An authority must satisfy themselves that these requirements are

met. Similarly, in determining the applicant's three year occupancy, an authority may wish to liaise with their Treasurer's Department to confirm resident status via the use of council tax records or refer to the electoral register. Exceptions to this are set out at section 78(2).

Payment, including Materials

20.   As soon as practicable after receipt of an application and no later than six months, the authority must inform the applicant whether they propose to give assistance, and give their reasons if they propose not to. They must indicate the nature and value of any materials they intend to provide and the likely amount of any grant (having regard to paragraph 6; or any subsequent Order) they intend to make.

21.   Where an authority has detailed specifications in regard to specific areas of work they should ensure that these are indicated at the application stage.

22.   The local authority should be satisfied that the works have been properly completed before paying grant or recording that the cost of assistance with materials has been properly made. Whether they decide to base this on any given case upon the contractor's (or, in DIY cases, householder's) certification that the work has been completed in accordance with any description in the application form is a matter for their professional judgement. The Regulations do not feature any time limit for dealing with claims, although the Secretary of State considers that work could typically be completed within about three months; and that authorities should normally aim to make an award within six weeks of receiving a claim.

23.   An authority must carry out inspections of the works or obtain certificates from any person carrying them out such as necessary to ensure that they are carried out to a reasonable standard.

Agency Services

24.   Agencies are often well placed to advise authorities on the potential scope of work and on priorities, as well as assisting in securing grant targeting and take up. For this reason the Secretary of State sees local authorities using agencies both in shaping policy and delivering grant and other assistance, particularly where agencies already in the locality provide help to the elderly. Accordingly, authorities may wish to reserve an identifiable part of their allocation to fund applications referred from an agency. The authority will wish to ensure the agency has clear guidelines on the priorities to be targeted and delivered so that an authority's statutory duties as set out in Part I, Chapter III of the Housing Grants, Construction and Regeneration Act 1996 are fulfilled. It is for individual authorities and agencies to work out the arrangements for delivering home repair assistance which best suit local needs and circumstances, within the statutory framework.

Manner and Content of Applications for Assistance

25.   An application for home repair assistance must be in writing and contain the following:

(a)   the name and address of the applicant;

(b)   the date of birth of the applicant;

(c)   whether the applicant is disabled or infirm;

(d)   whether the applicant or their partner is in receipt of income support, family credit, housing benefit, council tax benefit or disability working allowance;

(e)   whether the works are to adapt a dwelling to enable an elderly, disabled or infirm person, who lives or proposes to live in the dwelling as their only or main residence, to be cared for;

(f)   the address of the property to which the application relates;

(g)   whether the property is in a renewal area;

(h) whether the property is a dwelling, a house-boat or a mobile home;

(i) whether the applicant lives in the property as their only or main residence;

(j) whether the applicant has an owner's interest in the property; is a tenant; or occupies the property under a right of exclusive occupation granted for their life or for a period of more than five years;

(k) where the applicant is a tenant, confirmation that the applicant is not a tenant of:

a local authority; a new town corporation; an urban development corporation; a housing action trust; the Development Board for Rural Wales; a health authority, special health authority or NHS trust; a police authority established under section 3 of the Police Act 1964; a joint authority established by Part IV of the Local Government Act 1985; a residuary body established by Part VII of that Act; or an authority established under section 10(1) of that Act (waste disposal);

(l) where the applicant occupies the dwelling under a right specified in paragraph 10(c) of this Part, and where the purpose of the works is not one specified in paragraph 5 or paragraph 14 of this Part, or the property is not in a renewal area, whether the applicant has occupied the property as their only or main residence for a period of at least three years immediately preceding the date of the application;

(m) a description of the works;

(n) whether the works relate to means of escape from fire or other fire precautions;

(o) confirmation that the applicant has a duty or power to carry out all of the works;

(p) the name and address of the person who will carry out the works;

(q) an estimate of the cost to the applicant of the works and, if the works are to be carried out by the applicant, the cost of the materials to be used in carrying them out;

(r) confirmation that the works are not, so far as the applicant is aware, works for which a grant under Chapter I of Part I of the Housing Grants, Construction and Regeneration Act 1996 has been approved or for which an application for a grant is pending; or works which are specified in a group repair scheme approved under Chapter II of that Part or prepared and awaiting the approval of the Secretary of State;

(s) details of the amount or value of any home repair assistance given in respect of the property in the period of three years immediately preceding the date of application;

(t) the signature of the applicant or his agent.

In addition for house boats and mobile homes:

House-Boats

(a) whether the house-boat qualifies as a dwelling for the purpose of payment of council tax;

(b) whether the applicant is in lawful occupation of the house-boat;

(c) where the purpose of the works is not one specified in paragraph 5 or paragraph 14 of Part I, whether: the applicant has occupied the boat as their only or main residence for a period of at least three years immediately preceding the date of the application; the boat has for that period had its only or main mooring in the same locality on an inland waterway or in marine waters within the boundary of the authority; and the applicant had a right to moor their boat there.

Mobile Homes

(a) whether the mobile home qualifies as a dwelling for the purpose of payment of council tax;

(b) whether the applicant is in lawful occupation of the mobile-home;

(c) where the purpose of the works is not one specified in paragraph 5 or paragraph 14 of Part I, whether: the applicant has occupied the mobile home as their only or main residence for a period of at least three years immediately preceding the date of the application; the mobile home has for that period been on land forming part of the same protected site within the meaning of the Mobile Homes Act 1983; and the applicant occupied the mobile home under an agreement to which that Act applies or under a gratuitous licence.

Annex I

DISABLED FACILITIES GRANT

Disabled Facilities Grant

1. The disabled facilities grant provisions in the Housing Grants, Construction and Regeneration Act 1996 largely restate the provisions in the Local Government and Housing Act 1989. However, the 1996 Act introduces a number of important changes, the details of which are included in the guidance which follows.

Role of the housing authority

2. In meeting their responsibilities under section 8 of the Housing Act 1985 to consider housing conditions and provision in their area, local housing authorities must have regard to the special needs of chronically sick and disabled persons in their area under their powers in section 3 of the Chronically Sick and Disabled Persons Act 1970, including the provision or adaptation of existing accommodation for their own disabled tenants. Authorities therefore have wide responsibilities in identifying disabled people who need help with essential adaptations arising out of their disability. Authorities should consider the needs of the disabled person in the context of their wider life-style and desired activities. Housing authorities' responsibilities under the grants legislation in Part I of the 1996 Act complement those responsibilities.

3. The administration of the disabled facilities grants (DFGs) provisions in Part I, through all stages from initial enquiry (or referral by the social services authority) to post-completion, remains the responsibility of local housing authorities. However, it is important that where appropriate, other bodies, especially social services authorities, play a full and active part at different stages of the grant process.

4. While there is a duty to consult social services on the housing adaptation needs of disabled people seeking DFGs (see paragraphs 37 to 42) it is the housing authority who must decide what action should be taken on that advice and also whether or not the application is approved having regard to whether it is reasonable and practicable to carry out the proposed works. However, if both the social services and housing authorities collaborate effectively it should be a rare occurrence where a housing authority determines not to approve particular adaptations recommended by the social services authority.

Role of the social services authority to assist with adaptations

5. Social services authorities' responsibilities under section 2 of the Chronically Sick and Disabled Persons Act 1970 to make arrangements for home adaptations are not affected by the grants legislation. Where an application for DFG has been made, those authorities may be called upon to meet this duty in two ways:

    (a) where the assessed needs of a disabled person exceeds the scope for provision by the housing authority under section 23 of the 1996 Act; and

    (b) where an applicant for DFG has difficulty in meeting his assessed contribution determined by the means test and seeks financial assistance from the authority.

6. In such cases, where the social services authority determine that the need has been established, it remains their duty to assist even where the local housing authority either refuse or are unable to approve an application. Social Services authorities may also consider using their powers under section

17 of the Health and Social Services and Social Security Adjudications Act 1983 to charge for their services where appropriate.

Funding considerations

7.   It is for housing authorities and social services authorities between them to decide how particular adaptations should be funded either through CSDP Act or through a DFG.

8.   However, since DFGs were introduced in 1990 under the Local Government and Housing Act 1989, it has been common practice that equipment which can be installed and removed fairly easily with little or no structural modification of the dwelling is normally the responsibility of the social services authority.

9.   For larger items such as *stairlifts* and *through floor lifts* which require such structural works to the property, help is normally provided by housing authorities through DFG. However, some routine installations may not involve structural work. To ensure that such adaptations are progressed quickly, the respective authorities should jointly agree a standard line on the installation of lifts which will apply unless there are exceptional circumstances. Authorities will wish to include arrangements for routine servicing, maintenance, removal and possible re-use.

Limit on mandatory grant and discretionary payments above the limit

10.   The Disabled Facilities Grants and Home Repair Assistance (Maximum Amounts) Order 1996 places a limit of £20,000 on the amount of mandatory grant which may be given for works under section 23(1). The Order also provides for authorities to award discretionary grant above the limit for works qualifying for mandatory grant under those provisions. The purposes for which discretionary grant is available under section 23(2) is given in paragraphs 31 to 35.

Eligibility

11.   Broadly, the eligibility for DFGs remains unchanged. All owner-occupiers and tenants or licensees who are able to satisfy the criteria in sections 19 to 22 are eligible for disabled facilities grant. Landlords may also apply for a DFG on behalf of a disabled tenant but must also satisfy the requirements in those sections. Council tenants and housing association tenants continue to be eligible to apply for DFG and are assessed for needs on the same basis as private owners and tenants and under the same means testing arrangements as described in *Annex J2*. Where a council tenant is seeking help with adaptations, it is for the authority to decide whether to carry out the works under its own resources for capital works or to advise the applicant to apply for a DFG. If the local authority decide to undertake the works from their own resources they should be carried out on the same terms as if a DFG has been awarded.

12.   Where a disabled person is a council tenant residing in an overspill estate, it should be borne in mind that an application for DFG can only be made to the local authority in whose area the dwelling, which is the subject of the application, is situated and not to the particular council whose tenant the applicant is.

13.   Section 19(5) extends eligibility for a DFG to a range of licensees for example secure or introductory tenants who are licensees, agricultural workers, and service employees such as publicans.

Works eligible for mandatory grant

14.   The purposes for which mandatory disabled facilities grants may be given, set out in section 23(1), are largely unchanged but a new purpose has been added (see paragraphs 17 and 18). They fall into a number of categories.

Facilitating Access and Provision

15.   These include works to remove or help overcome any obstacles which prevent the disabled person from moving freely into and around the dwelling and enjoying the use of the dwelling and the facilities or amenities within it. In particular "facilitating access by the disabled occupant to (or providing for the disabled occupant)"

    i.   .... and from the dwelling or the building in which the dwelling or, as the case may be, flat is situated;

    ii.   .... a room used or usable as the principal family room;

    iii.   .... a room used or usable for sleeping, or alternatively providing such a room for the disabled occupant;

    iv.   .... a room in which there is a lavatory, a bath or shower (or both) and a washhand basin or providing a room in which there is such a facility or facilities;

    v.   .... the preparation and cooking of food.

16.   In considering applications for grant towards such works, the presumption should be that the occupant should have reasonable access into his home, to the main habitable rooms within the home - namely the living room and bedroom, and to a bathroom or shower room in which there are suitable facilities for washing and/or showering.

Making a dwelling or building safe

17.   Section 23(1)(b) is a new provision enabling grant to be given for certain works to the dwelling or building to make it safe for the disabled person and other persons residing with him. This maybe the provision of lighting where safety is an issue or for adaptations designed to minimise the risk of danger where a disabled person has behavioural problems which causes him to act occasionally or regularly in a boisterous or violent manner damaging the house, himself and perhaps other people. Where such need has been identified, grant is available to carry out appropriate adaptations to eliminate or minimise that risk.

18.   For those with hearing difficulties, an enhanced alarm system, which may be required in the dwelling to provide improved safety for the disabled occupant in connection with the use of cooking facilities or works to provide means of escape from fire could also qualify for mandatory grant under subsection (1)(b).

19.   It would be inappropriate to be prescriptive on the particular works covered under subsection (b) but they might include the provision of specialised lighting, toughened or shatterproof glass in certain parts of the dwelling to which the disabled person has normal access or the installation of guards around certain facilities such as fires or radiators to prevent the disabled person harming himself. Sometimes reinforcement of floors, walls or ceilings may be needed, as maybe cladding of exposed surfaces and corners to prevent self injury. The Community Learning Disability Team, local Challenging Behaviour Resource Team, or RNIB may be able to advise. In these cases it will be for housing and social services authorities between them to decide on the most appropriate adaptations to be provided.

Room usable for sleeping

20.   While in some cases a living room may be large enough to enable a second room for sleeping to be created, in smaller homes this will not be possible. The provision of a room usable for sleeping under section 23(1)(d) should therefore only be undertaken if the housing authority are satisfied that the adaptation of an existing room in the dwelling (upstairs or downstairs) or the access to that room is unsuitable in the particular circumstances. Where the disabled occupant shares a bedroom with

another person, mandatory grant may be given to provide a room of sufficient size so that the normal sleeping arrangements can be maintained.

Bathroom

21.   The provisions in section 23(1) relating to the provision of a lavatory and washing, bathing and showering facilities have been separated to clarify that a disabled person should have access to a wash-hand basin, a WC and a shower or bath (or if more appropriate, both a shower and a bath). Therefore subsections (e) to (g), provide that mandatory grant should be given to provide a disabled person with each of these facilities, and facilitating their use.

Facilitating preparation and cooking of food

22.   The provision in section 23(1)(h) covers a wide range of works to enable a disabled person to cater independently. Eligible works include the rearrangement or enlargement of a kitchen to ease manoeuvrability of a wheelchair and specially modified or designed storage units, gas, electricity and plumbing installations to enable the disabled person to use these facilities independently.

23.   Where most of the cooking and preparation of meals is done by another household member, it would not normally be appropriate to carry out full adaptations to the kitchen. However, it might be appropriate that certain adaptations be carried out to enable the disabled person to perform certain functions in the kitchen, such as preparing light meals or hot drinks.

Heating, lighting and power

24.   People with limited mobility who remain in one room for long periods usually need more warmth in the dwelling than able-bodied people. Section 23(1)(i) therefore provides for the improvement of an existing heating system in the dwelling to meet the disabled occupant's needs. Where there is no heating system or where the existing heating arrangements are unsuitable to meet his needs, a heating system may be provided. A DFG should not be given to adapt or install heating in rooms which are not normally used by the disabled person. The installation of central heating to the dwelling should only be considered where the wellbeing and mobility of the disabled person would otherwise be adversely affected.

25.   Section 23(1)(j) provides for works to enable a disabled person to have full use of heating, lighting and power controls in the dwelling. Such work includes the relocation of power points to make them more accessible, the provision of suitably adapted controls where a disabled person has difficulty in using normal types of controls and the installation of additional controls.

Dependent residents

26.   Section 23(1)(k) provides for works to a dwelling required to enable a disabled occupant better access and movement around the dwelling in order to care for another person who normally resides there whether or not they are related to the disabled person. This may include spouse, partner or family member, another disabled person or a child. Importantly the dependent being cared for need not be disabled. Such works could include adaptations to a part of the dwelling to which the disabled person would not normally need access but which is used by a person to whom they are providing care and therefore it is reasonable for such works to be carried out.

27.   It is the Secretary of State's view that the provisions of Section 23(1)(a)-(k) provide the flexibility to enable authorities to give help for the full range of adaptations to cover all the circumstances which may arise. These provisions enable authorities to provide mandatory grant to meet the adaptation needs of disabled people whose needs are less obvious, such as those with sight or hearing impairment. For instance, partially sighted people may require an enhanced form of lighting of a particular kind in the dwelling to enable them to carry out every day tasks and activities in the home. Such works may be required to facilitate access into and around the home and for such purposes as the

preparation and cooking of food, to improve the ability to use sources of power or to provide greater safety of the disabled occupant. Works for these purposes qualify for mandatory grant under section 23(1). Where safety is an issue, the works could qualify under subsection (1)(b).

28. However, decisions on whether such works are needed and if mandatory grant should be awarded in such cases are matters for the housing authority in consultation with social services in accordance with the provisions in Part I and will be based on individual circumstances. Where an applicant's prognosis implies that degeneration in the short term will occur, then this should be taken into account when considering the eligible works.

29. Section 23(1)(l) enables the Secretary of State to specify other purposes for which mandatory grant is approved.

Common parts

30. Housing authorities should bear in mind that disabled facilities grant is intended to assist towards works not only to dwellings but also to the common parts of buildings containing flats, where the disabled person is the occupant of one of the flats. The purposes for which grant is available for works to the common parts of such buildings are, in practice, limited to works to facilitate access to the dwelling through the common parts, or facilitating the use by the disabled person of a source of power, lighting or heating in the common parts.

Discretionary DFG

31. A DFG is available under section 23(2) at local authorities' discretion to make the dwelling or building suitable for the accommodation, welfare or employment of the disabled occupant in any other respect. Section 28(2) provides for a wide range of adaptation needs of a disabled person not covered by the mandatory grant provisions.

32. An example of *"accommodation"* might include works to provide more satisfactory internal living arrangements for a disabled occupant where the works are not of a description set out in subsection (1) of section 23 and where they would be of direct benefit to the disabled occupant rather than other members of the household. Such works might include extending or enlarging a dwelling which is already suitable for the disabled occupant in all other respects. However, works which are of direct benefit only to other household members, should be considered for discretionary renovation grant under section 12(1)(e).

33. Adaptations for the purpose of making the dwelling suitable for the *"welfare"* of the disabled occupant might include works to provide access to a garden adjacent to a property where the disabled person is unable to gain such access from the dwelling through existing doors or pathways. Authorities may wish to give discretionary grant in such cases or may consider there is sufficient merit in including the works within mandatory grant: section 23(1)(a): as access for the disabled person to and from the dwelling (defined at section 101).

34. Other adaptations to meet *welfare* needs may include the provision of a safe play area for a disabled child or where certain works of adaptation are required to provide for a disabled occupant to receive specialised care or medical treatment in their own home for which the disabled person is responsible for meeting the costs of works.

35. The most obvious works to make the dwelling suitable for the *"employment"* of the disable occupant could include adapting or providing a room to be used for a disabled person who is housebound but nevertheless is able to work from home.

36.   Where an application involves a combination of works qualifying for both mandatory and discretionary grant, the authority should consider the application in the same way administratively for both types of works assuming that the authority decides to approve the discretionary elements of the application.

Collaboration and Consultation

37.   Section 24 of the Housing Grants, Construction and Regeneration Act 1996 places a duty on housing authorities to consult social services authorities on the adaptation needs of disabled people seeking help through DFGs. For unitary authorities, the relevant department should be consulted on these matters. But housing authorities themselves must decide what action to take on the basis of that advice and therefore the level of adaptations, if any, for which grant is approved. The processing of grant applications is carried out by housing authorities and as such, it is the authority and not the occupational therapist who should be in the lead in playing a co-ordinating role for dealing with the grant applicant. However home improvement agencies and other agencies can provide a valuable service to elderly and disabled applicants in organising building works and raising finance to fund the works. Nevertheless, it is important that applicants are given the name of the officer of the authority who will act as the principal point of contact for the purposes of seeking information on progress with their application.

38.   The duty under section 24(3) to consult the social services authority relates solely to the matters concerned in section 24(3)(a). There is no reason why the procedures for consultation need to be carried out in a particular way. For instance, in many cases the assessment of adaptation needs will have been carried out by the social services authority prior to the disabled person being referred to the housing authority for DFG. This is especially the case where an assessment has already been carried out under the requirements of the NHS and Community Care Act 1990 through which it may be determined that all or some of a disabled person's needs may be met under CSDP Act. However the decision on grant assisted works remains a matter for the local housing authority.

39.   It is for social services authorities to decide in each case who should be involved in the assessment procedure in providing advise to the housing authority on the matters mentioned in section 24(3)(a). In most cases the assessment service will be provided by an occupational therapist employed by the social services department but it may be appropriate for others to be consulted in making the assessment. Above all however, it is important that the disabled occupant himself is involved in any discussions about an adaptation scheme. Others who may need to be involved will include:

- occupational therapist (OT) employed by health authority, private or voluntary organisation;
- applicant's GP;
- staff of health authority, including health professional;
- voluntary bodies;
- other household members
- home improvement agency or other agent appointed by the applicant

Where the housing authority employs its own occupational therapist, it will be important to maintain close collaboration with the social services authority to ensure an integrated approach to meeting the applicant's needs. Authorities should also bear in mind that, where such arrangements are in place the duty to consult social services authorities under section 24(3) still remains.

40.   The priorities and demands being made on both grants departments and social services departments (particularly for OT assessments) may cause delays and the adaptation needs of disabled people

not being met in a sufficiently timely manner. Authorities should jointly agree policies and procedures for delivering help through DFGs or Home Repair Assistance which ensure that the service provided is efficient and effective. Appropriate procedures and standards for dealing with routine minor adaptations, will enable housing authorities to respond to simple needs without a prolonged assessment process. Such approaches will be consistent with guidance given to social services authorities under the new community care arrangements to develop assessment procedures which are flexible and appropriate to levels of need.

41.   Where the housing authority is concerned that the adaptations are of an urgent nature or small but essential and it is aware of delays in obtaining an assessment by an OT, they may consider requesting the social services authority to ask others to carry out the assessment or requesting the social services department to accept a referral from another suitably qualified professional. This may include other health professionals with appropriate expertise, including the applicant's GP. This should help reduce delays and therefore speed up the grant process especially where more minor adaptations are required.

42.   The Housing Renewal Grants (Services and Charges) Order 1996 made under section 2(3) of the 1996 Act specifies the preliminary or ancillary services and charges which are eligible for grant. One category which applies only in relation to disabled facilities grants is fees for the professional services of an occupational therapist engaged by the applicant in relation to carrying out the works. This does not include the costs of an occupational therapist acting on behalf of the social services authority in the discharge of their responsibilities under section 24(3)(a) of the 1996 Act (or any other enactment).

Good practice

43.   Recent research commissioned for the Department indicates that there is wide disparity in the way local authorities deal with applications for DFG. Many of the difficulties associated with the involvement of separate authorities can be reduced if the respective authorities in a particular area adopt good practice in the administration of disabled facilities grant. Over the last few years, local authorities have developed innovative schemes in building up efficient and effective systems of co-operation and collaboration in the procedures for planning and assessment of those seeking help with adaptations through DFGs. There are a number of areas of good practice which local authorities should consider:

   a.   creation of a single team (one stop service) where everyone involved (grant team, OT and HIA staff) work together as one unit in dealing with all aspects of the application from initial enquiry through to grant approval. It is recognised that this might be more difficult to arrange in non-unitary authorities. The local housing authority must not delegate its authority under Chapter I, Part I of the 1996 Act to determine the grant application. They should also consider providing applicants with a named contact point in relation to their grant works and ensuring applicants are aware of any local support group or forum;

   b.   joint visits where adaptations to be provided are likely to be complex with high level of technical input;

   c.   joint training involving the staff of housing, social services authorities and health which helps everyone to gain a clear understanding of each others' responsibilities and problems and therefore fosters good working relationships for the future;

   d.   well documented policies and procedures on processing of grant applications as a ready source of reference available to staff in both authorities;

   e.   regular liaison group meetings between staff from neighbouring local authorities to discuss problems arising and possible solutions for dealing with them. This forges good contacts and helps to disseminate good practice and working methods more widely and quickly;

f. liaison committee involving more senior staff in the respective authorities meeting periodically to take a more strategic look at the operation of the housing adaptation services especially methods for prioritising demand under the new grant regime introduced by Chapter I, Part I of the 1996 Act. This might include discussion of policy areas across departmental responsibilities; and

g. development of common data systems providing up to date information on progress of DFG casework. This identifies problems and therefore helps reduce delays.

h. development of registers of adapted homes and of people looking for such properties.

44. The creation of the new unitary authorities provides a good opportunity for those authorities to review their present procedures to see whether improvements can be made to the current arrangements. It is appreciated that there will be more obstacles in setting up these arrangements in non-unitary authorities especially where housing and social services authorities are not situated in the same locality. Nevertheless, in these areas, authorities are urged to consider these options and seek to identify other good practice designed to improve the delivery of help to disabled people through DFGs.

Prioritising demand for DFGs

45. Advice on the setting of strategies for the use of DFG resources is given in *Chapter 7*. In setting their strategies for using those resources housing authorities will need to determine their priorities for meeting demand for mandatory disabled facilities grants. Many authorities already adopt a system of prioritising applications according to need and adopt a fast track approach to emergency cases where there is a clear need to provide early adaptations. Such cases will include applications for a disabled person whose disability arises following an accident and who is about to be discharged from hospital and therefore requires adaptations urgently. Local authorities should not use pre application tests as a way of delaying applications or avoiding their statutory duty to process applications within 6 months.

46. Some authorities have developed a priority system of ranking DFG applications under which those with a higher ranking are processed more speedily than others who have been given a lower ranking because their needs are less pressing. However, such decisions will not be taken easily and in some cases it will be difficult for the authority to determine that one person's needs are greater or more urgent than another's. In all cases authorities should keep the applicant fully informed of the date that they are likely to be notified of the outcome of their application.

Determination of whether works are necessary and appropriate

47. The local housing authority must satisfy itself that the works are necessary and appropriate to meet the needs of the disabled person under section 24(3)(a), and in doing so should consult the social services authority. They need to consider a number of factors. In particular whether the proposed adaptations or improvements:

● are needed to provide for a care plan to be implemented which will enable the disabled occupant to remain living in their existing home as independently as possible;

● would meet, as far as possible, the assessed needs of the disabled person taking into account both their medical and physical needs; and

● distinguish between what is desirable and possibly legitimate aspirations of the disabled person, and what is actually needed and for which grant support is fully justified.

48. In determining the needs of the disabled person consideration should be given to the particular household group in which the disabled occupant resides so that any adaptations being contemplated do not cause strain on the household which may lead to breakdown of the present care arrangements. For instance, a relevant factor might be the continued privacy of the disabled person or carer following completion of works.

49.   DFGs are designed to give disabled people a degree of independence in the home. Consideration therefore needs to be given to the impact of adaptations on the level of care given to the disabled person and whether those tasks will be reduced or eased. Adaptation works would not have achieved their objective within a care package if the disabled person does not gain an acceptable degree of independence, where possible, or, where the disabled person remains dependent upon the care of others, where the adaptation does not significantly ease the burden of the carer.

Determination of whether works are reasonable and practicable

50.   Section 24(3)(b) requires housing authorities to satisfy themselves whether it is reasonable and practicable to carry out the relevant works having regard to the age and condition of the dwelling or building.

51.   Under section 24(4) the question of the property's fitness for human habitation is a matter the local housing authority can take into account in determining the section 24(3)(b) question relating to reasonableness and practicality. This means that in a suitable case, the local housing authority can approve an application for DFG even where on the completion of the works the property is unfit for human habitation. Where, on inspection of a property in connection with a DFG application, it is found to be unfit to the extent that it would clearly be unreasonable and impractical to proceed with the proposed adaptations, the housing authority should, in consultation with the social services authority, consider alternative solutions in deciding the most appropriate course of action. Such considerations might include:

- urging the disabled occupant to seek a renovation grant to make the property fit following which the proposed adaptations can proceed;

- considering whether a reduced level of adaptations to the property, which would satisfy the needs of the disabled occupant and also satisfy the practicality considerations, would be appropriate;

- considering with the disabled person rehousing to other more suitably adapted accommodation in the locality, especially if the disabled person expresses such a preference. This would make sense if major expenditure on adaptations could be avoided and a suitably adapted house was available.

Age and condition of property

52.   There is no minimum age of a property which is the subject of a DFG application: section 4(1)(a). Nevertheless, housing authorities need to have regard to a number of factors in deciding whether it is reasonable and practicable to carry out the relevant adaptation works. Each case will present its own problems which need to be resolved in reaching decisions on grant approval but the following are issues which commonly arise in the processing of grant applications:

- (a)   the architectural and structural characteristics of the dwelling may render certain types of adaptation inappropriate;

- (b)   the practicalities of carrying out adaptations to smaller properties with narrow doorways, halls and passages which might make wheelchair use in and around the dwelling difficult;

- (c)   conservation considerations and planning constraints may prevent certain types of adaptation being carried out;

- (d)   the practicalities of carrying out adaptations to older properties with difficult or limited access e.g. steep flights of steps making access for wheelchair use difficult and therefore making continued occupation of the dwelling open to question;

- (e)   the impact on other occupants of proposed works which will reduce or limit the existing facilities or amenities in the dwelling.

Grant conditions

53.   Owner applicants for DFGs are required to provide an "owner's certificate" under section 21 in relation to future occupation. Where a tenant applies for a DFG, a "tenant's certificate" is required under section 22 - also an owner's certificate from the landlord is also required, unless the authority consider it is unreasonable in the circumstances to require it. Details of these provisions are given in *Annex F.*

54.   The conditions requiring repayment of grant on breach of occupation or letting requirements or the disposal of the dwelling under Part I do not apply to any application for disabled facilities grant.

Means testing

55.   The arrangements for means testing those applying for DFG is different from applications for renovation grants. The Housing Renewal Grants Regulations 1996 provide a definition of "relevant person" for the purposes of applications for DFG. This reflects the new policy that the test for DFG should take into account only the resources of the disabled occupant, where this is the applicant, their spouse and partner. Full details on the operation of the means test are given in *Annex J2.*

Successive applications

56.   For those disabled people whose conditions are degenerative, further adaptations to their home to cater for their deteriorating condition may become necessary at a later date. The grants legislation in Chapter I, Part I of the 1996 Act places no express restriction on successive applications for DFG on the same property. In such cases and depending on the time lapse between the two applications, provision is made in the Housing Renewal Grants Regulations to reduce the amount of an applicant's current contribution. The contribution will be reduced by any previous assessed contribution if the applicant went ahead with the previous adaptations. This means that existing commitments in respect of previous applications are disregarded if the most recent application is made within the lifetime of the notional loan assumed for the purposes of the test (five or ten years depending on whether the applicant is a tenant or an owner). For example, if the applicant's contribution was £8,000 and the amount of grant was £10,000 any contribution in a subsequent application within the time limits of five or ten years, would be reduced by £8,000. If, on the other hand the applicant's assessed contribution was £12,000 any contribution in a subsequent application would be reduced by £12,000.

57.   Authorities should explain to applicants the merits of pursuing an application through to completion even where it is clear the assessed contribution exceeds the cost of the present works and therefore the outcome will be that a "nil grant" is approved. In such cases, the current contribution will be reduced by an amount equivalent to the approved cost of works, not the assessed contribution which may have been greater. Where a local authority intends to approve a grant in such cases they should ensure that the works for which the original application was submitted were completed to a satisfactory standard.

Delayed payment of DFG

58.   The section 34 requirement to notify an applicant as soon as reasonably practicable and not later than six months after the date of the application, whether the application is approved or refused applies to DFG applications. However under section 36 the local authority may approve an application for mandatory grant on the basis that the grant, or part of the grant, will not be paid before a date specified in the notification of their decision. The date so specified must not be later than 12 months after the date of the application.

59.   The purpose of the provision is to provide authorities with discretion to delay payment of mandatory DFG for up to twelve months from the date when a valid application was made in exceptional circumstances where, because there is a particularly heavy caseload of applications involving works which attract mandatory grant, the approval of applications within the statutory six months

required by section 34 would present serious resource problems for the authority towards the end of the financial year.

60.   Section 36 provides a power and authorities are not obliged to use it. It is provided to ensure that where problems arise, authorities have the flexibility to schedule mandatory grant payments, particularly between financial years.

61.   An authority wishing to use the section 36 power may consider that it would be appropriate to defer payment of a mandatory DFG where, for example, particular adaptations are required for someone moving to a dwelling at a later date and therefore the works and payment can both be deferred to a later date without hardship to the applicant. However, it is the Secretary of State's view that the section 36 power should be used sparingly and not where it would cause hardship or suffering to an applicant whose adaptation needs have been assessed as urgent, for example where a disabled person will be leaving hospital or residential care to return home or to move into a new dwelling. It is also likely to be inappropriate to use the section 36 power where the long term costs of doing so would be disproportionate to the short term savings.

Insurance and legal claims

62.   Section 51 of the 1996 Act provides that a local housing authority, in approving an application may, with the Secretary of State's consent (*Annex J4*), impose a condition requiring the applicant to take reasonable steps to pursue a legal claim for damages in which the cost of the works to premises to which the grant relates is part of the claim.

63.   Authorities should consider imposing such conditions where the applicant has made or could make an insurance claim or a legal claim against another person for damages to the property, or (in the case of a legal claim) for damages where the costs of the works to the property was part of the claim. Further guidance on the provisions relating to insurance and legal claims in Section 51 is given in *Annex F*.

Recovery of equipment

64.   Section 52 allows local authorities with the consent of the Secretary of State to impose additional conditions on the approval of grant. Breach of any such condition will enable the local authority to demand repayment of the grant. Such conditions as authorities may impose may now cover matters occurring both before and after the certified date. There is a general consent, at *Annex J4*, and this includes imposition of a condition that specialised equipment such as a stairlift may be recovered by the local authority where it is no longer required. Where an applicant is making a significant contribution to the cost of the adaptations an authority should consider carefully any proposed conditions. In practice social services are best placed to recover the equipment so that it can be re-assigned to another person in need of such equipment. Where it is clear that the equipment will not be re-used because of age or condition a local authority may decide to waive their right to recovery.

Works zero-rated for VAT purposes

65.   The supply of the following works will be zero-rated for VAT where they are carried out to a person's private residence:

(a)   the construction of ramps or widening doorways or passages for the purpose of facilitating the disabled person's entry to or movement within the building, including any preparatory work or making good;

(b)   the installation of a lift for the purpose of facilitating the movement of the disabled person between floors of the building. Repair and maintenance or preparatory works, making good and restoring of decorations are also zero-rated;

    (c)   the providing, extending or adapting of a bathroom, washroom or lavatory where such provision, extension or adaptation is necessary by reason of the disabled person's condition. In addition, other work essential to the provision of these facilities can be zero-rated.

In order for this supply of goods or services to qualify for zero-rating the supplier or contractor must obtain a form of declaration from the disabled person.

Small adaptation works and Home Repair Assistance

66.   Where a disabled person requires help for small works of adaptation to their home, authorities should consider providing *home repair assistance* where the disabled person meets the eligibility criteria and where the costs can be contained within the cost limits imposed on that assistance. Steering disabled people to home repair assistance in appropriate cases will ensure they receive more speedy help than through the more complex procedures for DFG. Guidance on the use of HRA for this purpose is given in *Annex H*.

Annex J1

FINANCIAL MATTERS

A. *Allocation of Resources for Private Sector Renewal*

1. For the financial year 1997/98 onwards, the provision for private sector renewal and for disabled facilities grants will be made separately.

2. Local authorities will continue to be required to bid for resources for both disabled facilities grants and for other private sector renewal, as part of the HIP round. Ministers will have 100% discretion in the allocation of resources to each authority within each region. However, the allocations will be informed by indicators of local authority need and the content and quality of each authority's strategy and performance.

Disabled Facilities Grants

3. Subsidy towards expenditure on disabled facilities grants, both mandatory and discretionary, will continue to be paid as Specified Capital Grant (SCG), and resources will be allocated as a separate guideline figure in HIP, representing the maximum Supplementary Credit Approvals (SCAs) the Department can guarantee to provide to each authority to compensate for the need to reduce relevant credit approvals, pound for pound, on receipt of the SCG, in accordance with section 57 of the 1989 Act. Further information on SCAs and their distribution is given in *paragraphs 12 to 19 below*.

Other Private Sector Renewal Expenditure

4. Resources for other private sector renewal expenditure, ie renovation grants, slum clearance, group repair, renewal areas, relocation grants and improvement for sale, will be paid as Specific Grant, to be known as Private Sector Renewal Support Grant, and will be cash limited. This means that the allocation to local authorities in their HIP will be a capped amount above which no Exchequer contribution will be paid but there will be no requirement to reduce credit approvals.

5. The allocation represents the 60% of expenditure that is eligible for Exchequer contribution. Authorities must find from their own resources, the remaining 40%. They are not required to claim up to the limit of their allocation. If any authority will not require the full amount allocated in HIP, they should inform their local Government Office, preferably at second advance claim stage, so that the unused resources may be made available to other authorities in the region who have a need to spend more than their allocation will support.

6. However, before offering up specific grant resources, the authority must be certain that the resources will not be needed during that financial year. Should the authority have formally relinquished part of their allocation, the Department will not be able to pay subsidy on any additional expenditure that might be shown in the authority's final claim, where this exceeds the authority's reduced allocation.

B Method of Payment:

Specific Grant : Private sector renewal support grant

7. From 1 April 1997, payments of grant to authorities will continue to be made as ten monthly payments on account, paid as specific grant and based on the amounts claimed in the first and second advance claim forms. Adjustments will be made, where necessary, on receipt of final advance and audited claim forms.

8.   However, whereas previously the HIP allocation was a guide to the maximum SCAs authorities could expect to receive but they could claim Exchequer subsidy of 60% of whatever they needed to spend on private sector renewal during the year, the guideline Specific Grant allocation sets a limit on the amount of grant that may be paid to an authority during the year. No more subsidy will be payable once an authority has reached its limit. The authority will have to meet the full costs of any private sector renewal expenditure (except for expenditure on disabled facilities grants) in excess of the level of expenditure supported by the allocation.

9.   Apart from on-account payments in respect of the current year's expenditure, the annual allocation will also have to meet any additional payments made in respect of prior year adjustments. Where the final claim for the previous year shows a need for less than the total amount that has been paid on account for that year, the overclaim will be deducted from the next payment of specific grant to be made.

10.   In order to help authorities to keep within the annual cash limits, the grant determination will change from 17 December 1996, allowing for subsidy to be claimed on interim payments made to applicants (at present grant can only be claimed in the year in which the final payment is made to the applicant). Authorities will also be able to claim grant for expenditure incurred in the year for which there is an obligation to pay (ie where an acceptable receipt or invoice etc. has been received) even if it is not possible to make the payment in that financial year.

11.   Where there are credits payable to the Department, such as the recoupment of renovation grants and negative entitlement to slum clearance subsidy when the account is in profit, these will not increase an authority's allocation of specific grant.

Specified Capital Grant (Disabled Facilities Grants)

12.   From 1 April 1997, the arrangements for payment for both mandatory and discretionary disabled facilities grant will the same as at present. Subsidy will be paid as Specified Capital Grant (SCG), with the attendant requirement to reduce relevant credit approvals to match each pound received in Exchequer subsidy. Compensatory SCAs will be issued in two tranches, as at present, up to the level of the guideline HIP allocation for expenditure on disabled facilities grants. However, SCG may be claimed on 60% of whatever the authority spends on these grants during the year and, therefore, is not cash limited.

13.   Section 62(5) of the 1989 Act allows an authority to treat expenditure for capital purposes as temporary borrowing, where the expenditure has been defrayed by the authority and is due to be reimbursed out of grants, for up to 18 months after the expenditure is incurred and pending receipt of grant. The increase in the aggregate credit limit will allow the authority to borrow internally or to use revenue balances or usable capital receipts.

Reduction in Credit Approvals

14.   These arrangements apply only to disabled facilities grants and to other grants until the end of 1996/97. From the start of financial year 1997/98, Exchequer subsidy on all except mandatory and discretionary disabled facilities grants will be paid as specific grant and there will be no requirement to reduce credit approvals.

15.   Section 57 of the 1989 Act requires authorities to reduce relevant credit approvals by a pound for every pound they receive in Specified Capital Grant (SCG). In this context, a "relevant" credit approval is one issued for a capital purpose that includes the purpose of the SCG. Authorities are offered credit cover in the form of Supplementary Credit Approvals to match the SCG allocated for each year for private sector renewal in their HIP. From 1997/98 onwards, this will continue to apply for SCG allocated for expenditure on disabled facilities grants.

16.   While SCA cover may be available up to the level of the HIP allocation, the actual allocation of SCAs will be based on the amount of SCG paid to the authority during the current year. This will be based on the authority's first and second advance claim for the current year, adjusted to take account of any overclaim or under claim for previous years, as shown in the advance and audited final claims for those years.

17.   Where there has been an overclaim, the amount of SCG paid to the authority will be adjusted to take account of the overpayment in the previous year and the allocation of SCAs will be adjusted accordingly, as the authority's credit approvals will already have been reduced in the year the SCG was received. Where there was an under claim, no additional SCAs can be given as SCAs can only be given in respect of expenditure within the year in which they are issued.

18.   Where an authority's expenditure which attracts SCG exceeds the SCA allocated in HIP, additional SCG may be claimed but the authority must then reduce other relevant credit approvals. The Government Offices will re-distribute within their region, to authorities likely to have a need for additional SCAs, any SCAs given up by authorities which confirm that they will not use their full allocation for the year. Insofar as the authority's allocation together with any additional SCAs received, is insufficient to cover the amount of SCG claimed during the year, the authority must find the necessary reduction in any other relevant credit approvals that they have available or, where these are insufficient, from the first relevant approvals for the following year.

19.   These procedures will not compromise the status of those authorities which are debt-free, by increasing their credit ceilings. Procedures under section 57 of the 1989 Act are distinct from the "use" of a credit approval as set out under section 56, which is what increases the credit ceiling.

C. Transitional Arrangements

20.   Local authorities may continue to claim Exchequer subsidy on grant expenditure incurred under Part VIII of the 1989 Act and under Part XV of the Housing Act 1985, following commencement of Part I of the 1996 Act.

21.   Expenditure incurred under Part VIII of the 1989 Act will continue to be claimed in authorities' FH claim forms, on the same basis as previously. Grants under the 1985 Act will continue to be paid as at present. Those grants approved after 14 June 1989 and before 30 July 1990, should be claimed on the authority's FH claim form. Exchequer subsidy will be paid as SCG for all 1996/97 claims but, with the exception of expenditure on disabled facilities grants, from 1 April 1997, subsidy will be paid as Specific Grant and will be cash limited. Where the final claim for 1996/97 shows an additional entitlement to Exchequer subsidy, this will count against the cash limited allocation for 1997/98. It will be paid as specific grant and there will be no requirement to reduce credit approvals. Where the authority received subsidy in 1996/97 for which relevant credit approvals were not available in that financial year, the obligation to reduce credit approvals will remain and will count against the next available credit approvals in 1997/98. This will probably be the authority's 1997/98 BCA.

22.   Grants approved under Part XV of the 1985 Act, before 15 June 1989, should be claimed on form FED 0867A and will be paid as a commutation of notional loan charges over a twenty year period. This does not count as capital expenditure and will not count against the Specific Grant allocation.

D. Capital and Revenue Expenditure

23.   Capital expenditure is defined in section 40 of the 1989 Act, as extended by amendments to Regulation 2 of The Local Authorities (Capital Finance) Regulations 1990 (SI 1990 No. 432), made by Regulation 2(a) of the Local Authorities (Capital Finance) (Amendments) Regulations 1991(SI 1991 No.500).

24. Those items of expenditure which fall outside this definition should be claimed as non-capital expenditure. Because this is counted as revenue, and not capital, expenditure, no matching credit approval reduction is needed in respect of Exchequer contribution received. However, from 1997/98 onwards, contribution claimed in respect of expenditure on all but disabled facilities grants will count against the authority's Specific Grant allocation in HIP for the year.

25. There are no categories of expenditure under either Part VIII of the 1989 Act or under Part I of the 1996 Act, which necessarily fall outside the definition of expenditure for capital purposes. When examining an authority's claim for Exchequer subsidy towards expenditure on disabled facilities grants or other private sector renewal expenditure, the auditor will need to be satisfied that the costs are eligible for grant, irrespective of whether they are classified as capital or revenue expenditure. Where the auditor is satisfied that the costs are eligible for Exchequer subsidy but has doubts about the authority's classification of the expenditure, he may draw the Department's attention to the point. An authority claiming subsidy for revenue expenditure should be able to provide documentary evidence concerning the nature of the relevant expenditure to satisfy the auditor and the Department that the classification is defensible.

26. Types of qualifying expenditure which, depending on the circumstances, may fall outside the definition of expenditure for capital purposes include small works which do not substantially increase the extent to which a building can or will be used by a disabled person (discretionary disabled facilities grant). It may also include radon remedial works (discretionary renovation grant), some patch and mend grants (minor works assistance and home repair assistance) and the elements of slum clearance subsidy which cover the remuneration of the authority's own staff and the difference between the value of the land appropriated to slum clearance functions and the actual cost of the original acquisition, which must be claimed as revenue grant expenditure.

E. Fraud

27. The Department is responsible for ensuring that public funds are only available to subsidise local authorities' legitimate expenditure on grants. It is essential, therefore, that the Department should be made aware at the earliest opportunity of the possibility that a grant or grants may have been given ultra vires, or have otherwise been unlawfully obtained. The Secretary of State may then consider his position in the light of this information.

28. Accordingly, authorities are requested, in certifying their housing subsidy claims, to notify the Department immediately of any suspected or actual frauds involving grants approved under Part XV of the 1985 Act, Part VIII of the 1989 Act or Part I of the 1996 Act. Authorities should not delay notifying the Department of any such matter pending the report of the external auditor appointed by the Audit Commission on their final subsidy claim for the year. However, they should ensure that it is brought to the auditor's attention.

29. Authorities should continue to keep the Department informed of progress on the matter and of any action proposed or taken in bringing a case against any suspected person or persons. Under Part I of the 1996 Act, authorities are required to repay subsidy received in respect of grant recovered or that could reasonably have been recovered.

F: Ex-gratia Payments

30. Where a local authority feels that it has made a genuine mistake in the advice it gives to a grant applicant and that it is morally bound to pay grant in respect of expenditure which is not grant eligible but has been incurred by the grant applicant as a result of the local authority's mistake, application may be made to the Secretary of State for sanction under sections 19 and 20 of the Local Government Finance Act 1982 to make the payment.

31.   Because this is an ex-gratia payment, however, no part of it will be eligible for Exchequer subsidy.

32.   Application for sanction should be made to: The Department of the Environment, LGC2, Room P1/135, 2 Marsham Street, London SW1P 3EB (from January 1997, Eland House, Bressenden Place, London SW1E 5DU), giving details of the payment to be made, including the full amount of the grant, the amount of the ex-gratia payment and the reason for making the payment.

33.   Each application will be carefully considered on its merits and the Department will need to be persuaded that there is an obligation on the local authority to make the payment.

34.   Applications may also be considered in respect of "lost income" where an authority is required under Part VIII of the 1989 Act to demand repayment of grant, following a breach of condition, but the circumstances of the case are such that the authority considers it inappropriate to make such a demand. Application for sanction should be made to the address given in paragraph 32. Details required will be: details of the grant, including the full amount given, the amount to be repaid and the reasons for not issuing a demand for repayment. Each application will be considered on its merits but an application in respect of circumstances in which the authority would have discretion not to demand repayment under the 1996 Act, is likely to receive a favourable response.

G.   Miscellaneous Matters

Local Authority Overspill Estates

35.   As with other local authority tenants, tenants of overspill estates may be eligible to apply for disabled facilities grants. However, like all other grants, disabled facilities grants can only be paid by the local housing authority in whose area the dwelling is situated. The fact that the properties could be owned by a neighbouring housing authority does not alter the position.

36.   The disabled tenant, therefore, will be applying for grant to an authority other than the authority whose tenant he is. For this reason, the normal restrictions on Exchequer subsidy do not apply and the authority making the grant may include this expenditure in its claim for specified capital grant.

Local Government Boundary Changes

37.   Where a boundary change results in the transfer of dwellings from one local authority area to another, the new local housing authority is responsible for the administration and payment of grant under the house renovation grant system in respect of those dwellings, unless an agreement under section 68 of the Local Government Act 1972, on responsibility for grants already approved, has been reached between the two local authorities concerned, prior to the transfer.

38.   In these circumstances, the local authority making the grant payment will be eligible for 60% Exchequer subsidy on its inherited grant liabilities and may include the expenditure in its claim for private sector renewal subsidy.

Transfer of Local Authority Housing Stock to Housing Associations

39.   Where a local authority has approved an application for disabled facilities grant from a local authority tenant but, prior to payment of the grant, ownership of the property passes to a housing association on a freehold basis or by way of a lease of more than 21 years, the properties are no longer to be accounted for in the authority's HRA and, therefore, the grant costs must not be debited to the HRA.

40.   In these circumstances, the disabled facilities grant will attract the usual rate of Exchequer subsidy and may be included in the authority's claim for specified capital grant.

Annex J2

CALCULATION OF GRANT
Test of resources for owner occupiers and tenants

1. Following a review of the operation of the test of resources for owner occupiers and tenants provided for in the Housing Renovation etc. Grants (Reduction of Grant) Regulations 1994 (SI 1994/648) as amended, the Secretary of State has decided that the existing arrangements, based on regulations governing entitlement to housing benefit, will be retained for the purposes of determining grant applications made under the Housing Grants, Construction and Regeneration Act 1996.

2. Section 30 of the 1996 Act therefore provides, through regulations, for a test of resources to be undertaken for applicants for grant. It expands on section 109 of the Local Government and Housing Act 1989 in a number of ways. There is an extended definition of the qualifying interest of an owner-occupier's application; a new provision for prescribing applicants for disabled facilities grant; a new provision to enable the test of resources to be based on any other statutory means-testing regime; and a new provision enabling authorities to obtain information from certain persons. The details of the changes so far as they affect the test of resources are included in the following guidance.

3. The Housing Renewal Grants Regulations 1996, to a large extent restate the provisions in the Housing Renovation etc. Grants (Reduction of Grant) Regulations 1994 (SI 1994/648). They apply to all applications for renovation grant, disabled facilities grant, tenants' common parts applications and in the determination of individual participants' contributions to the costs of group repair schemes (see *Annexes D1-D3*). The regulations come into effect on 17 December 1996 to coincide with commencement of the provisions in Part I of the 1996 Act.

4. The regulations continue to mirror the rules which apply to housing benefit (HB) and council tax benefit (CTB) in the determination of the financial resources of an applicant in the calculation of the applicable amount (the assessment of needs and outgoings) and in the assessment of income and capital. Where the financial resources exceed the applicable amount, the regulations provide for grant to be reduced by a sum equal to a notional 'affordable loan'. However, these regulations contain some notable differences (which are discussed in greater detail below), and authorities should be cautious when comparing the similarities between the two systems, particularly as there are significant elements of the HB and CTB rules which have no parallel in the renovation grants system. Nevertheless, there will be occasions when discussions between local housing authorities and welfare authorities will prove beneficial ie concerning relevant disregards or premiums under HB or CTB.

5. More detailed guidance on the interpretation and application of HB and CTB premiums and allowances can be obtained from the Housing Benefit and Council Tax Benefit Guidance Manual which is issued by the Department of Social Security to all local housing and welfare authorities. However, authorities should initially address enquiries relating to these regulations to the Department of the Environment, *not* to the Department of Social Security.

Relevant persons

6. Regulation 5 provides that the test should be applied to the applicant for house renovation grant, and also to any other "relevant person" with an "owner's interest". However, there are now separate definitions of "relevant person" for the purposes of applications for renovation grant, common parts grant and for applications for disabled facilities grant.

7.   A relevant person for the purposes of an application for a *renovation grant* or a tenant's application for *common parts grant*, which is an owner's application accompanied by an owner-occupation certificate or a tenant's application, is defined in regulation 5 as anyone who:

- is an applicant; or

- has a grant eligible interest in the property (ie. as co-owner) and who lives, or intends to live in the property.

Relevant person for Disabled Facilities Grant

A relevant person for the purposes of an application for a *disabled facilities grant* (DFG) is defined as:

- the disabled occupant, for whose benefit the works are to be carried out; and

- his spouse or partner of the disabled occupant; or

- is the parent(s) of the disabled occupant who is less than 18 years of age.

8.   The more restrictive definition of a relevant person for DFG applications is the recognition of the fact that other members of the household gain no benefit from the provision of adaptations for a disabled occupant. It also recognises the care and support provided by other family members and carers which enables the disabled person to remain living in their home under community care policies. In such circumstances, only the disabled person and their spouse or partner will be treated as a relevant person, not other relatives or carers who live with them. However, where the disabled person is a child under the age of 18, the parents will be treated as relevant persons for the purposes of DFG. This is because a child is unable to make an application in his own right.

Assessment of resources

9.   For grant applications, the regulations provide for the income and capital of each relevant person, together with his or her partner (or, in the case of polygamous marriages, partners), to be taken into account in the assessment of financial resources. The income of any dependent child or young person is treated as possessed by the relevant person, up to an amount equivalent to the personal allowance awarded in respect of that child or young person in the calculation of the applicable amount (see regulation 32). However, any earnings of children are disregarded, as are those of young persons in most circumstances (see paragraphs 15 and 16 of Schedule 2 to the Regulations). The capital of children and young persons is only relevant to the award of personal allowances in respect of such dependents, and is not included in the assessment of the relevant person's capital.

Treatment of weekly income

10.   Unlike HB and CTB, the average weekly income, including earnings, of a relevant person is determined by reference to the income received over a period of up to 52 weeks immediately preceding the application (regulations 20 to 22). This gives authorities some flexibility in the way in which they can use the information supplied by applicants to determine more accurately the financial circumstances of each relevant person with respect to his or her ability to finance a loan at the time the assessment is made.

11.   Whilst there will be many cases where it is appropriate to calculate average weekly earnings by reference to earnings over the previous 52 weeks, authorities should not adopt this method as a hard and fast rule. Where there has been a significant change in a relevant person's circumstances during the previous 52 weeks, authorities should determine average weekly income by reference only to that period, up to the date of the application, which most accurately reflects his or her current situation. For example, the average weekly income of a relevant person currently in stable employment should not be diluted by including any previous periods of unemployment. Similarly, where a relevant person has recently been made redundant, it may not be appropriate to include periods of employment in the assessment of income.

12.   On the other hand, for those in casual or seasonal employment, it will often be more appropriate for authorities to assess income over the full 52 weeks in order to arrive at an accurate estimate of average weekly income. Authorities should note that they do not necessarily need to adopt the same assessment period for each of the three types of income (employed earnings, self-employed earnings, and other income) in respect of any particular relevant person. Authorities should note that there are no powers to anticipate changes to an applicant's circumstances once a valid application has been made.

Students

13.   The treatment of students' income (dealt with in Chapter X of Part II of the Regulations) is a greatly simplified version of that which is currently in force for HB and CTB. A student's grant income, including any assessed contribution, is taken into account subject to certain disregards in respect of fees, books, travel etc, but there are no special rules relating to covenanted income.

Capital

14.   The value of a relevant person's savings and other capital assets is determined in much the same way as HB and CTB. However, the lower capital threshold for grant purposes is £5,000, and tariff income at a rate of £1 per week per £250 is applied to any capital in excess of this value. There is no upper threshold for capital. Where the capital of a dependent child or young person, determined in the same manner as for a relevant person, exceeds £5,000, no personal allowance in respect of that dependent child or disabled person is to be included in the determination of the applicable amount (regulation 14(b)), and any income of that child or young person is not to be treated as income of the relevant person (regulation 32(2)).

15.   Most of the standard HB disregards of income and capital are applicable. However, some of the rules have been modified to take account of the one-off nature of the assessment. Authorities should note that there is no power to adopt 'local schemes', such as those authorised for HB by section 28(6) of the Social Security Act 1986, in respect of additional disregards of war disablement and war widow's pensions. This reflects the different nature of the grants system compared to HB and avoids possible inequity of treatment between those applicants receiving a full disregard and those only receiving the statutory amount. The financial resources in respect of an application is calculated by adding together the average weekly income, including tariff income from capital, of each relevant person.

Assessment of needs (the applicable amount)

16.   With a few exceptions, each relevant person's applicable amount (the assessment of basic needs) is determined in the same way as HB by the award of personal allowances in respect of the relevant person, his or her partner and any dependent children. A variety of premiums may also be awarded in respect of special needs such as lone parenthood, old age or disability. The amounts of the various allowances and premiums are identical, but in some cases the rules have been slightly modified, in particular where, in HB, they deal with continuity of entitlement. The applicable amount (or 'lower threshold') in respect of an application is calculated by adding together the weekly applicable amounts of each relevant person, and then adding the £40 'grant premium' (regulation 10(b)) in recognition of general overall housing costs. Authorities should note that only one grant premium can be awarded per application, regardless of the number of relevant persons.

Tapers and calculation of affordable loan

17.   Where the financial resources in respect of an application do not exceed the applicable amount, grant will be equal to the cost of the approved works. Regulation 12 provides that where the financial resources are greater than the applicable amount, a staggered taper to produce an appropriate 'loan generation factor' is applied to the excess amount to arrive at the notional 'affordable loan'. This is the amount by which grant is to be reduced. The loan generation factors are designed to match the size of the available income to the size of an affordable loan that could be raised based on the current

standard national rate of interest, over repayment periods of 10 years for owner-occupiers and 5 years for tenants. The factor is revised, by way of amending regulations, to reflect changes in the standard national rate.

18.   Regulation 13 provides for the notional loan (the amount by which grant is to be reduced) to be abated by an amount equivalent to any loan assumption made in respect of any previous applications for grant under Part I of the 1996 Act or Part VIII of the Local Government and Housing Act 1989 by any one or more of the relevant persons in respect of works to the same property, within the 'lifetime' of that assumption (ie. 5 years for tenants' applications or 10 years for owner-occupiers' applications). Similarly, a deduction is made in respect of any contribution made to a group repair scheme within the previous 10 years.

'Nil Grant' approvals

19.   Where a previous application has been approved, but no grant was paid because the cost of the works was less than the applicant's contribution and the works concerned were actually carried out to a satisfactory standard, a deduction of an amount equivalent to the approved cost of the works (not the notional loan, as this will be greater in such cases) should be made. It is for the local authority to judge what is a satisfactory standard although it would normally be that which would have been acceptable to the authority for the purposes of paying grant. The production of receipts and/or an inspection of the property should normally be sufficient for these purposes. Authorities should note that the effective operation of the test in relation to successive grant applications will require adequate records of all applications to be kept for a period of at least 5 years where they relate to tenanted properties and 10 years where they relate to owner-occupied properties and group repair schemes. Authorities should inform applicants of the practical benefit of proceeding with an application which is likely to result in a "nil grant" award, explaining what will happen in the case of subsequent applications.

Joint owners and tenants

20.   Where the property, which is the subject of the application is jointly owned and occupied, or tenanted, the regulations provide that, except in the case of an application for a DFG, the test of resources is applied individually to each person (or couple) with an eligible owner-occupier's or tenant's interest in the property, regardless of whether or not they are a party to the application. Their individual applicable amounts are added together and (with the addition of the £40 grant premium) subtracted from their total average weekly income (including tariff income from any capital). The loan generation factor is then applied to the difference (if any) to give the joint affordable loan. The amount of grant payable to the applicant(s) is then calculated as the cost of the approved works less the joint affordable loan. It is entirely a matter for the joint owners or tenants as to how they apportion the balance of the costs between themselves. Couples (married or otherwise) who are joint owners or joint tenants should never be subject to separate tests, but treated as a single unit in the normal way (ie. as applicant/relevant person and spouse or partner).

Treatment of persons on income support

21.   Where a relevant person, or his or her partner, is in receipt of income support (IS), all of their income and capital is completely disregarded. This means that 100% grant will automatically be available as long as all other relevant persons in the application (or their partners) are also on IS. In these circumstances it follows that it is not necessary to calculate the relevant person's applicable amount. This will, however, be necessary for any other relevant persons in the application who are not on IS.

Uprating

22.   The various allowances and premiums specified in the regulations will continue to be reviewed and uprated annually in line with HB and CTB. The "grant premium" will also be kept under review.

Prescribed forms

23.   Section 2(4) of the 1996 Act provides for the Secretary of State to make regulations to prescribe an application form. The Housing Renewal Grants (Prescribed Form and Particulars) Regulations 1996 set out the prescribed particulars to be included in an application for grant and the forms of application to be used. Applications which are not made in the prescribed form, or a form substantially to the like effect, will not be validly made. It is the Secretary of State's view that an application should be regarded as being made where it is in the form prescribed, or substantially the form, and on the date on which it is submitted to the authority. Where information required in the form itself is missing or incomplete, it is the Secretary of State's view that an application should be treated as made when that information has been supplied. It is for each authority to decide what additional information or evidence may be required, if any, to verify the information given in the application. Under section 34(1), local authorities must notify a grant applicant whether the application has been approved within six months of the date it is made.

Preliminary applications

24.   In order to filter out ineligible applicants or those who are likely to be unsuccessful when making a formal application, it might be in the interests of both applicants and authorities if an effective preliminary enquiry system is established. One way to do this is for authorities to use a preliminary enquiry form. However, it should be made clear that completion of these forms does not constitute a formal application. Authorities should also avoid using a preliminary enquiry system to delay unreasonably a formal application and thus postpone the start of the six month decision period which runs from the receipt of a valid application. Further advice on the question of a preliminary enquiry system is given in *Annex F*.

The Housing Renewal Regulations 1996

25.   These Regulations bring into effect the new test of resources under section 30 of the Housing Grants, Construction and Regeneration Act 1996. As well as introducing some changes to the test, they largely consolidate the Housing Renovation etc. Grants (Reduction of Grant) Regulations 1994 (SI 1994/648) and subsequent amendments (SI 1995/838 and SI 1996/1331) and introduce further changes as described below.

26.   Regulation 2(1) includes new definitions of *earnings top-up* and the *Earnings Top-up Scheme*. Earnings top-up is a new weekly payments like Family Credit but for single people and those without dependent children. It is initially available in six areas in England and is normally payable for 26 weeks at a time. Where payments are made, under paragraph 56 of Schedule 3 and paragraph 9 of Schedule 4, they should be disregarded as income other than earnings and as capital respectively.

27.   Regulation 2(3) provides for the new *jobseeker's allowance* which replaced income support for the unemployed and unemployment benefit with effect from 7 October 1996. These references are to "income-based jobseeker's allowance" and a reference to the qualification for a person on an income-based jobseeker's allowance.

28.   Regulation 3 provides for the *exclusion from grant eligibility*, certain persons, who under Home Office immigration rules are given leave to remain in the country but must have no recourse to public funds. It includes a provision which treats certain asylum seekers and sponsored immigrants as 'persons from abroad' and not eligible for house renovation grant.

29.   Regulation 7(6) contains a reference to *income-based jobseeker's allowance* in the definition of remunerative work to ensure that the earnings of a relevant person on receipt of income-based jobseeker's allowance in paragraph 12 of Schedule 2 will be disregarded. Paragraphs 4 and 6 of Schedule 3 also include references to ensure that relevant persons in receipt of such an allowance, and any compensatory payments made for the non-payment of the allowance, will have their payments or income

other than earnings disregarded. Paragraph 50(2) of Schedule 3 also ensures that, where an addition is made to the allowance in respect of a dependant who is not a member of a relevant person's family, that additional amount is disregarded. Paragraphs 6 and 9 of Schedule 4 also ensure that such an allowance is disregarded as capital.

30.   Regulation 12 provides for the following revised loan generation factors to be applied to excess income over and above the applicable amount as the basis for calculating the "affordable loan" based on a standard rate of interest of 6.87 per cent.

	Owner-Occupiers (10 year repayment period)	Tenants (5 year repayment period)
5p in £ for first £47.95 per week of excess income	18.46	10.77
10p in £ for next £47.95 per week of excess income	36.92	21.54
40p in £ for next £95.90 per week of excess income	147.68	86.16
100p in £ for all remaining income ...	369.21	215.40

31.   The *child care disregard* in regulation 18(1)(d) is uprated from £40 to £60 in accordance with housing benefit changes.

32.   Regulation 31(6)-(8) allows the authority to require the applicant to provide the name and address of the pension fund holder and any other relevant information, and provides the pension fund holder to provide relevant information as to the *personal pension scheme or retirement annuity contract.*

33.   Regulation 41 contains additional definitions in relation to the assessment of *students.* The new definitions are for "college of further education", "education authority", "the FEFC", "full-time course of study", "last day of the course" and redefined definitions of "contribution", "course of study", "full-time student", "grant", "sandwich course" and "student".

34.   Regulation 43(2)(f) has been amended to update the amount to be excluded in the *calculation of a student's grant* to meet the costs of books and equipment to £280.

35.   The reference to the treatment of *student loans* in regulation 46(2) has been amended in accordance with the change to housing benefit to clarify the position so that student loans are taken into account provided the student would be entitled to one if he took reasonable steps to apply.

36.   Regulation 47 is amended to clarify the position where a *student's partner's income* is taken into account for the purposes of assessing a contribution to the student's grant. In these cases an amount equal to the contribution should be disregarded when determining the income of the person who is assessed for the contribution.

37.   Schedule 1 updates the allowances and premiums in line with the annual "Rossi Index" used to uprate housing benefit and other income-related benefits. The relevant allowances and premiums are set out in the *Appendix 1 to this Annex.*

38.   The reference to *severe disability premium* in paragraph 13 of Schedule 1 has now been amended commensurate with the change to housing benefit. The amendment will mean that a person who is a member of a couple should be treated as being in receipt of attendance allowance (AA) or the care

component of disability living allowance (DLA) at the highest or middle rate if the only reason that he has stopped receiving it is because he has been in hospital for more than 28 days. Where only one member of a couple is in hospital, the single rate of severe disability premium can continue to be awarded in respect of the person who remains at home although AA or DLA may have ceased to be paid to the person in hospital.

39.   Paragraph 9 of Schedule 3 amends the position where, in 1995, annuities paid to *holders of the Victoria Cross or the George Cross* were increased to £1,300. Paragraph 9 wholly disregards these payments. From this April, medal holders will have the option to commute the annuity into a one-off lump sum payment of £6,000. The amendment emulates the change to housing benefit so that a total capital disregard is made of the lump sum payment for all time.

40.   Paragraph 12 of Schedule 3 has been amended to increase the amount by which regular *charitable and voluntary payments* are disregarded in the determination of income other than earnings from £10 to £20, in accordance with changes to housing benefit. A similar change in paragraph 31 of Schedule 3 has been made to certain pensions mentioned in paragraph 13.

41.   Paragraph 19(b) of Schedule 3 uprates the amount to be disregarded in the *determination of income other than earnings* in cases where a relevant person's home is occupied by certain person's who have a contractual liability to make payments to the relevant person. Where such payments include heating costs, the amount to be disregarded should be increased in line with changes to housing benefit to £9.25.

42.   Paragraph 49 of Schedule 4 is an additional disregard of capital for payments of *Back to Work Bonus*, including that payable under the equivalent Northern Ireland provisions.

The Housing Renewal Grants (Prescribed Form and Particulars) Regulations 1996

43.   These Regulations introduce a new prescribed form under section 2(4) of the 1996 Act for applications for house renovation grant. The Regulations consolidate three of the four forms in the Housing Renovation etc Grants (Prescribed Forms and Particulars) Regulations 1994 (SI 1994/565) and subsequent amendments (SI 1995/839 and SI 1996/1332) and replaces them with one form.

44.   Schedule 1 of the Regulations prescribes a form for applications by owner-occupier's and tenant's for housing renovation grants, for applications (other than landlord's applications) for disabled facilities grants, and for tenant's applications for common parts grants. **Part 1** seeks preliminary and general information from applicants and **Part 2**, which asks information specific to the type of application, is split into **Part 2A** (renovation grant), **Part 2B** (disabled facilities grant) and **Part 2C** (tenant's applications for common parts grant). **Part 3** requires financial information about the applicants and their families. A declaration follows at the end of this part, and **Part 4** guides an applicant on the supporting documents needed to accompany their application.

45.   The form in general largely replicates and consolidates the questions and notes in the first three forms of SI 1994/565 as amended. Of the more significant changes, there is a new question seeking the address of the relevant person's pension fund holder where applicable (**Q3.28 and Notes 72 and 73**), and there are now requests for details of contribution- and income-based jobseeker's allowances (**Q3.29 and Note 48**). It is intended that this form will be easier for authorities to reproduce than ones based on the 1994 Regulations and, although it is larger, it is hoped that the clear signposting throughout will not prove too difficult for applicants to follow.

46.   There is no longer a prescribed form for a landlord to apply for an HMO grant; authorities will now have to consider a range of factors in dealing with such applications and these are set out in *paragraphs 48 to 52 of this Annex.*

Calculation of grants for landlords

47.   The Department has reviewed the operation of the test of resources for applications for grant under the provisions of Part VIII of the 1989 Act for applications where a certificate of intended letting has been provided. It has become clear that the test does not adequately reflect the ability of a landlord to contribute to the cost of works or the benefit of public investment in his business. The test under the 1989 Act has proved difficult for authorities to operate in practice especially where authorities have taken the view that the works in respect of which an application has been made, would not provide the landlord with additional rental income.

48.   The powers in section 31(3) therefore provides for a general power to enable a local authority to use its discretion in deciding the level of any grant offered in respect of a landlords' application. Section 31(3) requires authorities to have regard to the extent to which the landlord is able to charge a higher rent for the premises following the completion of the works.

49.   While section 31(3) also provides for the Secretary of State to direct that regard be taken of particular matters, it is not intended to exercise this power on introduction of the new grant system. However, this will be reviewed if there is evidence that authorities are experiencing problems in the use of their discretionary powers. The particular applications to which the discretionary test of resources applies are set out in section 31(1).

50.   It is the Department's view that a local authority should, in the main, use grant to secure strategic objectives. A local authority should commence consideration of grant from the premise that a landlord is operating a business in which he should be able to make sufficient investment to ensure the product offered, ie accommodation, meets the fitness requirement. However there will be circumstances where it could be unreasonable to expect a landlord to secure improvement eg properties let on regulated rents, empty properties and conversions requiring significant investment to make them habitable. In such cases an authority may wish to consider an offer of a level of grant which will make it economic for the owner to undertake the necessary works. Local authorities should give careful consideration to the level of any grant offered where a property is let at a market rent under an assured shorthold tenancy. In such cases the rental flow should be adequate to ensure the owner investing in the upkeep of his property.

51.   It should be remembered that an owner is primarily responsible for the upkeep of his property, and grant should only be an option where market forces are not operating effectively. Care should be taken to ensure an authority's grant policy does not leave the impression that grant has been used to reward poor management. In establishing a framework for determining the amount of grant awarded in landlords' applications, authorities may consider that the following factors are relevant in its deliberations. This list is not exhaustive and local authorities may wish to apply other criteria:

- whether the cost of relevant works are such that they should be affordable from the current rental income;

- nature of the works; in this respect work related to safety improvements, such as to provide fire precautions, may well be seen to justify priority or a higher level of grant than other repairs or improvements;

- type of tenancy held by tenants; with regulated rents less likely to provide surplus resources to meet the costs of improvement of the property;

- current rents charged by landlords; it might be appropriate to award higher grant to a landlord who has set his rents at a reasonable level than to one whose rents are high compared to other comparable properties in the locality;

- age of property e.g. older properties are likely to warrant more grant;

- possible contribution to the strategic objectives of the authority; an authority might consider it important that repairs to a landlord's property goes ahead because it contributes to a wider scheme of improvements to the area;

- increase in the capital value of the improved property and the ability of the owner to realise the capital value;

- expectation of works taking place without grant aid; it may be inappropriate to award grant where authorities believe the works should proceed without grant aid. In determining such matters, authorities are likely to need to establish whether the landlord and tenants have a reserve fund or sinking fund to meet the cost of ongoing maintenance and repair works to the property;

- additional conditions attached to grant under section 52; in particular, where an authority enters into an agreement with a landlord under which grant is given on condition that the authority receives tenant nomination rights;

- landlord's record either in respect of the property for which grant is sought or more widely within the authority, e.g. whether the landlord has a good record in keeping his property or properties in good repair, whether the council have had to take enforcement action or prosecute or whether the authority have had to carry out repairs in default, may have a bearing in an authority's decision to award grant.

52.   Section 31(4) provides for authorities to seek and act upon advice from rent officers on matters concerning rents, if they think it appropriate. Such matters might include:

- the amount of rent which would normally be expected to be payable on a similar tenancy for similar dwellings in the locality in a similar state of repair;

- the amount of rent which might reasonably be expected to be obtained for the tenancy taking account of the relevant works;

- the amount of any increase in rent payable which the landlord might reasonably be expected to obtain following completion of the relevant works either under a statutory tenancy or on the open market under an assured tenancy;

- the likely rent possible for the building on completion of the works where the building was not a dwelling before commencement of the works.

53.   This information will then help an authority judge the appropriateness of the rent currently charged for the dwelling and possibility for the owner to have made provision from the rental stream to meet the cost of the relevant works. While it is discretionary whether authorities seek such advice from rent officers, the Department urges authorities to use the service, especially where information about rent levels is less clear.

54.   Authorities must always exercise their discretion under section 31 reasonably. Each case should be treated on its merits and authorities should therefore avoid adopting a blanket approach in determining grant applications such as awarding grant of a certain percentage of cost of works in every case. In all cases, as resources will always be finite authorities should not award more grant than that necessary to ensure the landlord is able to proceed with the scheme of works.

Application forms for landlords' grants

55.   Authorities have a wide discretion to determine the amount of grant payable in respect of an application to which section 31 of the 1996 Act applies (landlord's applications). Consistent with this discretion, the Secretary of State for the Environment has not prescribed particulars or a form of application for landlord's applications for housing renewal grant.

56.   Authorities may nevertheless find the form set out in *Appendix 2 to this Annex* helpful in designing their own application form(s) for landlord's applications for grant. It is a recommended form, not a prescribed one. Authorities are encouraged to adopt or amend it, or such parts of it, as they see fit.

57.   The recommended form draws on *paragraphs 47 to 54* above and on the questions relating to landlords' applications contained in the now-superseded prescribed forms for housing renovation etc grants made under Part VIII of the Local Government and Housing Act 1989. The style of the recommended form reflects that of the prescribed form for owner-occupier's and tenant's applications for housing renewal grant under section 30 of the 1996 Act.

Annex J2 (Appendix 1)

RENOVATION AND DISABLED FACILITIES GRANTS: TEST OF RESOURCES: UPRATED ALLOWANCES AND PREMIUMS WITH EFFECT FROM 17 DECEMBER 1996

Note: There are no changes to the premiums and benefits since they were last uprated on 17 June 1996, the effective date of the amendments to the 1994 regulations made by SI 1996/1331.

	Existing rate £
Personal Allowances	
Single person aged -	
(a) less than 25	37.90
(b) not less than 25	47.90
Lone parent aged -	
(a) less than 18	37.90
(b) not less than 18	47.90
Couple -	
(a) where both members are aged less then 18	57.20
(b) where at least one member is aged not less than 18	75.20
Child or Young Person aged -	
(a) less than 11	16.45
(b) not less than 11 but less than 16	24.10
(c) not less than 16 but less than 18	28.85
(d) not less than 18	37.90
Premiums	
Lone parent premium	11.50

The higher of whichever of the following may be applicable:

	Existing rate £
Pensioner premium for persons aged 60 to 74 -	
(a) single	19.15
(b) couple	28.90
Enhanced pensioner premium for persons aged 75 to 79 -	
(a) single	21.30
(b) couple	31.90
Higher pensioner premium for persons aged 80 or over, or aged 60 or over and disabled -	
(a) single	25.90
(b) couple	37.05

Existing rate
£

Disability premium for persons aged under 60 and disabled -
    (a) single   20.40
    (b) couple   29.15

Additional Premiums

Severe disability premium (for persons receiving Attendance Allowance or the higher or middle rate of the care component of Disability Living Allowance):
    (a) single   36.40
    (b) couple:
        (i) single rate   36.40
        (ii) double rate   72.80
Disabled child premium   20.40
Carer premium   13.00

Family premium (for persons with at least one child aged under 19):   10.55

To qualify for these premiums, a disabled person must be in receipt of Attendance Allowance, Disability Living Allowance, Disability Working Allowance, Mobility Supplement, Long Term Incapacity Benefit or Severe Disablement Allowance, or be registered as blind or incapable of work.

Annex J2 (Appendix 2)

PRIVATE SECTOR HOUSING RENOVATION GRANTS: FORM OF APPLICATION FOR A LANDLORD'S APPLICATION

(Name and address of Council)

In these instructions and the accompanying form and notes, "the Act" means the Housing Grants, Construction and Regeneration Act 1996 and, unless otherwise stated, all references to sections etc are to sections etc in the Act.

This is the form to use if you are making one of the following applications:-

Renovation grant

– a conversion application where all the accompanying certificates are certificates of intended letting;

– any other owner's application which is accompanied by a certificate of intended letting.

Disabled facilities grant

– any landlord's application for disabled adaptations to a dwelling or to the common parts of a building containing one or more flats.

Common parts grant

– a landlord's application;

– an application as a participating landlord in a tenants' application.

HMO grant

– any application.

When you have completed this form, please send it to the Council.

If you are uncertain how to answer any of these questions, please contact:

(Name, address and telephone number of contact in the Council)

PART 1
PRELIMINARY AND GENERAL INFORMATION

Throughout this form and the accompanying notes, "the Act" means the Housing Grants, Construction and Regeneration Act 1996 and, unless otherwise stated, all references to sections etc are to sections etc in the Act.

Please answer each question unless directed elsewhere. Please read the notes (set out at the end of the form) before answering the questions to which they relate.

If a question does not provide enough space for your answer, please continue your answer on a separate sheet of paper and mark the sheet with your name (or, if yours is a joint application, with all the applicants' names) and the question number. Please make sure you enclose all additional sheets with your application.

Addresses and other preliminaries

1.1   Please give the following details for each grant applicant:

Full name: ....   **Note 1**

Title: Mr / Mrs / Miss / Ms / Other (please specify) ....

Address: ....

....

....

Address for correspondence (if different from above):

....

....

Telephone numbers: (home) ....

(work) ....

1.2   Please give your (or the applicant's) age and date of birth:.........   **Note 2**

Date of birth: ....

Age: .... years

1.3   Do you, or does this applicant, have limited leave to remain in the United Kingdom under Home Office immigration procedures?   **Note 3**

<table>
<tr><td>Yes</td><td>No</td></tr>
<tr><td>❏</td><td>❏</td></tr>
</table>

1.4   If someone else (e.g. a friend or an organisation) is handling this application on your behalf, please give the name, address and telephone number of the person to be contacted about this application.

Name: . ...

Title: Mr / Mrs / Miss / Ms / Other (please specify) ....

Address: ....

....

....

Telephone numbers: (home) ....

(work) ....

1.5 Please give the name, address and telephone number of the person who may be contacted to gain access to the property (e.g. to carry out an inspection).

Name: ....

Title: Mr / Mrs / Miss / Ms / Other (please specify) ....

Address: ....

....

....

Telephone numbers: (home) ....

(work) ....

Parsonages, charities etc

1.6 Are you applying-   Yes   No

- in respect of the residence house
  of an ecclesiastical benefice?   ❏   ❏

- in respect of glebe land?   ❏   ❏

- as a charity?   ❏   ❏

Note 4

The property where the works are to be carried out

1.7 Please give the address of the property at which the works are to be carried out:

....

....

....

....

....

Is this a house or a flat? (please delete as appropriate): *house / flat*   **Note 5**

1.8 Was the property built, or provided by conversion, **less** than 10 years ago?

Yes   No

❏   ❏

Note 6

1.9 Have you or has anyone else been served with a notice under section 189, 190 or 352 of the Housing Act 1985 regarding the property?   **Note 7**

Yes ❏

Please give details, including the date the notice was served:

....

....   No ❏

1.10 Have you or has anyone else been served with a notice under section 81 or 84 of the Act, or section 264, 265 or 289 of the Housing Act 1985, regarding the property?   **Note 8**

Yes ❏

Please give details, including the date the notice was served:

....

....   No ❏

Your interest in the property where the works are to be carried out

1.11 Do you (alone or jointly with others), own the freehold of the property or hold a tenancy of it with at least 5 years still to run?   **Note 9**

Yes ❏

Please indicate which interest you own (please delete as appropriate):

Freehold / tenancy with at least 5 years still to run

If you own the interest jointly with other people, please give the names and addresses of your co-owners:

....

....

....

....   No ❏

1.12 Do you (alone or jointly with others) propose to acquire the freehold of the property or a tenancy of it with at least 5 years still to run?   **Note 10**

Yes ❏

Please indicate which interest you propose to acquire (please delete as appropriate):
Freehold / tenancy with at least 5 years still to run

When do you propose to acquire the interest? ....   **Note 10**

If you propose to acquire it jointly with other people, please give the names and addresses of the other proposed co-owners:

....

....

....

....   No ❏ **Note 11**

Previous applications for grant or assistance

1.13 Have you previously made an application for any type of grant or assistance for this property? Please give the date of your application and Council reference (if known):   **Note 12**

Yes ❏

Date: .... Reference number: ....   No ❏

1.14 Do you know of any previous application for grant or assistance made by another person for this property? Yes ❏

Please give details (if known):

....
.... No ❏ **Note 12**

Planning permission and building regulations approval

1.15 Have you applied for planning permission for the works? **Note 13**

Yes ❏

Please give the date, reference number and outcome of your application:

Date: .... Reference number: ....

Outcome (please delete as appropriate):

granted / refused / no decision yet No ❏

1.16 Have you applied for building regulations approval? **Note 13**

Yes ❏

Please give the date, reference number and outcome of your application:

Date: .... Reference number: ....

Outcome (please delete as appropriate):

granted / refused / no decision yet No ❏

Who will carry out the works?

1.17 Will you or a member of your family carry out the works? **Note 14**

Yes No

❏ ❏

1.18 Do you agree for any grant approved to be paid to your builder (either directly or by cheque made out to your builder)? **Note 15**

Yes No

❏ ❏

Preliminary or ancillary services and charges

1.19 Please give details of any preliminary or ancillary services or charges which you wish to have considered for grant: **Note 16**

....
....
....
....

1.20   Have you already begun or finished the works for which you are applying for grant?

    - begun the works?   Yes ❑   No ❑ **Note 17**

    - finished the works?   Yes ❑   No ❑ **Note 17**

Which grant and which kind of application?

1.21   Which grant are you applying for and by which kind of application? Please tick **one** box only:

Renovation grant

A landlord's application:

    - a conversion application where all the accompanying   ❑   **Notes**
       certificates are certificates of intended letting   **18 & 19**

    - any other owner's application accompanied by a   ❑ **Note 19**
       certificate of intended letting

(Please go to **Part 2A**)

Disabled facilities grant

A landlord's application for disabled adaptations to: **Note 20**

    - a dwelling   ❑

    - the common parts of a building containing one or more flats   ❑

(Please go to **Part 2B**)

Common parts grant

    - a landlord's application   ❑ **Note 21**

    - a landlord participating in a tenants' application   ❑ **Note 22**

(Please go to **Part 2C**)

HMO grant

    - any application   **Note 23**

(Please go to **Part 2D**)

PART 2
INFORMATION SPECIFIC TO THE APPLICATION YOU ARE MAKING

Please answer only the questions which relate to the particular grant(s) for which you are applying, and to the particular type(s) of application which you are submitting.

PART 2A
RENOVATION GRANT

2A.1   Is the property currently unoccupied?   Yes ❑   No ❑

2A.2   Which certificate(s) are you providing with your application?

Conversion application

–   .... certificate(s) of intended letting*   ❑   **Note 19**

(**Please state how many of each certificate you are providing*)

Other application

–   Certificate of intended letting   ❑   **Note 19**

2A.3   Will the works involve-   Yes   No

–   converting the property to provide one or more dwellings?   ❑   ❑

–   improving and/or repairing an existing dwelling?   ❑   ❑   **Note 24**

2A.4   If you are making a conversion application, please describe the conversion to be carried out and say how many dwellings will be provided by the conversion: **Note 25**

Description of conversion works:

....
....
....
....
....

Number of dwellings to be provided by the conversion: ....

2A.5   If you are applying for grant for improvement/repair works to an existing dwelling, please describe the repairs and/or improvements to be carried out to the dwelling: **Note 25**

Description of repairs/improvements:

....
....
....
....

2A.6   Please give the name and address of everyone (whether or not the person is also named under question **1.11** or **1.12**) who proposes to reside in the dwelling or, in the case of a conversion application, the dwelling(s) to be provided by the conversion:

....

....

....

If this is the only landlord's application you are making, please go to **Part 3**

If you are making any other landlord's application, please complete **Part 2B, 2C** *or* **2D** *(as appropriate) before going to* **Part 3**

PART 2B

DISABLED FACILITIES GRANT

2B.1   Is the property currently unoccupied?   Yes ❏   No ❏

2B.2   Are you providing an owner's certificate with your application?   **Note 26**

Yes ❏   No ❏

2B.3   Who is the disabled occupant, or who are the disabled occupants, for whose benefit the adaptations are proposed (please tick as appropriate)?   **Note 27**

Please give each such disabled occupant's name and describe his or her disability (giving the medical name of the condition, where known):

....

....

....

....

2B.4   Are the works, for which disabled facilities grant is sought:

(a)   works to a dwelling (i.e., a house or flat)?   Yes ❏   No ❏

(b)   works to the common parts of a building
containing one or more flats?   Yes ❏   No ❏   **Note 28**

2B.5   Please describe the works briefly:

....

....

....

....

2B.6   Are you also applying for a renovation grant?   Yes ❏   No ❏   **Note 29**

2B.7   Please give the name and address of everyone (whether or not the person is also named in any of questions **1.11**, **1.12** or **2B.3**) who resides or proposes to reside in the dwelling or (in the case of an owner's application for disabled adaptations to the common parts of a building) in the relevant flat(s) in the building:

....

....

....

If this is the only landlord's application you are making, please go to **Part 3**

If you are making any other landlord's application, please complete **Part 2A, 2C** *or* **2D** *(as appropriate) before going to* **Part 3**

PART 2C

COMMON PARTS GRANT

		Yes	No	
2C.1	Are you-			
	– making a landlord's application for common parts grant?	❏	❏	Note 21
	– a participating landlord joining in a tenants' application for common parts grant?	❏	❏	Note 22

2C.2   Which certificate is being submitted with your application?

	Yes	No	
– a landlord's certificate under section 16(1)	❏	❏	Note 30
– a section 16(2) certificate (certificate for tenants' application)?	❏	❏	Note 31

2C.3   How many flats are there in the building?

Please state number: .... flats

2C.4   Which flats are occupied by "occupying tenants"?

Please give details for each flat so occupied: **Note 32**

....

....

....

2C.5   Which of the works to the common parts of the building do you have a **duty or power to carry out?**   **Note 33**

	Yes	No
All of the works	❏	❏

Please give details of your duty or power:

....

....

....

	Yes	No
Some of the works	❏	❏

Please give details of your duty and specify the works for which you have **no such duty or power**:

....

....

....

	Yes	No
None of the works	❏	❏

If this is the only landlord's application you are making, please go to **Part 3**

If you are making any other landlord's application, please complete **Part 2A, 2B** *or* **2D** (*as appropriate*) *before going to* **Part 3**

PART 2D

HMO GRANT

2D.1   Are you providing a certificate of future occupation with your application?   **Note 34**

Yes ❏   No ❏

2D.2   Will the works involve-   Yes   No

– providing a house in multiple occupation by
the conversion of a house or other building?   ❏   ❏

– improving and/or repairing an existing
house in multiple occupation?   ❏   ❏   **Note 35**

CONVERSION APPLICATIONS FOR HMO GRANT

2D.3   Please describe the HMO which will be provided by the conversion (saying in particular what
accommodation will be provided):   **Note 25**

Description of conversion works:

....

....

....

....

Description of the accommodation to be provided by the conversion: **Note 36**

....

....

....

....

Please go to question **2D.13** *(fire amenities)*

APPLICATIONS IN RESPECT OF WORKS OF REPAIR OR IMPROVEMENT TO AN EXISTING HMO

2D.4   Please describe the accommodation currently provided in the HMO (giving number and type of units of accommodation):

....

....

....

....

2D.5   Is any part of the house occupied, or capable or being occupied, as a self-contained dwelling by persons forming a single household?   **Note 36**

Yes ❏

How many such dwellings are there? ....   No ❏

2D.6   How many households in total does the house contain accommodation for?   **Note 37**

.... households in total

2D.7   How many people in total currently reside in the house?

.... people in total reside in the house

2D.8   Has a direction under section 354 of the Housing Act 1985 been given in relation to the property, specifying the maximum number of individuals or households who may occupy the property?

Note 38

Yes ❏

Please give details, including the date on which the direction was given:

....

....   No ❏

2D.9   Has an overcrowding notice under section 358 of the Housing Act 1985 been served on the property, specifying in relation to rooms in the property the maximum number of persons by whom each room is suitable to be occupied as sleeping accommodation?   **Note 39**

Please give details, including the date on which the notice was served:

Yes ❏

....

....   No ❏

2D.10   Have you given an undertaking under section 368 of the Housing Act 1985, which has been accepted by the Council, that part of the house will not be used for human habitation?   **Note 40**

Yes ❏

Please give details, including the date on which the undertaking was accepted:

....

.... No ☐

2D.11   Please describe the repairs or improvements to be carried out, and the accommodation which will be provided after the repairs/improvements have been completed: **Note 25**

Description of repairs/improvements: .

....

....

....

....

....

....

Description of the accommodation after repair/improvement of the HMO: **Note 36**

....

....

....

....

2D.12   Please state what standard amenities are provided in the house for the exclusive use of the occupants, and what amenities are to be added or replaced (if any) as a result of the proposed works:

Note 41

	Number of amenities	
	(a) already provided	(b) to be added or replaced
(a) satisfactory facilities for storing, preparing and cooking food including a sink with a satisfactory hot and cold water supply	....	....
(b) a suitably located water closet	....	....
(c) a suitably located fixed bath or shower with a satisfactory hot and cold water supply	....	....
(d) a suitably located wash-hand basin with a satisfactory hot and cold water supply	....	....

FIRE PRECAUTIONS AND MEANS OF ESCAPE FROM FIRE

Please answer the following questions, whichever type of application you are making for HMO grant

2D.13   Please describe what provision already exists in the property in relation to-

(a)   giving warning in case of fire:

....

....

....

(b)   preventing the spread of fire:

....

....

....

(c)   aiding escape from fire:

....

....

....

2D.14   Please give details of any works proposed-   **Note 25**

(a)   to give warning in case of fire:

....

....

....

(b)   to prevent the spread of fire:

....

....

....

(c)   to aid escape from fire:

....

....

....

2D.15   To your knowledge, has a notice requiring any of these works to be carried out ever been served by the Fire Authority?   **Note 42**

Yes   ❏

Please give details, including the date the notice was served:

....

....   No   ❏

If this is the only landlord's application you are making, please go to **Part 3**

If you are making any other landlord's application, please complete **Part 2A, 2B** or **2C** (as appropriate) before going to **Part 3**

PART 3

FINANCIAL INFORMATION

Please complete the appropriate section(s) of this Part. In the case of joint applications, each applicant should answer this Part separately.

PARSONAGES, CHARITIES ETC

If your application is in respect of the residence house or glebe of an ecclesiastical benefice, or you are applying as a charity (as defined by the Act: see Note 4), please fill in both the questions in this section and the section(s) dealing with the particular grant(s) you are applying for.

3.1 Is the application made in respect of the residence house of an ecclesiastical benefice?

Yes ❑

No ❑ (Please go to question **3.3**)

3.2 Please supply any other information as to your circumstances which may be relevant to your application:

....

....

....

....

3.3 Is the residence house currently let? Yes ❑ (Please go to question **3.9**)

No ❑ (Please go to **Part 4**)

3.4 Are you applying as a charity, or is the application in respect of glebe land? **Note 4**

Yes ❑ No ❑

3.5 Are you under any obligation, or is it your practice, to let dwellings at a rent which is less than a market rent? Yes ❑

Please give details:

....

....

.... No ❑

3.6 Are any financial resources available to you in addition to the rent from the dwelling(s) which are the subject of your application? **Note 43**

Yes ❑

Please give details:

....

....

.... No ❑

3.7 Are you under any obligation, or is it your practice, to dispose of buildings improved by you within a period of five years of carrying out those works?   Yes ❑

Please give details:

....

....

....   No ❑

3.8 Please supply any other relevant information as to your circumstances: **Note 44**

....

....

....

RENOVATION GRANT AND DISABLED FACILITIES GRANT

3.9 Please give the following details for each dwelling or flat which is the subject of your application:

Address: ....   **Note 45**

Type of tenancy/licence: ....   **Note 46**

When the current rent/licence fee was set: ....

The current rent/licence fee and the period in respect of which it is paid:

£ .... per ....

Whether any of the following are included in the rent (please tick appropriate boxes):

	Yes	No
– water charges	❑	❑
– board	❑	❑
– furniture	❑	❑
– other services	❑	❑

Please give details:

....

....

3.10 Please give any other information concerning the tenancy/licence which may be relevant to your application: **Note 47**

....

....

....

....

COMMON PARTS GRANT

3.11 Please give the following details for each flat in the building:

Address: ....   **Note 45**

Type of tenancy/licence: ....   **Note 46**

The date the current rent was set: ....   **Note 48**

The current rent/licence fee and the period in respect of which it is paid:

£ .... per ....

Whether any of the following are included in the rent (please tick appropriate boxes):

		Yes	No
–	water charges	❏	❏
–	board	❏	❏
–	furniture	❏	❏
–	other services	❏	❏

Please give details:

....

....

3.12 Do any of the tenants/licensees in the building have-   **Note 49**

– a duty to carry out any of the relevant works?   ❏

– a duty to make a contribution in respect of the carrying   ❏
out of any of the relevant works?

Note 50

Please give details:

....

....

....

3.13 In the last 3 years, have you, or has any other person, either demanded or received any service charges under the provisions of any lease, tenancy agreement or licence agreement relating to a flat in the building?   **Note 51**

Yes ❏(Please go to question **3.14**)

No ❏(Please go to question **3.15**)

3.14 Please summarise and document all service charge income and expenditure for the building over the last 3 service charge years of account: **Note 52**

....

....

....

....

....

3.15   Please give any other information concerning the tenancy of or licence agreement for each flat in the building which may be relevant to your application:

....

....

....

....

....

HMO GRANT

3.16   Please give the following details for each unit of accommodation in the HMO (**excluding** self-contained accommodation):   **Note 36**

Address: ....   **Note 45**

Type of tenancy/licence: ....   **Note 46**

The date the current rent was set: ....

The current rent/licence fee and the period in respect of which it is paid:

£.............................. per ....

Whether any of the following are included in the rent (please tick appropriate boxes):

	Yes	*No*
– water charges	❑	❑
– board	❑	❑
– furniture	❑	❑
– other services	❑	❑

Please give details:

....

....

3.17   Please give any other information concerning the tenancy/licence of each unit which may be relevant to your application: **Note 47**

....

....

....

....

....

GENERAL

This section must be completed by each applicant.

3.18   Are you the landlord of any other residential property within the Council's area?

Yes   ❑

Please give the full address of each such property:

....

....

....

....   No ❏

3.19   Please give any other information in support of your application: **Note 53**

....

....

DECLARATION

WARNING: IF YOU KNOWINGLY MAKE A FALSE STATEMENT YOU MAY BE LIABLE TO PROSECUTION

I declare that to the best of my knowledge, information and belief the information in this application is correct.

Signature: ....

Date: ....

NOW GO TO PART 4

PART 4

DOCUMENTS TO BE SUBMITTED WITH YOUR APPLICATION

4.1   Please indicate which documents you are enclosing with your application:

		Yes	No	
(a)	Two estimates from different contractors of the cost of carrying out the works (unless otherwise instructed by the Council)	❑	❑	**Note 54**
(b)	Particulars of any preliminary and ancillary services and charges	❑	❑	**Note 55**
(c)	The certificate(s) required for your application (please indicate which certificates you are enclosing and, for renovation grant conversion applications only, how many of each):			

Renovation grant

	Yes	No
.... owner-occupation certificate(s)	❑	❑
.... certificate(s) of intended letting	❑	❑
Tenant's certificate	❑	❑

Disabled facilities grant

	Yes	No
Owner's certificate	❑	❑
Tenant's certificate	❑	❑

Common parts grant

	Yes	No
Section 16(2) certificate	❑	❑

You must submit these documents with your application in any event. The Council may require you to submit, or you may wish to submit, other documents (for example, copies of planning permissions, building regulations approvals, tenancy/licence agreements, certified accounts (or summaries) relating to service charges) in support of your application. The questions and notes draw your attention to points on which supporting documentation may be required or helpful.

If you are in any doubt, the Council will be pleased to guide you.

NOTES

In these notes, "the Act" means the Housing Grants, Construction and Regeneration Act 1996 and, unless otherwise stated, all references to sections etc are to sections etc in the Act.

1. If the applicant is a company or similar body, give the official (registered) address.

2. You cannot apply for a grant unless you are aged 18 or over on the date of your application. In the case of joint applicants, any applicant aged under 18 on the date of the application will be left out of account. See section 3(1).

3. The Council is not allowed to pay a grant to someone who is a "person from abroad" within the meaning of regulation 7A of the Housing Benefit (General) Regulations 1987 (S.I. 1987/ 1971 as amended): regulation 3 of the Housing Renewal Grants Regulations 1996 (S.I. 1996/).

If you answered "Yes" to question **1.3**, you should not be making an application for grant. If you are unable to answer "No" to this question, do not proceed any further with this application.

Regulation 7A of the Housing Benefit (General) Regulations 1987 can be summarised as follows:

(1) Subject to paragraphs (2) and (3), a "person from abroad" is a person who has limited leave to enter or remain in the United Kingdom which was given in accordance with any provision of Home Office immigration rules relating to -

(a) there being, or there needing to be, no recourse to public funds, or

(b) there being no charge on public funds, during that limited leave.

(2) "Person from abroad" does not include a person who -

(a) is a national of a European Economic Area State, a state which is a signatory to the European Convention on Social and Medical Assistance signed in Paris on 11th December 1953 (Cmd.9512), a state which is a signatory to the Council of Europe Social Charter signed in Turin on 18th October 1961, the Channel Islands or the Isle of Man; or

(b) has, during any period of limited leave, supported himself/herself without recourse to public funds but is temporarily (i.e., for no more than a total of 42 days during any period of limited leave) without funds because remittances to him/her from abroad have been disrupted; provided that there is a reasonable expectation that his/her supply of funds will be resumed; or

(c) is an asylum seeker, that is, a person who submits on his/her arrival (other than on his/her re-entry) in the United Kingdom from a country outside the Common Travel Area (i.e., the United Kingdom, the Channel Islands, the Isle of Man and the Republic of Ireland collectively) a claim for asylum to the Secretary of State and that claim is recorded by the Secretary of State as having been made; or

(d) becomes, while present in Great Britain, an asylum seeker; or

(e) is a sponsored immigrant (see paragraph (3)(f) below) and the person or persons who undertook to provide for his/her maintenance and accommodation has or have died; or

(f) is in receipt of income support; or

(g) is on an income-based jobseeker's allowance.

(3) "Person from abroad" **includes** any person, other than a person to whom any of sub-paragraphs (c) to (g) of paragraph (2) applies, who -

(a) having a limited leave to enter or remain in the United Kingdom, has remained without further leave beyond the time limited by the leave; or

(b) is the subject of a deportation order requiring him/her to leave and prohibiting him/her from entering the United Kingdom, except where his/her removal from the United Kingdom has been deferred in writing by the Secretary of State; or

(c) is adjudged by the immigration authorities to be an illegal immigrant who has not subsequently been given leave to enter or remain in the United Kingdom except a person who has been allowed to remain in the United Kingdom with the consent in writing of the Secretary of State; or

(d) is a national of a European Economic Area State and is required by the Secretary of State to leave the United Kingdom; or

(e) is not habitually resident in the United Kingdom, the Republic of Ireland, the Channel Islands or the Isle of Man, but no person shall be treated as not habitually resident in the United Kingdom who -

   (i) is a worker for the purposes of Council Regulation (EEC) No. 1612/68 or (EEC) No. 1251/70 or a person with a right to reside in the United Kingdom pursuant to Council Directive No. 68/360/EEC or No.73/148/EEC; or

   (ii) is a refugee within the definition of Article 1 of the Convention relating to the Status of Refugees signed at Geneva on 28th July 1951 (Cmd.9171), as extended by Article 1(2) of the Protocol relating to the Status of Refugees signed at New York on 31st January 1967 (Cmnd.3906); or

   (iii) has been granted exceptional leave to remain in the United Kingdom by the Secretary of State; or

   (iv) falls within paragraph (1)(b) above; or

   (v) is the subject of a deportation order requiring him/her to leave and prohibiting him/her from entering the United Kingdom, and whose removal from the United Kingdom has been deferred in writing by the Secretary of State; or

   (vi) is adjudged by the immigration authorities to be an illegal immigrant, has not subsequently been given leave to enter or remain in the United Kingdom but has been allowed to remain in the United Kingdom with the consent in writing of the Secretary of State; or

(f) has been given leave to enter, or remain in, the United Kingdom by the Secretary of State upon an undertaking given by another person or persons in writing to be responsible for his/her maintenance and accommodation; and he/she has not been resident in the United Kingdom for a period of at least 5 years beginning from the later of date of entry or the date on which the undertaking was given in respect of him/her; or

(g) while he/she is a person to whom paragraph (1) or any of sub-paragraphs (a) to (d) and (f) of this paragraph applies, submits a claim to the Secretary of State, which is not finally determined, for asylum under the Convention relating to the Status for Refugees.

4. Under section 95, "charity" does not include a registered social landlord but otherwise has the same meaning as in the Charities Act 1993.

5. A flat is a dwelling which is a separate set of premises, whether or not on the same floor, divided horizontally from some other part of the building.

6. Under section 4, the Council is not allowed to entertain an application for a grant if the property was built or was provided by conversion less than 10 years ago. This general rule does not apply to:

(a) any application for a disabled facilities grant; or

(b) an application for an HMO grant in respect of an HMO that was provided by conversion.

7. A notice under section 189 of the Housing Act 1985 is a repair notice for premises which are unfit for human habitation. A notice under section 190 of the 1985 Act is a repair notice for premises which, although fit for human habitation, require substantial repair. A section 189 or 190 notice specifying works to the common parts of a building may be served on a person who is an owner of that part of the building (or the building as a whole) who, in the opinion of the Council serving the notice, ought to carry out the works.

A notice under section 352 of the 1985 Act requires works to be carried out to render an HMO (house in multiple occupation) fit for the number of occupants. The notice may be served on the person having control of, or the person managing, the HMO; and any owner, lessee, occupier or mortgagee of the house, of whom the Council are aware, should be informed of the fact that the notice has been served.

8. Sections 81 and 84 provide respectively for deferred action notices, and notification of reviews of such notices.

Sections 264 and 265 of the Housing Act 1985 deal with closing orders and demolition orders respectively. Under section 289 of the 1985 Act, the Council may declare a clearance area (i.e., an area which is to be cleared of all buildings).

9. These are the "owner's interests" as defined by section 101. If you do not own one of these interests on the date of your application, you cannot make a landlord's application, or join as a participating landlord in a tenants' application, for common parts grant: section 15(1)(a) and (4).

For renovation grant, disabled facilities grant and HMO grant, you can make a landlord's application either if you have an owner's interest in the property on the date of your application or if you propose to acquire such an interest in the property: sections 7(1)(a), 19(1)(a) and 25(1). See also question **1.12** and note **10**.

10. You can make a landlord's application for renovation grant, disabled facilities grant or HMO grant on the basis that you propose to acquire an owner's interest in the property. Please note that in such cases the Council is not allowed to approve the application until they are satisfied that you have acquired the interest: sections 13(3), 24(2) and 28(3).

If you have exchanged contracts on a purchase give the date that the purchase is to be completed. The Council cannot approve an owner's application for renovation grant until they are satisfied that you have acquired an owner's interest.

11. If you have answered "No" to both questions **1.11** and **1.12**, you are not eligible to make a landlord's application for any of the housing renewal grants. If you cannot answer "Yes" to one of these questions, do not proceed any further with this application.

If you are in this position, you will also be unable to make an owner-occupier's application. However, if you have a tenancy (other than a tenancy with at least 5 years still to run) of, or (in some cases) a licence to occupy, the dwelling or a flat in the building, you may be able to make a tenant's application for renovation grant or disabled facilities grant or to join in a tenants' application for common parts grant. Please ask the Council for further information or consult the separate form, which you can obtain from the Council, for owner-occupier's and tenant's applications.

12. Please give details of all previous grant applications of which you are aware, and of any contribution notified under a group repair scheme (if known to you). Please also mention any minor works assistance and home repair assistance you have received. Previous grant approvals may affect the works for which a grant may be given - and also, in the case of previous approvals of applications made by you, the amount of grant payable.

13. Planning permission or building regulations approval may or may not be required. If you are not sure whether permission or approval is required, contact the relevant department of the Council. Where permission or approval has already been obtained, please enclose a copy with your application.

14. Under section 37(4), payment of grant can be made only against an invoice, demand or receipt for payment for the works which is acceptable to the Council; and an invoice given by you or a member of your family is not acceptable. Thus, for example, where you or a member of your family carry out the works, an invoice (which can be authenticated) from a third party will be needed for the cost of the materials.

Section 98(1) defines "member of a family" by reference to section 113 of the Housing Act 1985. The definition includes spouses; persons who live together as husband and wife; parents; grandparents; children; grandchildren; brothers; sisters; uncles; aunts; nephews; and nieces.

15. Under section 39, the Council may pay a grant (or part of a grant) either directly to the contractor or by cheque made out to the contractor but given to the grant applicant. The Council can do this only if, before approving the grant application, they informed the applicant that this would or might be the method of payment.

16. Examples of preliminary or ancillary services and charges which may be included in a grant application are: technical and structural surveys; design and preparation of plans and drawings and preparation of schedules of works; obtaining of estimates; applications for building regulations approval and planning permission; supervision of the works; disconnection and reconnection of electricity, gas, water and drainage utilities made necessary by the works (but not charges arising from non-payment of bills); advice on contracts and on financing the cost of the works, including such services given by home improvement agencies. The Council can give full details of what charges and services would be eligible.

Please see note **14** for the documentation which the Council will require from you before they can pay any grant.

17. Under section 29, grant will not normally be paid if you, or anyone acting on your behalf, begin works before you receive written approval of this application. An exception may be made where the Council is satisfied that there were good reasons for beginning the works before the application was approved; but the application will be treated as excluding any works already completed. Where all the works have been completed, the Council is not allowed to approve the application.

Section 29 does not apply to grant approval for works required to comply with a notice under section 189, 190 or 352 of the Housing Act 1985: section 29(5) and (6).

18. A conversion application, in relation to an application for a renovation grant, means an application for works to provide one or more dwellings by the conversion of a house or other building: section 58.

If you are making a conversion application for renovation grant and any of the certificates accompanying the application is an owner-occupation certificate, you must make an owner's application: section 30(2). Please do not use this form, but instead fill in the separate form for owner-occupier's and tenant's applications. You can obtain this form from the Council.

19. A certificate of intended letting for renovation grant certifies that you -

    (a) have or propose to acquire an owner's interest in the dwelling or building, and

    (b) intend that, throughout the period of 5 years beginning with the date when the Council certify the works as completed to the Council's satisfaction, the dwelling will be let or available for letting as a residence (and not for a holiday) to a person who is not connected with the owner for the time being of the dwelling. See section 8(3).

In (b), "letting" includes the grant of a licence to occupy premises, but does not include a letting on a long tenancy (a tenancy for a term of over 21 years): section 8(4). Under section 98(2), a person is "connected with" the owner of a dwelling if he/she is a member of the owner's family (see note **14**) or if he/she has a beneficial interest in the dwelling, or the proceeds of sale of the dwelling, under a will or trust.

20. A landlord's application for disabled facilities grant means an owner's application for works to a dwelling which is or is intended to be let, or to the common parts of a building in which a flat is or is intended to be let, by the applicant(s): section 31(2).

21. A landlord's application for a common parts grant is an application by a person who has an owner's interest in the building and a duty or power to carry out the relevant works: section 15(1)(a) and (2).

22. A participating landlord in a tenants' application for common parts grant is a person who has an owner's interest in the building and a duty or power to carry out any of the relevant works, and who joins in a tenants' application: section 15(4).

This form - not the form for owner-occupier's and tenant's applications - should be completed by a participating landlord. This applies even to landlords who also have a tenancy of a flat in the building and the tenancy is of a kind that would entitle them to join in a tenants' application for common parts grant as a tenant.

23. An applicant for an HMO grant must have or propose to acquire an owner's interest in the premises on which the works are to be carried out: section 25(1). For "owner's interest", see question **1.11** and note **9**.

24. If you have answered "No" to questions **2A.3** and **2A.4** you should not be applying for a renovation grant. If you cannot answer "Yes" to one of these this questions, do not proceed any further with this application.

25. Give as full a description as you can of the proposed works. It will help you to supply plans and in the case of works of improvement or conversion these should be of the property before and after the works have been carried out.

26. Under sections 21 and 22, the Council is not allowed to entertain an application for disabled facilities grant unless the application is accompanied (in the case of an owner's application) by an "owner's certificate". This certifies that the applicant-

(a) has or proposes to acquire a qualifying owner's interest in the property on which the relevant works are to be carried out, and

(b) intends that the disabled occupant will live in the dwelling or flat as his only or main residence throughout the grant condition period or for such shorter period as his health and other relevant circumstances permit.

27. The disabled occupant, in relation to an application for disabled facilities grant, means the disabled person for whose benefit it is proposed to carry out any of the relevant works: section 20.

Section 100 gives the meaning of "disabled person" for the purposes of the housing main grants legislation.

28. If you have answered "No" to both questions (a) and (b) of question **2B.4,** you cannot apply for disabled facilities grant.

29. Under section 24, a property's fitness for human habitation is one of the matters which the Council can take into account in assessing whether the proposed disabled adaptation works would be "reasonable and practicable" (which is a requirement of the section). Where the property is unfit for human habitation and/or in serious disrepair, you should consider also making an application for renovation grant (which is the appropriate grant for works to remedy unfitness or disrepair) as well as for disabled facilities grant.

30. A section 16(1) certificate is signed by the applicant and-

(a) specifies the interest of the applicant in the building, and

(b) certifies that the required proportion of the flats in the building is occupied by occupying tenants.

The Council is not allowed to entertain a landlord's application for common parts grant unless it is accompanied by a section 16(1) certificate.

31. A section 16(2) certificate is signed by each of the applicants and-

(a) specifies the interest of each of the applicants in each flat in the building, and

(b) certifies that the required proportion (i.e., two-thirds) of the flats in the building is occupied by "occupying tenants" (for the meaning of which please see note **32**).

Only one such certificate need be submitted for all the individual applications comprising a tenants' application. The Council is not allowed to entertain a tenants' application for common parts grant unless it is accompanied by a section 16(2) certificate.

32. Section 14(2) defines "occupying tenant" as a person who has in relation to the flat (alone or jointly with others)-

(a) a long tenancy at a low rent to which section 1 of the Landlord and Tenant Act 1954 or Schedule 10 to the Local Government and Housing Act 1989 applies;

(b) an assured tenancy under Part I of the Housing Act 1988;

(c) a protected tenancy under the Rent Act 1977;

(d)   a secure tenancy under the Housing Act 1985;

(e)   a statutory tenancy under the Rent (Agriculture) Act 1976 or the Rent Act 1977; or

(f)   a protected occupancy under the Rent (Agriculture) Act 1976 or an assured agricultural occupancy under Part I of the Housing Act 1988.

Please give full details as requested, whether you are making a landlord's application or are applying as a participating landlord. You need not give these details on the form if they are set out in the section 16(1) or 16(2) certificate accompanying the application.

33.   The Council is not allowed to entertain a landlord's application for common parts grant unless they are satisfied that the applicant has a duty or power to carry out all the works for which grant is sought (the "relevant works"): section 15(1)(a). A participating landlord's duty or power is sufficient if it relates to only some of the relevant works: section 15(4).

Please attach copies of any documentation (e.g., the relevant part(s) of your lease or tenancy agreement) containing or evidencing your duty or power. If other people share your duty or power, please state how many people do so. For this purpose, an interest held jointly by two or more people should be counted as if it were held by one person.

34.   Under section 26(2), a "certificate of future occupation" certifies that the applicant-

(a)   has or proposes to acquire a qualifying owner's interest in the house, and

(b)   intends that throughout the grant condition period the house or a part of it (specified in the certificate) will be residentially occupied, or available for residential occupation, under tenancies or licences by persons who are not connected with the owner for the time being of the house.

35.   If you have answered "No" to both parts of question **2D.2**, you should not be applying for an HMO grant. If you cannot answer "Yes" to one part of question **2D.2**, do not proceed any further with this application.

36.   By virtue of section 101, for the purposes of the housing renewal grants legislation "house in multiple occupation" has the same meaning as in Part XI of the Housing Act 1985 (houses in multiple occupation), except that it does not include any part of such a house which is occupied as a separate dwelling by persons who form a single household.

As a result, HMO grant cannot be approved for works to a self-contained dwelling situated within the house. Renovation grant is the appropriate grant to apply for in relation to such works. If you are in doubt as to the correct application to make, please consult the Council.

37.   Examples of a "household" could be a person living on his or her own or persons living together as a family (whether or not they are related).

38.   A direction given under section 354 of the Housing Act 1985 sets a maximum number of occupants who may live in the house. The Council will serve prior notice of their intention to make such a direction on every owner and lessee of the house of whom they are aware, and post the notice in a position in the house where it is accessible to those living there.

39.   A notice under section 358 of the Housing Act 1985 is an overcrowding notice stating that an excessive number of persons is being, or is likely to be, accommodated on the premises, having regard to the number of rooms available. The Council will serve prior notice of their intention to serve such a notice on the occupier of the premises, or the person who appears to be managing them, and will take reasonable steps to inform every person living in the premises of their intention.

40. A notice under section 368 of the Housing Act 1985 is served where, in order to ensure that means of escape from fire are adequate, part of the house is not to be used for human habitation. The notice forbids human habitation of the relevant part of the house and the Council may, if they think fit, consult with the owner or mortgagee of the house before serving the notice.

41. The amenities listed in question **2D.12** are the basic standard amenities for an HMO (apart from fire precautions works, dealt with in questions **2D.13 to 2D.15**), set out in section 352(1A) of the Housing Act 1985. A notice under section 352 requires the execution of works to render an HMO fit for the number of occupants or, alternatively, a reduction of the number of occupants living in the HMO. The notice can be served on the person having control or managing the house and the Council must notify any occupier, of whom they are aware, that the notice has been served.

42. If notices have been served by the Fire Authority (under the Fire Precautions Act 1971 or other legislation), it is possible that your property would not qualify for HMO grant. You should check this with the Council.

43. Details given may include information about resources made available by the Diocesan Board of Finance, for example, an extract from the annual budget of the Board. If you are not making this application as a representative of the Board, please give the address of the Board.

44. A summary or copy of the charity's trust deed or similar document should be provided in addition to any other information. In the case of glebe land, please indicate whether the property (or part of it) is currently occupied rent-free by a licensed minister or layworker.

45. Please give the exact address (e.g. Flat C, 25 Anystreet).

46. If you are not sure of the type of tenancy or licence to occupy, please consult the Council or your own solicitor, the Citizens Advice Bureau or a legal aid centre.

47. For example, whether the tenant or licensee is responsible for any repairs.

48. "Rent" includes ground rent. Please give the weekly / monthly / quarterly / annual amount as appropriate.

49. Under section 15(1)(b) and (2), a tenants' application for common parts grant may be made by three-quarters of the "occupying tenants" (see note 32) who under their tenancies have a duty to carry out, or to make a contribution in respect of the carrying out of, some or all of the relevant works. This is subject to the overriding requirement, under section 14(1), that at the date of the application at least the required proportion of the flats in the building is occupied by "occupying tenants".

If you are making a landlord's application for common parts grant (rather than joining in a tenants' application as a participating landlord: see notes **21** and **22**) and a tenants' application could have been made in respect of the relevant works, please explain why such an application (with you joining in as participating landlord) has not been made.

50. The details given should include a full copy of each of the relevant leases or licence agreements. Please do not submit extracts: the Council needs to see the full text of the lease or agreement.

51. You should treat as a "service charge" any amount payable, directly or indirectly, under the tenancy or licence agreement as part of or in addition to the rent/licence fee for services, repairs, maintenance or insurance or the landlord's costs of management, and the whole or part of which varies or may vary according to the costs incurred or to be incurred in relation to those matters: c.f., the definition of "service charge" in section 18(1) of the Landlord and Tenant Act 1985.

52. You should document your service charge income and expenditure by submitting to the Council certified accounts for the last 3 service charge years of account. Certified accounts prepared as summaries of relevant costs in compliance with section 21 of the Landlord and Tenant Act 1985 will be appropriate for this purpose.

53. An important point on which the Council will require a full explanation is why the relevant works cannot be fully financed from your income as landlord of the property. You are encouraged to submit with your application any documentation which you think will illustrate or support your explanation on this point.

54. The Council will normally ask for two estimates of the costs of works from different contractors; but they may require more or fewer than two estimates in any particular case. The estimates should be itemised. See also note 14.

55. The particulars of any preliminary or ancillary services and charges are for the services and charges identified in question 1.19 (see note 16). Please include estimates.

Annex J3

Housing renewal grants etc.
(Exchequer contributions) (England) Determination 1996

The Secretary of State for the Environment, in exercise of the powers conferred on him by section 92 of the Housing Grants, Construction and Regeneration Act 1996 and section 96(3) of the Local Government and Housing Act 1989 (as applied by section 132(4) of that Act) and section 132 of that Act and of all other powers enabling him in that behalf, and with the consent of the Treasury, hereby makes the following determination and imposes the following conditions-

Citation, commencement and interpretation

1.—(1) This Determination may be cited as the Housing Renewal Grants etc. (Exchequer Contributions) (England) Determination 1996 and shall have effect, subject to paragraph 4, after 16th December 1996 in respect of all local housing authorities in England.

(2) In this Determination -

"the 1989 Act" means the Local Government and Housing Act 1989, and

"the 1996 Act" means the Housing Grants, Construction and Regeneration Act 1996.

Exchequer contribution

2.—(1) The Secretary of State shall pay contributions to local housing authorities towards the expenditure incurred by them under Part VIII of the 1989 Act or Part I of the 1996 Act as follows.

(2) Subject to sub-paragraph (3) and paragraph 4, the contribution to a local housing authority shall be at the rate of 60 per cent. of the aggregate of -

(a) the amount of renovation grants, common parts grants and HMO grants approved under Part VIII of the 1989 Act or Part I of the 1996 Act which either have been paid by the authority or are outstanding;

(b) the amount of disabled facilities grants approved under Part VIII of the 1989 Act or Part I of the 1996 Act which either have been paid by the authority or are outstanding, excluding any paid in respect of an application made by a tenant relating to -

(i) a dwelling let to him by a local authority, or

(ii) a building containing such a dwelling;

(c) the costs of works and fees incurred by the authority in executing group repair schemes approved by the Secretary of State, excluding any contributions towards those costs met by persons or bodies participating in a scheme as assisted or unassisted participants; and

(d) the amount of assistance under section 131 of the 1989 Act or section 76 of the 1996 Act which either has been given by the authority or is outstanding.

(3) For the purposes of sub-paragraph (2) -

(a) grants are outstanding only where acceptable invoices, demands or receipts have been submitted for payment to a local housing authority in accordance with section 117(3) and (4) of the 1989 Act or section 37(4) of the 1996 Act;

(b) the reference to the costs of works and fees in relation to group repair schemes includes any payments which are outstanding where invoices, demands or receipts have been submitted for payment to a local housing authority and are acceptable to the authority but not otherwise; and

(c) assistance is only outstanding where invoices, demands or receipts have been submitted for payment to a local housing authority and are acceptable to the authority; and

where a contribution has been paid in full in respect of an amount which is outstanding, no further contribution shall be payable in respect of that amount.

Manner of payment

3.—(1)   Subject to sub-paragraphs (2) and (3), contributions shall be payable in 10 instalments on account on the basis of an authority's estimated expenditure in respect of each financial year, and the balance will be payable on receipt of an authority's claim after the end of the financial year to which it relates, subject to any adjustment, if necessary, once the claim has been examined by an auditor appointed by the Audit Commission.

(2)   For the purposes of sub-paragraph (1), expenditure means the aggregate of the amounts, costs and fees referred to in paragraph 2 in respect of that year, excluding (unless the local authority otherwise determine) any amounts, costs and fees in respect of the invioces, demands or receipts referred to in paragraph 2(3) where it would not be reasonably practicable for the authority to make the payment in that year.

(3)   For the purposes of sub-paragraph (1), after 31st March 1997, the cash limit provided for in paragraph 4 shall be applied rateably.

Cash limit

4.—(1)   After 31st March 1997, -

(a) the aggregate of contributions referred to in paragraph 2(2)(a), (c) and (d), and

(b) any payment made to the local housing authority as a result of a prior year adjustment to contributions already received by the authority, excluding any made in relation to disabled facilities grants,

in any financial year (when aggregated with relevant payments) shall not exceed the total provision allocated to the local housing authority towards relevant expenditure for that financial year.

(2)   In sub-paragraph (1) -

"allocated" means allocated in exercise of the powers in section 132 of the 1989 Act or section 92 of the 1996 Act or any of the powers under which relevant payments are made.

"relevant expenditure" means expenditure incurred by the local housing authority under -

(a) section 429 of the Housing Act 1985 (improvement for sale schemes),

(b) Part IX of the Housing Act 1985 (slum clearance),

(c) Part VII of the 1989 Act (renewal areas),

(d) Part VIII of the 1989 Act (grants towards costs of improvements and repairs etc.), other than in relation to desabled facilities grants,

(e) Part I of the 1996 Act (grants etc. for renewal of private sector housing), other than in relation to disabled facilities grants; or

(f) section 132 of the 1996 Act (relocation grants); and

"relevant payments" means contributions and subsidies paid in that financial year under section 429 of the Housing Act 1985 (contributions for improvement for sale schemes), section 96 of the 1989 Act (contributions relating to renewal areas), section 165 (3) to (9) of the 1989 Act (slum clearance subsidy) or section 139 of the 1996 Act (relocation grants).

The conditions

5. The conditions imposed on the payment, under section 92 of the 1996 Act or under section 132 of the 1989 Act, of Exchequer contributions towards the expenditure incurred in giving renovation grants, common parts grants, HMO grants, disabled facilities grants, minor works assistance and home repair assistance and towards expenditure incurred in relation to group repair schemes under Part VIII of the 1989 Act or under Part I of the 1996 Act shall be as provided for in the following paragraphs.

General condition : keeping records

6. Each local housing authority shall maintain adequate records of expenditure to facilitate the completion of claims for payments of Exchequer contributions. Information shall be provided in such form and at such times as may from time to time be required by the Secretary of State.

General condition : allowing access to records

7. Each local housing authority shall permit the auditor appointed by the Audit Commission, or any other officer authorised by the Secretary of State, to have access to and inspect the registers, records and certificates referred to in this determination and, where necessary, accounts, plans, contracts and other relevant documents and vouchers.

General condition : keeping registers

8. Each local housing authority shall keep, as detailed below, registers of properties provided, repaired, improved or adapted with grant aid, or as part of a group repair scheme, under Part I of the 1996 Act or Part VIII of the 1989 Act. These registers shall be kept separately from any other registers which are being, or have been, kept relating to grants or other assistance towards the cost of improvements, repairs, conversions and adaptations of properties.

Renovation grants register

9. The register to be maintained in respect of dwellings for which renovation grants have been paid by the local housing authority under section 13 of the 1996 Act, or under sections 112, 113 or 115 of the 1989 Act, shall contain the following particulars of each dwelling or group of dwellings improved, repaired or provided by conversion -

(a) Name and address of applicant;

(b) Address of dwelling or dwellings;

(c) Statement as to whether applicant(s) is/are owner(s), or tenant(s);

(d) Statement as to whether works were to comply with a statutory notice (type and reference of notice);

(e) Statement as to whether the property was fit/unfit for human habitation prior to commencement of works;

(f) Estimated expense calculated in respect of the eligible works, both in total and identifying separately -

(i) the amount relating to the execution of the eligible works; and

(ii) the amount relating to preliminary or ancillary services and charges;

(g) The amount by which the grant was reduced in accordance with section 30(3) or section 31(3) of the 1996 Act, or section 109 or section 110 of the 1989 Act;

(h)   Amount of grant paid;

(i)   Date of completion of works;

(j)   Reference to certificate of completion (see paragraph 16 below);

(k)   Date of payment of grant.

Disabled facilities grants register

10.   The register to be maintained in respect of dwellings for which disabled facilities grants have been paid by the local housing authority under section 24 of the 1996 Act, or under section 114 of the 1989 Act, shall contain the following particulars of each dwelling or building to which adaptation works are carried out -

(a)   Name and address of applicant;

(b)   Address of dwelling or building;

(c)   Statement as to whether applicant(s) is/are owner(s), landlord(s) or tenant(s);

(d)   Estimated expense calculated in respect of the eligible works, both in total and identifying separately -

(i) the amount relating to the execution of the eligible works; and

(ii) the amount relating to preliminary or ancillary services and charges;

(e)   The amount by which the grant was reduced in accordance with section 30(4) or section 31(3) of the 1996 Act, or with section 109 or section 110 of the 1989 Act;

(f)   Amount of grant paid;

(g)   Date of completion of works;

(h)   Reference to certificate of completion (see paragraph 16 below);

(i)   Date of payment of grant.

Common parts grants register

11.   The register to be maintained in respect of buildings for which common parts grants have been paid by the local housing authority under section 18 of the 1996 Act, or under sections 113 or 115(2) of the 1989 Act, shall contain the following particulars of each building improved or repaired -

(a)   Name and address of applicant;

(b)   Address of building;

(c)   Statement as to whether application is landlord's or tenant's common parts application;

(d)   Statement as to proportion of dwellings in the building occupied by occupying tenants;

(e)   Statement as to whether works were to comply with a statutory notice (type and reference of notice);

(f)   Estimated expense calculated in respect of the eligible works to the building, both in total and identifying separately -

(i) the amount relating to the execution of the eligible works; and

(ii) the amount relating to preliminary or ancillary services and charges;

(g)   Costs attributed to applicant (amount and as a percentage of (f) above);

(h) Amount by which the grant was reduced in accordance with section 31(3) or section 32 of the 1996 Act, or with section 109 or section 110 of the 1989 Act;

(i) Amount of grant paid;

(j) Date of completion of works;

(k) Reference to certificate of completion (see paragraph 16 below);

(l) Date of payment of grant;

(m) Reference number(s) of associated application(s).

HMO grants registers

12. The register to be maintained in respect of properties for which HMO grants have been paid by the local housing authority under section 28 of the 1996 Act, or under sections 113 or 115 of the 1989 Act, shall contain the following particulars of each house in multiple occupation improved, repaired or provided by conversion -

(a) Name and address of applicant;

(b) Address of property;

(c) Statement as to whether works were to comply with a statutory notice (type and reference of notice);

(d) Statement as to whether, prior to commencement of works, the property was fit/unfit -

(i) for human habitation; and

(ii) fit for the number of occupants;

(e) Estimated expense calculated in respect of the eligible works, both in total and identifying separately -

(i) the amount relating to the execution of the eligible works; and

(ii) the amount relating to preliminary or ancillary services and charges;

(f) Amount by which the grant was reduced in accordance with section 31(3) of the 1996 Act, or with section 110 of the 1989 Act;

(g) Amount of grant paid;

(h) Date of completion of works;

(i) Reference to certificate of completion (see paragraph 16 below);

(j) Date of payment of grant.

Group repair schemes register

13. The register to be maintained in respect of group repair schemes carried out under section 63 of the 1996 Act, or section 127 of the 1989 Act shall contain the following particulars in respect of each scheme completed -

(a) Statement as to whether or not the scheme is located within the boundaries of a Renewal Area declared under section 89 of the 1989 Act;

(b) Statement of the date on which -

(i) the scheme was approved by the Secretary of State; and

(ii) any variation of the scheme was approved by the Secretary of State;

and in a case where the scheme or a variation of a scheme was not submitted for specific approval the date of approval of the scheme or, as the case may be, the variation of a scheme shall be taken to be the date on which the authority decided that the scheme fulfilled the criteria for general approval of a group repair scheme or, as the case may be variation of a group repair scheme;

(c)   Statement of the works carried out under the scheme;

(d)   Date of completion of the scheme;

(e)   Schedule setting out for each of the properties included in the scheme -

    (i) the address of the property;

    (ii)   the name of the person or body having an owner's interest in the property;

    (iii)   an indication of whether the owner participated as an assisted or as an unassisted participant;

    (iv)   the costs of works attributable to the property;

    (v)   the amount (if any) of the owner's contribution.

Minor works assistance register

14.   The register to be maintained in respect of dwellings for which minor works assistance has been paid by the local housing authority under section 131 of the 1989 Act shall contain the following particulars of each dwelling assisted -

(a)   Name and address of applicant;

(b)   Address of dwelling;

(c)   Statement of the nature of the works carried out, specifying for which of the purposes (a) to (e) in section 131 of the 1989 Act the assistance was given;

(d)   Total cost of the works eligible for assistance;

(e)   Value of any materials provided;

(f)   Amount of any grant given;

(g)   Total amount of assistance given;

(h)   Date of completion of works;

(i)   Reference to certificate of completion (see paragraph 16 below);

(j)   Date of payment of grant.

Home repair assistance register

15.   The register to be maintained in respect of dwellings for which home repair assistance has been paid by the local housing authority under section 76 of the 1996 Act shall contain the following particulars of each dwelling assisted -

(a)   Name and address of applicant;

(b)   Address of dwelling;

(c)   Statement of the nature of the works carried out;

(d)   Total cost of the works eligible for assistance;

(e)   Value of any materials provided;

(f) Amount of any grant given;

(g) Total amount of assistance given;

(h) Date of completion of works;

(i) Reference to certificate of completion (see paragraph 16 below);

(j) Date of payment of grant.

Certificates

16. The certificates referred to above shall include the heading-

(a) "Housing Grants, Construction and Regeneration Act 1996"

where payment is under Part I of the 1996 Act; or

(b) "Local Government and Housing Act 1989"

where payment is under Part VIII of the 1989 Act.

and all certificates shall be in the following form -

" Certificate of completion of improvement, repair, conversion or adaptation works

This is to certify that in respect of each of the dwellings, buildings, house-boats, mobile homes or houses in multiple occupation described in the schedule below the works of improvement, repair, conversion or adaptation were completed to the satisfaction of the Council, and acceptable invoices, demands or receipts for payment were provided in respect of those works, before the date set opposite their description in that schedule.

SCHEDULE

Address of dwellings, buildings, house-boats, mobile homes or houses in multiple occupation	Date	Reference number for register

Date of certificate_____ Signed _____

Surveyor or other authorised officer of the._____Council."

Signed by authority of
the Secretary of State

2 December 1996

C.L.L Braun
Assistant Secretary
Department of the
Environment

Annex J4

Renovation grant – specifications, directions and consents

The Housing Renewal Grants (Owner's Interest) Directions 1996

The Secretary of State for the Environment, in exercise of the powers conferred on him by sections 7(3), 19(3), 25(2) and 146 of the Housing Grants, Construction and Regeneration Act 1996[1] and of all other powers enabling him in that behalf, hereby gives the following directions -

Citation and commencement

1.   These directions may be cited as the Housing Renewal Grants (Owner's Interest) Directions 1996 and shall come into force on 17 December 1996.

Owner's interest condition

2.—(1)   A local housing authority may treat the condition in sections 7(1)(a), 19(1)(a) and 25(1) of the Housing Grants, Construction and Regeneration Act 1996 as fulfilled by a person who has, or proposes to acquire, an owner's interest in only part of the land to which an application for a grant relates if -

(a) the relevant works include specified works which are to be carried out (in whole or in part) on land which is not the applicant's land; and

(b) the applicant has the power to carry out the works.

(2)   In sub-paragraph (1) "specified works" means -

(a) works to connect the applicant's land with a gas, electricity, water or drainage utility at the nearest practicable point so as to provide to the applicant's land -

(i)   adequate lighting;

(ii)   adequate heating;

(iii)   an adequate piped supply of wholesome water; or

(iv)   an effective system for draining of foul, waste or surface water;

(b) works described in section 23(1)(a) of the Housing Grants, Construction and Regeneration Act 1996; or

(c) works to repair or replace (in whole or in part) any of the works described in paragraph (a) or (b).

(3)   In sub-paragraph (2) "applicant's land" means land in which the applicant has, or proposes to acquire, an owner's interest.

Application

4.   These directions -

(a) shall apply to local housing authorities in England only; and

---

(1) 1996 c 53

(b) shall not apply in a case where the application for a grant was made before the date on which these directions come into force.

Signed by authority of
the Secretary of State

2 December 1996

C L L Braun
Assistant Secretary
Department of the
Environment

The Housing Renewal Grants (Radon) (England) Specification 1996

The Secretary of State for the Environment, as respects England, in exercise of the powers conferred on him by sections 12, 17 and 27 of the Housing Grants, Construction and Regeneration Act 1996[1], hereby makes the following Specification:-

Citation, commencement and interpretation

1.   This specification may be cited as the Housing Renewal Grants (Radon) (England) Specification 1996 and shall come into force on 17 December 1996.

Maximum level of radon gas

2.   For the purposes of sections 12(1)(g), 17(1)(h) and 27(1)(h) of the Housing Grants, Construction and Regneration Act 1996 (renovation grant, common parts grant and HMO grant: compliance with specified requirements as to construction or physical condition of dwelling, building or house), the annual average level of radon present in a dwelling, building or house shall not exceed 200 Becquerels per cubic metre (Bq/m3,).

Application

3.   Paragraph 2 shall not have effect in relation to applications for grant made before 17 December 1996.

Signed by authority of
the Secretary of State

2 December 1996

C L L Braun
Assistant Secretary
Department of the
Environment

The Housing Grants Construction and Regeneration Act 1996 (Grant recovery) general consent 1996

The Secretary of State for Environment in the exercise of his powers under sections 45, 46, 47 and 94 of the Housing Grants, Construction and Regeneration Act 1996 and of all other powers enabling him in that behalf, hereby gives to all local housing authorities in England the following general consent -

Citation and Commencement

1.   This consent may be cited as the Housing Renewal Main Grants (Grant Recovery) General Consent 1996 and shall come into force on 17 December 1996.

Interpretation

2.   In this consent "disponor" means the person who, were it not for this consent, would be liable under sections 45, 46 or 47 of the Housing Grants, Construction and Regeneration Act 1996 (condition for repayment on disposal) to repay to the local housing authority on demand the amount of grant that has been paid.

---

(1) 1996 c 53

Consent

3.—(1) Subject to sub-paragraph (2), where a local housing authority have a right to demand repayment of a grant under sections 45, 46 or 47 of the Housing Grants, Construction and Regeneration Act 1996 upon a relevant disposal (which is not an exempt disposal), they may determine not to demand repayment or to demand a lesser sum where they are satisfied that -

    (a) the disposal is made with the intention of enabling the disponor to move to other accommodation for the purpose of -

        (i)   the disponor or his partner accepting employment where either of them is or would otherwise become unemployed, or

        (ii)   enabling the disponor or his partner to continue in employment where either of them is required by his employer to move to another place of work, or

    (b) the disposal is made by a mortgagee in exercise of his power of sale and the mortgage was entered into before the application for the grant was made.

(2)   Where the grant is a common parts grant or an HMO grant, the local housing authority must also be satisfied that the whole or part of the building or house has been the disponor's only or main residence from the date on which -

    (a) the disponor was notified that his application for a grant was approved, or

    (b) in the case of an HMO grant which was approved for the purpose of complying with a notice under sections 189, 190 or 352 of the Housing Act 1985, the relevant works were completed.

Signed by authority of the Secretary of State	C L L Braun Assistant Secretary Department of the
2 December 1996	Environment

The Housing Renewal Main Grants (Recovery of Compensation) General Consent 1996

The Secretary of State for the Environment, in the exercise of the powers conferred upon him by sections 51 and 94 of the Housing Grants, Construction and Regeneration Act 1996[1] and of all other powers enabling him in that behalf, hereby gives to all local housing authorities in England the following general consent -

Citation and Commencement

1.   This consent may be cited as the Housing Renewal Main Grants (Recovery of Compensation) General Consent 1996 and shall come into force on 17 December 1996.

Consent

2.   Where a local housing authority approve an application for grant under Part I of the Housing Grants, Construction and Regeneration Act 1996 they may impose a condition requiring the applicant to take reasonable steps to pursue any relevant claim to which section 51 of that Act applies and to repay the grant, so far as is appropriate, out of the proceeds of such a claim.

Signed by authority of the Secretary of State	C L L Braun Assistant Secretary Department of the
2 December 1996	Environment

---

(1) 1996 c 53

The Housing Renewal Grants (Additional Conditions) (England) General Consent 1996

The Secretary of State for the Environment, as respects England, in exercise of the powers conferred on him by sections 52 and 94 of the Housing Grants, Construction and Regeneration Act 1996[1], hereby gives the following Consent:-

Citation, commencement and interpretation

1.—(1)　This specification may be cited as the Housing Renewal Grants (Additional Conditions) (England) General Consent 1996 and shall come into force on 17 December 1996.

(2)　In this Consent,-

"the Act" means the Housing Grants, Construction and Regeneration Act 1996;

"authority" means a local housing authority;

"applicant", without more, means an applicant for a grant under Chapter I of Part I of the Act (private sector housing renewal: main grants) and includes any person who is for the time being an owner of the property;

"the property" means the dwelling, house or building which is grant-aided.

Additional Conditions

2.　Where an authority approves an application for a grant under Chapter I of Part I of the Act, they may impose such of the conditions set out in paragraphs 3 to 7 as appear to them appropriate.

Notice of relevant disposal

3.—(1)　The applicant shall forthwith notify the authority of his intention to make a relevant disposal of any dwelling, building or house in multiple occupation with respect to which there is in force, as a grant condition, any condition under sections 45 to 52 of the Act and shall furnish to the authority any information reasonably requested by them in connection with such notification.

(2)　This condition shall have effect during the grant condition period.

Nomination of tenants to the property

4.—(1)　In the case of an application to which any of paragraphs (a), (c) and (d) of section 31(1) of the Act (determination of amount of grant in case of landlord's application for renovation grant, disabled facilities grant or HMO grant) applies, the authority shall be entitled to nominate tenants to the property (or a relevant part of the property) throughout the grant condition period.

(2)　The applicant agrees not to offer the property (or a relevant part of the property) for letting, and the authority agrees not to make nominations to it, in such manner (including as to timing and the terms of any offer or nomination) as would prevent this condition being, or continuing to be, operable fairly and reasonably.

(3)　Without prejudice to the generality of sub-paragraph (2), the applicant agrees-

(a) if the property (or part of it) is or becomes vacant on the date of approval of the application, or

(b) if (and every time that) the property (or part of it) becomes vacant between that date and the end of the grant condition period,

---

(1) 1996 c 53

forthwith to hold the property (or the vacant part of it) available for letting by persons nominated by the authority and to notify the authority of its availability for that purpose and of the terms upon which it is so available.

(4) Subject to the applicant's strict compliance with sub-paragraph (3), this condition shall not have effect while the property (or each of its several parts) is occupied under a tenancy or tenancies satisfying the requirements of such certificate of intended letting, owner's certificate or certificate of future occupation as was submitted with the application (or, in a case where the requirement for such certificate was waived by the authority, would meet that certificate's requirements had one been so submitted).

(5) Where the authority approve a conversion application for a renovation grant, they may apply this condition to one or more only, or to a proportion, of the total number of dwellings to be provided by the conversion; provided that the dwellings, or the proportion of dwellings, in the house or other building and to which this condition is to apply shall be identified to the applicant in writing when the application is approved.

(6) Where the authority approve a landlord's application for a disabled facilities grant for adaptations to the common parts of a building containing one or more flats, and the application is for the benefit of more than one flat in the building, they may apply this condition to one or more only, or to a proportion, of the flats which the application is intended to benefit; provided that the flats, or the proportion of the flats, to which this condition is to apply shall be identified to the applicant in writing when the application is approved.

(7) In this condition,-

"a relevant part of the property" means a part of the property which is or becomes vacant as described in sub-paragraph (3);

"tenancy" includes a licence arrangement satisfying the certificate of intended letting, owner's certificate or certificate of future occupation in question, and related expressions shall be construed accordingly.

Recovery of specialised equipment for the disabled

5.—(1) Where an application for disabled facilities grant has been approved under section 23(1) or (2) (disabled facilities grant: purposes for which grant must or may be given) and the eligible works consist of or include the installation in the property of specialised equipment for the disabled occupant(s), the applicant shall notify the authority if and as soon as the equipment is no longer needed.

(2) For the purposes of this condition-

(a) the authority shall, on approving the application, specify in writing the equipment to which this condition is to apply and the period (being a reasonable condition period for the equipment in question) during which it is to apply, and shall serve on the applicant a copy of such written specification; and

(b) the authority, or the social services authority on their behalf, shall be entitled, upon reasonable prior written notice given to the applicant either following the giving of the notification under sub-paragraph (1) or at any time during the condition period specified under paragraph (a), to inspect the equipment and, subject to complying with sub-paragraph (3), to remove it.

(3) The authority agrees, within a reasonable time following an inspection of the equipment,-

(a) to notify the applicant in writing whether the equipment is to be removed; and

(b) if the equipment is to be removed, to remove it or arrange for it to be removed and forthwith to make good any damage caused to the property (whether by the authority themselves or the social services authority) by its removal.

(4) The authority further agrees, where the applicant has contributed to the cost of carrying out the eligible works, to pay to him, within a reasonable time of the removal of the equipment, the reasonable current value of that proportion of its original cost which represents the proportion of his contribution to the cost of carrying out the eligible works.

(5) For the purposes of sub-paragraph (4), the reasonable current value of the equipment shall be its value at the time of removal from the property.

(6) Subject to the authority giving prior written notice in accordance with sub-paragraph (2)(b) or, as the case may be, (3)(a), the applicant agrees to afford, or to use his best endeavours to arrange for the affording of, reasonable access to the property to the authority or the social services authority for the purposes of inspection and removal of the equipment.

Insurance for grant-aided property

6. Where the applicant has an insurable interest in the grant-aided property, he shall arrange and maintain in effect adequate insurance for the property, subject to and with the benefit of the completed works, throughout the grant condition period.

Repair of grant-aided property

7. Where the applicant has a duty or power to carry out works of repair to the grant-aided property, he shall ensure that, to the extent that his duty or power allows, the property remains fit for human habitation throughout the grant condition period.

Repayment of grant

8. In the event of a breach of any of the conditions set out in paragraphs 3 to 7, the authority may demand repayment from the applicant of a sum equal to the amount of the grant paid or, as the case may be, any instalments of grant paid and the same shall become repayable to the authority in accordance with section 52 of the Act.

Application

9. Paragraphs 2 to 8 shall not have effect in relation to applications for grant made before 17 December 1996.

Signed by authority of
the Secretary of State

C L L Braun
Assistant Secretary
Department of the
Environment

2 December 1996

The Housing Renewal Grants (Landlord's Applications) (England) Direction 1996

The Secretary of State for the Environment, as respects England, in exercise of the powers conferred on him by sections 31(3)(b) and 146(1) and (2) of the Housing Grants, Construction and Regeneration Act 1996[1] ("the Act"), hereby makes the following Direction:-

Citation and commencement

1. This direction may be cited as the Housing Renewal Grants (Landlord's Applications) (England) Direction 1996 and shall come into force on 17 December 1996.

---

(1) 1996 c 53

Determination of landlord's grants

2.   In determining the amount of grant (if any) where they approve an application to which section 31 of the Act applies (determination of amount of grant in case of landlord's application), the local housing authority shall take into account, in addition to the matters referred to in section 31(3)(a) of the Act, such other matters as seem to them to be relevant in all the circumstances, having regard in particular to any relevant policy contained in their published renewal strategy (if any) for private sector housing in their area.

Application

3.   Paragraph 2 shall not have effect in relation to applications for grant made before 17 December 1996.

Signed by authority of
the Secretary of State

2 December 1996

C L L Braun
Assistant Secretary
Department of the
Environment

Annex J5   Not allocated

Annex J6

COMMON PARTS GRANT - CALCULATION OF GRANT WORKED EXAMPLES

A.   Tenants' application for grant in respect of works to a small privately built block of 8 flats located in East London.

Cost of relevant works

Replacement of steel windows and repair of roof = £27,000

Tenants' liabilities

All flats are let on long leasehold and all 8 tenants are required by the terms of their lease to contribute to the costs of carrying out the work. 4 tenants are each liable for 15% of the costs, the remaining 4 are each liable for 10%.

Attributable cost

Only 6 tenants are applying for grant, 4 with 15% liability and 2 with 10% liability. Their total liability is thus for 80% of the costs.
Attributable cost = £21,600

Calculation of Grant

The attributable cost is apportioned between the 6 applicants according to individual liability:

Those with 15% liability = £4,050 per applicant (x4)
Those with 10% liability = £2,700 per applicant (x2)

The test of resources is then applied to each applicant in relation to his share of the costs. For the purpose of this example it is assumed that the affordable loans of those with 15% liabilities are £1,000, £2,000, £3,000 and £500 respectively. Those with 10% liabilities are on income support. Total grant in respect of this application will therefore be £15,100.

B.   Tenants' application with a participating landlord in respect of the same building as in example A above.

Cost of relevant works

Replacement of steel windows and repair of roof = £27,000

Liabilities

6 of the flats are on long leasehold, 1 is vacant and 1 is let on a regulated tenancy. The long leaseholders are required to contribute to three quarters of the cost of the works, 3 at 10% and 3 at 15%. The landlord is liable for the remaining 25%.

Attributable Costs

All tenants are applying for grant. Together with the participating landlord, the total liability is for 100% of the costs.

Attributable cost = £27,000

Calculation of Grant

Apportionment of attributable cost:

Tenants with 15% liability = £4,050 per applicant (x3)
Tenants with 10% liability = £2,700 per applicant (x3)
Landlord with 25% liability = to be determined by the local authority.

The test of resources is then applied to each tenant. For the purpose of this example it is assumed that the affordable loans of those with 15% liability are £2,000, £1,500 and £500 respectively. Two of those with 10% liability are on income support, the remaining tenant is assessed as having an affordable loan of £1,000. Tenants' grants therefore amount to £15,250.

The landlord's grant is determined by the local authority in accordance with the provisions of section 31 of the 1996 Act.

Annex J7

COMMUTATION OF SPECIFIC GRANTS ON LOAN CHARGES

HOME IMPROVEMENT GRANTS

GUIDANCE NOTES

1. In accordance with the Government announcement of 6 November 1991, specific loan charge grants for Home Improvement Grants approved before 15 June 1989 were commuted on 1 October 1992, 1 March 1994 and 14 March 1995. It is accepted that there will continue to be new entitlements arising, although in greatly diminishing numbers, and that these will need to be commuted as they arise and paid as a lump sum; also, that there will be repayments of grants recovered following commutation. These guidance notes explain how the commutation will be achieved and the implications for the local authority capital finance system. *Appendix 1 to the Annex* explains in detail how the commutation will be carried out.

2. Powers to enable the Secretary of State to commute Exchequer contributions are contained in section 157 of the Local Government and Housing Act 1989 (the 1989 Act).

Summary of Procedures

3. All payments will be made on an *ad hoc* basis as and when claims are received. Payment of the commuted sum will be made to the authority and must be set aside as provision for credit liabilities (PLC), even if the authority is debt-free. The authority's credit ceiling will be reduced by the amount of the payment received.

4. The commuted sum on the outstanding loan charge grants remaining to be paid will be calculated using the information provided on the claim form enclosed with this note, submitted by authorities and certified by their Audit Commission appointed auditors. 100% of the commuted payment will be paid to the authority concerned as soon as possible after receipt of the audited claim form. The 1989 Act makes provision for later adjustments for any underpayments or overpayments.

Implications for the Capital Finance System

5. When a commuted payment is made to a local authority for the redemption of debt, the authority's credit ceiling is reduced by the amount of the reduction in debt (Schedule 3, paragraph 14(1) of the Local Government and Housing Act 1989). When the payment is made to a debt-free local authority, they are required to set aside an equal amount as provision for credit liabilities (section 63(2) of the 1989 Act); and their credit ceiling is reduced by the same amount (Schedule 3, paragraph 12(1)).

Calculation of the Commuted Sum

6. The method of calculating the commuted sum for the grants concerned is set out in detail in *Appendix 1 to this Annex.*

Grant Claims

7. Powers for the Secretary of State to obtain information for commutation are contained in section 157(9) of the 1989 Act. The Department will obtain the necessary information by means of commutation claim form (FED 0867A), copies of which are available from: **Housing Renewal Policy Division, Department of the Environment, 2 Marsham Street, London SW1P 3EB (from January 1997 : Second Floor, Eland House, Bressenden Place, London SW1E 5DU.**

8.   The claim form should be prepared in duplicate. Each authority should send the copy to the Department, while the original should be sent for certification to the authority's Audit Commission auditor who should return it to the Department as soon as possible and, in any event, no later than the certification date for the authority's final claim for housing subsidies and grants, if payment is to be made within the financial year. The local authority will bear the cost of the certification in the normal way.

9.   The Department will rely on section 157(7) of the 1989 Act to rectify any underpayments or overpayments.

Annex J7 (Appendix 1)

COMMUTATION OF NEW ENTITLEMENTS TO HOME IMPROVEMENT GRANTS APPROVED BEFORE 15 JUNE 1989

1.   The Department proposes to pay to local authorities a Commuted Sum in respect of expenditure by local authorities on Home Improvement Grants completed since the 1992 and subsequent commutation exercises.

2.   In order to calculate this Commuted Sum, the Department will assume that, but for commutation, the Department would have paid to the local authority a grant based on 20 years notional loan charges on the eligible capital expenditure incurred. It will be assumed that the notional loan charges would have been based on annuity loans for 20 years and that the interest rate would be the weighted average of PWLB interest rates for the non-quota A annuity loans for 20 years for the calendar year: eg, the 1994 weighted average will be used for 1994/95 loan charges.

3.   The Department will assume that it would have made 10 equal payments in May to February inclusive for 20 years from May of the year in which the loan charge grant would first have been claimed, e.g. for 1994/95 entitlements the 20 year period would run from May 1994 - February 1995 to May 2013 - February 2014.

Commutation Factor

4.   The Commutation Factor is used to determine the present value, compounding or discounting to the date the payment instruction is issued, of the 200 monthly payments arising from expenditure in the claim year.

5.   The Commuted Sum equals the *monthly* payment times the Commutation Factor. The Commutation Factor is:

$$\frac{a + a^{11}}{1 - a} \times \frac{1 - b^{20}}{1 - b} \times (1 + r)^{(n/12)}$$

where

r = the interest rate expressed as a decimal; for example, $8\frac{3}{8}$ =.08375. The interest rate used will be the PWLB non-quota A annuity rate for over 15 but not over 25 years on Commutation Day.

$$a = (1 + r)^{-1/12}$$

$$b = (1 + r)^{-1}$$

n = the number of months between the April preceding the first May payment and the Commutation Month.

6.   The derivation of the Commutation Factor is available from the Department on request.

Information Required From Local Authority

7.   Details of the grants completed, giving the year in which the expenditure was incurred, the full amount of the grant given and the rate of contribution: Factor sheets will not be provided. The Department will calculate the annual subsidy by applying the appropriate factor, as part of its calculation of the commuted sum payable.

Annex K

HOUSING GRANTS, CONSTRUCTION AND REGENERATION ACT 1996 – GRANT LEGISLATIVE PROVISIONS BY SECTION

Subject	Renovation Grant	Common Parts Grant	Disabled Facilities Grant	HMO Grants	Home Repair Assistance	Group Repair	Relocation Grants
Preliminary Conditions							
Eligibility of Applicants/dwelling	s 3(1)	s 3(1)	s 3(1)	s 3(1)	s 3(1)	s 61 / s 64(1)–(2)	s 133
Eligibility of Bodies	s 3(2)	s 3(2)	s 3(2)	s 3(2)	s 3(2)	s 64(6)	–
Age of Property	s 4	s 4	s 4	s 4	s 4	–	–
Qualifying Conditions							
Resolution to pay relocation grants	–	–	–	–	–	–	s 131
Owners Interest in Property	s 7(1)–(6)	s 15(1)–(4)	s 19(1)–(5)	s 25(1)–(3)	s 77(1)–(5)	s 64(1)–(5)	s 133(1)
Occupying Tenants Condition and required	–	s 14(1)–(3)	–	–	–	–	–
proportion	–	s 15(1)(b) / s 15(2)+(3)	–	–	–	–	–
Definition of Disabled Occupant	–	–	s 20 and s 100(1)–(5)	–	s 100(1)–(5)	–	–
Certificate Owner Occupation/Interest in property	s 8(1)–(2)	s 16(1)–(2)	s 21(1)–(2)	–	–	s 64(3)	s 132(2)+(5)
Certificate for/tenants application	s 9(1)–(4)	s 16(1)–(2)	s 22(1)–(3)	–	–	–	
Certificate of intending letting	s 8(3)	s 16(1)–(2)	s 22(3)	–	–	s 64(4)	–
Certificate of future occupation	–	–	–	26(1)–(2)	–	s64(5)	–

Subject	Renovation Grant	Common Parts Grant	Disabled Facilities Grant	HMO Grants	Home Repair Assistance	Group Repair	Relocation Grants
Prior Qualifying Period	s 10	—	—	—	s77(4) s 78(3)+(4)	—	—
Disapplying Prior Qualifying Period	s 10(3)–(6)	—	—	—			
Conditions relating to prior qualifying period	s 11	—	—	—	s 77(4) s 78(2)		
Purpose for which grant may be given	s 12(1)–(5)	s 17(1)–(3)	s 23(1)–(3)	s 27(1)–(4)	s 76(1)+(3)	s 60+ 62	
Approval of Application/Scheme consent	s 13(1)–(6)	s 18(1)–(5)	s 24(1)–(5)	s 28(1)–(6)	s 76(2)	s 63	
Fitness on Completion of	s 13(4)–(5)	s 18(3)–(4)	s 24(3)+(4)	s 28(4)–(5)	—	s 66	
Works/Certification completion Date	s 59	s 59	s 59	s 59	s 80	s 75	
Defined Expression	s 58	s 58	s 58	s 58			
Minor Definitions	s 101	s 101	s 101	s 101	s 101	s 101	s 140
Definition of family and connected person	s 98	s 98	s 98	s 98	s 98	s 98	
Definition of owner	s 99	s 99	s 99	s 99	s 99	s 99	s 140(2)
Restrictions on Grant Aid							
Restrictions on grants for works commenced	s 29	s 29	s 29	s 29	s76(3)	s 98	
Means Testing owner occupier or tenant	s 30	s 30 s 32	s 30(1)(b) 30(4)	—	s 76(2)	s 67	s 134(4)–(8)
Means Testing Landlords	s 31	s 31	s 31	s 31	—	s 67	—
Grant Maximum	s 33(1)+(2)	s 33(1)+(2)	s 33(1)–(4)	s 33(1)+(2)	s 76(2)	—	s 134(1)–(3)

Subject	Renovation Grant	Common Parts Grant	Disabled Facilities Grant	HMO Grants	Home Repair Assistance	Group Repair	Relocation Grants
Decision							
Decision/Notification Period	s 34(1)+(2)	s 34(1)+(2)	s 34(1)+(2)	s 34(1)+(2)	s 79	–	–
Details to be notified	s 34(3)+(4)	s 34(3)+(4)	s 34(3)+(4)	s 34(3)+(4)	s 79	–	–
Redetermination of grant	s 34(5)	s 34(5)	s 34(5)	s 34(5)	–	s 68	–
Payment of Grants							
Payment of Grants and Delayed Payment	s 35	s 35	s 35 s36	s 35	s 79	–	–
Payment of grant period for carrying out works	s 37	s 37	s 37	s 37	–	–	–
Extension of period for completion of works	s 37(2)	s 37(2)	s 37(2)	s 37(2)	–	–	–
Works complete to LA satisfaction/ specification	s 37(3)+(4)	s 37(3)+(4)	s 37(3)(4)	s 37(3)+(4)	–	–	–
Works by family members	s 37(4)	s 37(4)	s 37(4)	s 37(4)	–	–	–
Conditions as to contractors employment and payment of grant to contractor	s38 & 39	s 38 & 39	s 38 & 39	s 38 & 39	–	–	–
Change of circumstances before grant payment	s 40(1), (2), (3)	s 40(1)(2), (6)	s 40(1), (2), (4) s 41	s 40(1), (2), (5)	–	–	–
Circumstances recalculation, withholding/repayment of grant before completion of works	s 42	s 42	s 42	s 42	–	–	–

Subject	Renovation Grant	Common Parts Grant	Disabled Facilities Grant	HMO Grants	Home Repair Assistance	Group Repair	Relocation Grants
Repayment where there is no entitlement	s 43(1), (2), (3)	s 43(1),(2), (6)	s 43(1), (2), (4)	s 43(1), (2), (5)	-	-	-
Grant Conditions and Repayment							
General meaning and provision of period	s 44 / s 44(3)	s 44 / s 44(3)	s 44 / s 44(3)	s 44 / s 44(3)	-	s 69 / s 69(2)	s 140
Repayment on Disposal including local land charge on property	s 45	s 46	-	s 47	-	s 70	s 135 / s 138
Conditions where demand made or a lesser amount demanded	s 45(4), (5), (6)	s 46(4)+ (5)	-	s 47(4)+(5)	-	-	s 135(3)+(4)
Conditions for residency, including owner occupation and letting	s 48 & 49	-	-	s 50	-	s 71	s 136
Discretion not to recover breach on residents condition	s 48(5) / s 49(5)		-	s 50(5)	-	s 71(5)	-
Discretion not to recover on breach conditions	s 51(4) / s 52(4)	s 51(4) / s 52(4)	s 51(4) / s 52(4)	s 51(4) / s 52(4)	-	-	-
Tenancy nominations, maintenance, etc, recovery of equipment	s 52	s 52	s 52	s 52	-	-	-
Insurance Claim	s 51	s 51	s 51	s 51	-	-	-
Additional Conditions							
Definition of relevant disposal	s 53	s 53	s 53 in respect of s 51 and 52	s 53	-	s 72 [s 53]	s 135(6) [s 53]
Definition of Exempt Disposal	s 54(1)	s 54(1)	s 54(1) in respect of s 51 and 52	s 54(1)	-	s 72 [s 54(1)]	s 135(7) [s 54(1)]

Subject	Renovation Grant	Common Parts Grant	Disabled Facilities Grant	HMO Grants	Home Repair Assistance	Group Repair	Relocation Grants
Definition of Qualifying Person for exemption disposal	s 54(2)	s 54(2)	s 54(1) in respect of s 51 and 52	s 54(2)	–	s 72 [s 54(2)]	s 135(7) [s 54(2)]

Supplementary Provisions

Subject	Renovation Grant	Common Parts Grant	Disabled Facilities Grant	HMO Grants	Home Repair Assistance	Group Repair	Relocation Grants
Circumstances where grant conditions cease to apply	s 55(1),(3), (4)	s 55(1), (2), (4)	s 55(1),(3),(4) in respect of s 51 and 52	s 55(1),(3) (4)	–	s 73	s 137
Treatment of grant payment where applicant died before certified date	s 56	s 56	s 41+s 56	s 56	–	–	–
Power for housing authority to undertake grant works	s 57(1)+(2)	57(1)–(3)	s 57(1)+(2)	s 57(1)+(2)	–	–	–
Definition of Tenant	s 7(5)	s 14(2)	s 19(5)	–	s 77(3)	s 75 (s 101)	–
Works to houseboats and mobile homes where Section 7 does not apply	–	–	–	–	s 78	–	–
Scope of Secretary of State consents	s 94	s 94	s 94	s 94	–	–	–
Recovery of Secretary of State contributions	s 93	s 93	s 93	s 93	s 93	s 93	s 137
Contributions by Secretary of State	s 92	s 92	s 92	s 92	s 92	s 92	s 139
Scope of Orders, regulations and directions Applications in respect of parsonages and charities	s 146 s 95(1)–(3)	s 146 s 95(1)–(3)	s 146 s 95(1)–(3)	s 146 s 95(1)–(3)	s 146 s 95(5)	s 146 s 95(4)	s 146 –
Meaning of Reasonable Repair and Interpretation of fitness standard	s 96 + 97	s 96+97	s 96+97	s 96+97	s 96+97	s 96	–
Transitional Provisions	s 102	s 102	s 102	s 102	s 102	s 102(1)	–
Power for Secretary of State to modify group repair scheme provision	–	–	–	–	–	s 74	–

Annex L

HOUSING GRANTS, CONSTRUCTION AND REGENERATION ACT 1996 - STATUTORY INSTRUMENTS MADE UNDER PART I

Housing Renewal Grants (Services and Charges) Order - SI 1996 No. 2889

The order is made under section 2(3). It specifies the "preliminary or ancillary services and charges", such as preparation of schedules of work, which are eligible for grant.

Housing Renewal Grants (Prescribed Form and Particulars) Regulations - SI 1996 No. 2891

The regulations are made under section 2(4) prescribing a form of grant application which all applicants applying for grant must complete. The regulations set out the particular details that applicants will be required to provide to enable authorities to determine grant applications.

Housing Renewal Grants Regulations - SI 1996 No. 2890

The regulations are made under section 30(5) to (9) and set out the detailed rules for means testing of applications by owner-occupiers or tenants.

Disabled Facilities Grants and Home Repair Assistance (Maximum Amounts) Order - SI 1996 No. 2888

The order is made under sections 33 and 76 specifying a grant maximum of £20,000 in England and £24,000 in Wales for mandatory DFGs; and a maximum of £2,000 per application and £4,000 in any period of three years for home repair assistance.

Group Repair (Qualifying Buildings) Regulations - SI 1996 No. 2883

The regulations are made under section 61 and prescribe the conditions for qualifying buildings, primary buildings and additional buildings in relation to a group repair scheme.

Home Repair Assistance Regulations - SI 1996 No. 2887

The regulations are made under section 79 and set out the way in which applications for home repair assistance are to be made and the procedure for dealing with those applications.

The Housing (Fitness Enforcement Procedures) Order - SI 1996 No. 2885

The order is made under section 86 and specifies certain pre-formal enforcement procedures to be followed by local authorities. Authorities are not prevented by the order from taking immediate enforcement action in cases where such action appears to them to be necessary.

The Housing (Maximum Charge for Enforcement Action) Order - SI 1996 No. 2886

The order is made under section 87 and specifies the maximum charge a local authority can make for enforcement action in accordance with subsection (5) of that section. A maximum of £300 is specified.

The Housing (Deferred Action and Charge for Enforcement Action) (Forms) Regulations SI 1996 No. 2884

The regulations are made under section 89 and prescribe a suite of forms for use by local authorities in applying the new deferred action notice enforcement option under section 81 and in making a charge for enforcement action under section 87.

The Housing Grants, Construction and Regeneration Act 1966 (Commencement No. 1) Order 1996 - SI 1996 No. 2352

The order commences a number of provisions in Part I and other parts of the 1996 Act which confer powers on the Secretary of State to make orders, regulations and determinations, to give directions or guidance or to do other things.

The Housing Grants, Construction and Regeneration Act 1996 (Commencement No. 2 and Revocation, Savings and Supplementary and Transitional Provisions) Order 1996 - SI 1996 No. 2842

The order provides for the private sector renewal provisions in Part I of the 1996 Act to commence on 17 December 1996. It also makes provision under sections 102 and 150 so that transitional provisions are made adapting Part VIII of the 1989 Act so as to disapply, as appropriate, sections 112 and 113 of that Act (under which certain applications for grant, other than disabled facilities grant, must be approved). This allows the applications for mandatory grant under Part VIII, identified in section 102(3) - (4) of the 1996 Act, to be treated as applications under Part VIII for discretionary grant (ie, for purposes which previously attracted mandatory grant). The order is also used as the vehicle for revoking the current subordinate legislation.

All the statutory instruments listed in this Annex are published by Her Majesty's Stationery Office (now known as "The Stationery Office") from whom copies can be obtained.

Bibliography

PUBLICATIONS ARISING FROM DEPARTMENT OF THE ENVIRONMENT SPONSORED RESEARCH ON PRIVATE SECTOR RENEWAL

Published research reports and other guidance

Neighbourhood Renewal Assessment - HMSO 1992 (ISBN 0 11 752456 5)

Local House Condition Surveys - Guidance Manual - HMSO 1993 (ISBN 0 11 752830 7)

Housing Associations, Rehabilitation & Urban Renewal: Part 2 - The Consequences of Changes in the Rehabilitation Activities of Housing Associations - DOE 1995 *(available from DOE Sales Unit, Block 3, Spur 7, Government Buildings, Lime Grove, Eastcote, Ruislip, Middx HA4 8SF. From 1 January 1997 contact 0171 276 0900 our Public Enquiry Helpline.)*

In from the Cold - Working with the Private Landlord - DOE 1995 *(available from DOE Sales Unit - see address details in the above entry)*

Private Landlords in England - HMSO 1996 (ISBN 0 11 753 239 8)

Home Owners & Clearance: An Evaluation of Rebuilding Grants - HMSO 1996 (ISBN 0 11 7531731)

Vacant Dwellings in the Private Sector - HMSO 1996 (ISBN 0 11 753 214 2)

An Evaluation of the Disabled Facilities Grants System - HMSO 1996 (ISBN 0 11 753242 8)

Monitoring the Actions of Unsuccessful Renovation Grant Enquirers - HMSO 1996 (ISBN 0 11 7533068)

Houses in Multiple Occupation

DOE free publication covering:

    a)   Establishing Effective Local Authority Strategies

    b)   Local Authority Houses in Multiple Occupation - Survey Report

Copies available from Peter-tomas Gray, Building Stock Research division, Room P3/169, 2 Marsham Street, London SW1P 3EB, Tel: 0171 276 3194 (from January 1997 the address will change to Eland House, Bressenden Place, London SW1E 5DU).

Forthcoming publications

The following are expected to be published over the next:

    - 6 months

Repairs and Improvements to Private Rented Dwellings in the 1990s
Monitoring Housing Renovation Standards

    - 12 months

Repair in the Owner Occupied Sector

Flats Over Shops

Neighbourhood Renewal Assessment and Renewal Areas

Development of Private Renewal Strategies.

The majority will be TSO (formerly HMSO) publications. Further information on publication details can be obtained by contacting *Peter-tomas Gray, Building Stock Research division, Room P3/169, 2 Marsham Street, London SW1P 3EB, Tel: 0171 276 3194 (from January 1997 the address will change to Eland House, Bressenden Place, London SW1E 5DU).*

Printed in the United Kingdom for The Stationery Office
Dd.0303366, 12/96, C35, 3400, 5673, 363387.